WALKING
THE MAZE

Other books by Loren Cruden

The Spirit of Place: A Workbook for Sacred Alignment
*Coyote's Council Fire: Contemporary Shamans on
  Race, Gender, & Community*
*Compass of the Heart: Embodying Medicine Wheel
  Teachings*
Medicine Grove: A Shamanic Herbal

WALKING THE MAZE

The Enduring Presence of Celtic Spirit

Loren Cruden

Destiny Books
Rochester, Vermont

Destiny Books
One Park Street
Rochester, Vermont 05767
www.InnerTraditions.com

Destiny Books is a division of Inner Traditions International

Library of Congress Cataloging-in-Publication Data
Cruden, Loren, 1952–
     Walking the maze : the enduring presence of Celtic spirit / Loren
Cruden
        p.   cm.
     Includes bibliographical references.
     ISBN 0-89281-623-6 (pbk. : alk. paper)
     1. Celts—Religion—Miscellanea. 2. Indians of North America—
Religion—Miscellanea. I. Title.
BL900.C78   1998
299′.16—dc21   98-39936
                                                   CIP

Grateful acknowledgment is made to the follwing for permission to reprint
these excerpts:
   "The Incitement to Battle from the Headship of the Gael," the Clan
      Donald Lands Trust.
   "It Belongs to Us" by Dougie MacLean, published by Limetree Arts and
      Music, © 1994 by Dunkeld Records.

Printed and bound in Canada

10 9 8 7 6 5 4 3 2 1

Text design by Bill Brillmayer
This book was typeset in Palatino with Baker Signet and Willow as the
   display typefaces

To ancestors, family, and children yet to come—
may there continue a love of the land

CONTENTS

Acknowledgments

M ANY PEOPLE ENTHUSIASTICALLY PITCHED IN to suggest and loan books for my research of the Celts. Special thanks to Jim and Tames Alan for help in that quarter, to my son Gabriel for borrowing and shipping books from Western Washington University's fine collections, and to Walter Dudar and the helpful ladies at Nakusp, British Columbia's tiny but gem-stocked library. Gratitude to my mother, Barbara Lyman Cruden, for allowing use of her poem and for reminders about focusing on experience, not personality, when writing about personal experience.

The editors and the production staff at Inner Traditions are not only wizards at their jobs but also have been invaluable teachers and warm cultivators of the writer's art; thank you Susan Davidson, Rowan Jacobsen, Jon Graham, and Lee Wood. Thank you Larry Hamberlin and Robin Dutcher-Bayer for early encouragement.

Leigh Cruden, on whom falls the vital but underpaid task of transferring manuscripts to disks, deserves most earnest gratitude; thanks also to her busy husband, Bill Kuhn, for ironing out computer speed bumps and promoting book sales in unlikely quarters. Heartfelt thanks to Dougie MacLean and Dunkeld Records for permitting use of the lyrics to "It Belongs to Us," and to Lewis Sawaquat for allowing inclusion of his vision-quest song.

Gratitude to family and friends whose names or deeds appear in this text; I hope verity and love are clearly conveyed in what is written. Living alone, there is no one to thank for patience with my preoccupations except a dog and two cats, and thank them I do. For inspiration, delight, solace, and proper atmosphere, keen gratitude is extended for the music of Ireland's Davy Spillane and Scotland's Andy Stewart and Silly Wizard, Battlefield Band, Capercaille, and Dougie MacLean: beautiful, always.

The Scottish National Library in Edinburgh, the Clan Donald Library and the Heritage Council's library on Skye, and the Gairloch Heritage Museum's archives in Gairloch were of particular help during my months in Scotland. I'm grateful to Rob MacDonald Parker of the Clan Donald Trust for conversation and rides; thanks also to him for generous permission to use Clan Donald's Incitement to Battle. Gratitude to Peter MacDonald of Skye for exemplary Celtic sensibility, sensitivity, and sentimentality; to Susan Watson for making my time in Perthshire so relaxed; to Camille Dressler for information about Eigg; to Archie and Penny of Golspie for inclusive Highland friendliness; and to the Scottish bus drivers for their memorable skill and good humor.

Special thanks to Skye's Gavin Scott Moncrieff for patience with my endless, sometimes prying questions, for passion about Scottish independence, for gallantry and wit, and for the days of walking and evenings of whiskey and "crack"; and gratitude also to Colin of Caithness for the unforgettable waltz.

Coyote Celt

When Coyote comes in she has a plaid, none too clean, slung round her shoulders. "Are you here to wish me a happy birthday?" I ask, as it is that occasion.

"Could be. Are those treats on the table for guests?"

"Sure," I say. "But tell me, Coyote; what do you see looking at me?"

"Not difficult, that. I see a woman, fair, tall, red haired, angular, long handed, hazel eyed, freckled, willful and canny. . . . Are there poppy seeds in those cakes?"

"Some. I heard you singing last night, Coyote. Can you tell me, what was it made you sing?"

"Not difficult, that. It was a snowfield twinkling in moonlight; it was the heart-shaped prints of deer hooves between dark cedars; it was the gliding owl, warm breasted, cold taloned; and the river of life in my veins, fierce and free."

"Your song woke me, Coyote. In the night, alone in my bed, I shivered from wildness so near."

Coyote smiles, adjusts her plaid. "And were you afraid in your strong stone house, in your soft warm bed?"

"Oh, yes! But I saw snow twinkling in the moonlight, and rose and went outside. Did you hear me singing, too?"

Coyote eyes the cakes. "Maybe."

INTRODUCTION

AMBER FIRELIGHT PATTERNS A FLICKERING DANCE on the circle of friends seated on stumps around a crackling blaze. A few yards away, the mounded shape of a sweat lodge hunkers between cedar trees, waiting with open doorflaps for the ceremony to begin.

There are no American Indians present, though one of the men sundances on the Crow reservation; the ceremonial leader's mentor is a Potawatomie medicine man; one of the women is involved with a tribal member of the northern Diné, and another has ties with an Apache shaman. During a pause in the drumming, a discussion about ancestry reveals that everyone in the circle this night is descended from Scot's heritages. It seemed a congenial coincidence then, but as years passed I began to reflect on the nature of resonance between American Natives and Celts, affinities that in early times manifested in intermarriage and, today, in the interest many Celtic Americans feel in Native spirituality. Four aspects of traditional life appear as taproots of commonality between Celtic and Native people: orientation to tribe or clan; high regard shown women; a fluid perspective of reality; and an integrated spiritual relationship with the land.

It is often forgotten, despite present-day "Troubles" in Northern Ireland and the undying Scottish autonomy movement, that Celts suffered invasion, religious persecution, and removal from their lands.

Ireland went from being the most densely populated country in Europe to the least, losing three-quarters of its people. Vikings invaded in the eighth century, Normans conquered in the twelfth; in the sixteenth century Elizabethans cut down Ireland's forests in pursuit of Irish (and Norman-Irish) guerrilla fighters, and the Calvinist Cromwellians came close to committing genocide of the Irish in the seventeenth century.

Oliver Cromwell obliterated one-third of the Irish. One hundred thousand others were shipped as indentured servants (slaves) to the New World, particularly to Barbados. In 1654, Irish were forced to a reservation west of the river Shannon in Connacht; resisters were immediately executed. Sir William Parsons, seventeenth-century Master of the Court of Wards, noted that "We must change the Irish course of government, apparel, manner of holding land, language, and habit of life. It will otherwise be impossible to set up in them obedience to the laws and to the English empire."

In the eighteenth century, English penal laws denied Irish Catholics the right to purchase or lease land, become educated, practice their religion, own a horse worth more than five pounds, keep profits from rented land, or speak Gaelic. The people were sequentially stripped of the vitality of their paganism and the acceptability of their Christianity. To the Protestant conquerors, Catholicism was an intolerable relic of the past.

A century later, attitudes had not changed. An English official traveling in Ireland during the potato famine (in which nearly one million died while England turned its back) referred to the people as "chimpanzees," and mused about how strange it was that, though the Irish looked like white people, they were not really human.

One and one-half million Irish emigrated during the famine. By 1914 another four million were gone, and the total population was less than four and one-half million. Scotland's Highland population evaporated also; the Highlands are one of the only areas in the world once containing a larger population than it now sustains. Famine and the merciless Clearances of the late 1700s and 1800s emptied the glens and replaced people with sheep. After centuries of warfare with England, the battle of Culloden in 1746 brought a final shattering of the Scottish clans. Celtic culture was proscribed: the playing of bagpipes, wearing of tartan, carrying of weapons, and speaking of Gaelic were banned. Today, in some parts of the Highlands, one-third to one-half of all properties are either vacant or are holiday homes for non-Highlanders.

Recall of these tribulations is not meant to divert attention from or absolve Celtic Americans from participation in wrongs perpetrated on Natives in North America. Between 1778 and 1871 the United States' government ratified 371 treaties with American Indians. Every one of those treaties was either broken or annulled. As Chief Red Cloud of the Lakota said, "They made us many promises, more than I can remember, but they never kept but one; they promised to take our land and they took it."

There is much oppression to be addressed. Healing occurs in an immediacy that takes into account past as well as future. Understanding where we have been offers insight and perspective on how to unfold an honest future; not a return to or perpetuation of the past, but a flowering of the most honorable potentials held within our roots.

In the spring of 1997, Dr. Joseph McDonald, president of the Salish Kootenai College on Montana's Flathead reservation, gave a talk at Sabhal Mor Ostaig, the Gaelic business college on Scotland's Isle of Skye. Dr. McDonald's ancestors include Glencoe's MacDonald chiefs. Earlier in the spring of 1997, members of the Nez Perce tribe met in Assynt, Scotland with crofters who had made history by buying their land back, as a community, from the lairds holding it. The meeting of crofters and Native Americans, like Dr. McDonald's talk, was to discuss commonalties and to share experiences and perspectives. At Assynt it was noted that crofters' ancestors, coming to North America as a result of displacement from their own lands, were among those who displaced ancestors of the Nez Perce now sitting with the crofters. The realization brought not guilt or blame, but a sense of history's patterns and how things can change when human relationships align with commonalties of principle and heart.

This book touches on similarities between American Indians and Celts, but its purpose and focus is not to legitimize Celticism's value by comparing it to Native culture. The aim is to present the spirit of Celtic culture in its own light and strength, in its uniqueness as well as its relationship to other ancient ways of life.

It is an exploration of Celtic heritage that seeks both rootedness and transcendent evolution. That quest, reflected in many Celtic American lives, was apparent in the firelit circle of friends preparing to enter the sweat lodge. We ask ourselves: What and where is homeland and the continuity of ancestral spirit?

Return

In dreams forever walking
moors and shores in Hebridean wind,
forever seeking leeward reception,
inbreath of heritage: "Take me,"
to quivering heather, promiscuous wind,
the eyes of working people—peat cutters,
bus drivers, plain-dressed women
with satchel handbags.
Not tartan but stone,
curling North Sea breakers, the Cuillin,
the wind—Oh, the wind!—streaming
in centuries as though history
is a sea journey.
In dreams Gaelic-greeted, curlews
and the panic of grouse wings,
evening's silk in stillness over the firth.
"Come back," whispered (never aloud)
to disappearances and white-sailed ships
making me tourist
in this homeland.

PART I

CLAN AND CULTURE

THERE IS A SMALL, UNPRETENTIOUS PLACE on Scotland's eastern coast, above Aberdeen, called Cruden Bay. A nearby plain, now a golf course, is where Scots living in that area in the first millennium regularly battled marauding Danes. The story is that so many people on both sides were killed over the centuries that a Danish chieftain initiated peace between his warriors and the Scots occupying that land.

When the truce was arranged, a huge pile of stones was massed as a memorial to the slain warriors on both sides, and as a symbol of lasting peace. This truce may have happened following a major battle fought in A.D. 1012. The stones remained for centuries until perhaps one hundred fifty years ago, when farmers, and then the builders of the golf course, dismantled this ancient monument.

My uncle, Donald Graeme Cruden, on a visit to Scotland, researched the Cruden name and came up with four possible derivations: Croih Dain (battle between Scots and Danes, 1012); Cruithan (name of the first Pictish King); Cro-Dun (the circle on the hill); or Croo-Dane (circle of standing stones or enclosure of the Danes). During research for a novel I chanced on references to the Cruithins or Cruithni, the name ancient Irish called the Picts as a whole. This bit of information invited imagination of a time when all Scotland's inhabitants were "Crudens," a privately satisfying notion.

My older brother carries the traditionally passed family name of Alexander Burgess Cruden (one of the earlier A. B. Crudens arrived in Virginia from Aberdeen in 1792). My sister-in-law, Dedria, relates a story about the time she and Alex went to a pub in Cruden Bay. Readying to leave, my tall, quiet-spoken brother addressed the room at large, saying, "I'm a Cruden from the States and I'd like to buy a round of drinks for everyone." He deposited money on the bar and departed, leaving the locals to drink their pints in peace.

I was with my mother and thirteen-year-old son the first time I visited Cruden Bay, so we eschewed the pubs. But never having met a Cruden or encountered the name outside my own family, it was enough to stand where the river—the Burn of Cruden—empties into the North Sea and, for once, have my name be ordinary and indigenous. I used to look for Crudens in phone books wherever I lived, but never came across one. Now, experiencing Cruden Bay, there was this: a link of lineage and land, an old name that speaks of stones and warriors and the wisdom to make peace; worth a toast.

Where do Celtic people in Great Britain come from? For, in this book, it is at the Celts of Great Britain—in particular, those of Scotland— that we'll most closely peer. We first catch sight of them in lands west of the Urals and north of the Black Sea, where Indo-European language is thought to have originated. They moved in waves from the Middle East and the southwest plains and mountains of the Ukraine into central and northern Europe. The Greeks called them Keltoi and the Romans described them as restless, fearsome, tall, fair, having great pride and insolence. Celtic women were particularly alarming to Romans unused to encountering female warriors and assertive women.

Some of these Celts remained in Asia Minor (the Galatians) and northern Italy. In France and southern Germany they became known as the Gauls; in Spain, as Iberian Celts, great sea-traders who may have been the first Europeans to settle in North America. Ógham-inscribed stones in New England have been dated to 800 B.C., and there are numerous crossovers in Celtic and Algonquin place-names. Celts crossed to Britain as early as 400 B.C. from Brittany and Gaul and became Britons. Later in the century they were pushed by the Germanic Angles and Saxons west into Cornwall and Wales (there to become King Arthur's Celts).

Around 350 B.C. (though proposed dates range from then through the third century B.C.) Celts from Brittany and Iberia arrived in Ireland, displacing the legendary Tuatha de Danand, the Celt-Iberians becoming the dominant group in Ireland.

Celts in Wales, Cornwall, and Brittany are considered the Brythonic branch, and those in Ireland, Scotland, and the Isle of Man the Goidelic branch, so designated for the types of Gaelic spoken. Evidence indicates that Goidelic Celtic languages are extremely ancient. One hypothesis is that a common Celtic linguistic group, originating in the steppes of southern Russia in the third millennium B.C., divided into two distinct dialects. The older Goidelic branch was carried to Spain and later to Ireland, while the Brythonic branch developed in Gaul and spread to southern Britain. There are only two and one-half million speakers of Celtic languages today, a dramatic indication of cultural loss. But, unlike other ancient civilizations, the Celts survived, their language a cornerstone of that endurance.

Sally M. Foster, in *Picts, Gaels, and Scots*, diagrams the Celtic language groups as follows:

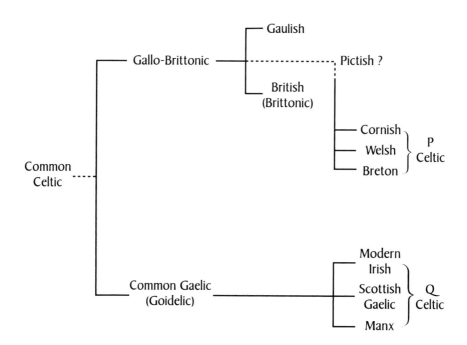

Many Celts arriving in Scotland came there from Ireland between the final two centuries B.C., to the northern and western isles and the extreme south of Scotland, and to Lowland Scotland during the first two centuries A.D. These Irish Celts (known as Dal Riadans, for their kingdom of Dal Riada, established in what is now Argyll) competed with and intermarried with the Picts, whose culture was similar to that of the Irish. Both Pictish and Irish cultures were kin-based, tribal, and heroic, and both were Celtic.

Theories abound about the origins of the Picts, but most modern scholars consider them Celts from earlier migrations to Scotland. The northwest *broch* (circular stone tower) builders on the upper rim of the Highlands likely predated the Picts, though were perhaps Celts also; it is possible that in the far northwest was a mix of indigenous Picts and seafaring immigrants from western Europe. There is evidence of German Celts on the Isle of Skye in 2000 B.C. Dal Riadans and Picts were both predated by neolithic and mesolithic peoples, about whom little is known. The neolithic people built such astonishing structures as Britain's Stonehenge (2950 B.C.) and Ireland's Newgrange (3200 B.C.). There are still middens on the Isle of Skye dating to 6500 B.C., and evidence of habitation going back 8000 years on the Isle of Rhum.

It became increasingly difficult to distinguish between Picts and Dal Riadans as the groups integrated. The tribal Picts themselves confederated earlier to repulse the Romans. Between the fifth and ninth centuries there was a gradual centralization of authority in Scotland. During the push and pull, sometimes there were Pictish kings ruling Dal Riadans (A.D. 741–50) and sometimes Dal Riadans ruling Picts. Pictish King Óengus (A.D. 729–61) had Dal Riadan blood. Britons and Angles also competed with Dal Riadans; Scotland during that period was a jostle of four kingdoms: Picts, Dal Riadans, Angles, and Britons. The four groups unified to fight the Norse and Danish Vikings, however, who appeared on Scotland's coasts starting around A.D. 794 and who, with difficulty, were defeated (except in Orkney and Shetland) by 1264.

The Pictish kingdom was at its height during the eighth century, before the Vikings eroded its edges. Early Pictish power was in the north; by the seventh century it had moved south to the agriculturally rich Perthshire area. During the period of immigration that eclipsed Pictish culture, Celtic Britons settled around Strathclyde while Angles and Saxons—and, later, Normans—gradually pushed into the southeast Lowlands. T. W. Rolleston, in his book *Celtic Myths and Legends,* is of the opinion that current use of the term Anglo-Saxon in reference to British people is misleading:

> There is nothing to justify this singling out of two Low German tribes when we wish to indicate the race-character of the British people. . . . The true term for the population of these islands, and for the typical and dominant part of the population of North America, is not Anglo-Saxon, but Anglo-Celtic.

Cináed mac Ailpín (Kenneth MacAlpine), who gave his sons alternating Pictish and Roman names and who had a Pictish wife and Pictish blood himself, used organized military and religious means to found the first Scottish royal dynasty in 843. MacAlpine's center was in Scone, the heart and spiritual capital of Pictland, and in Dunkeld, an important power center. His ascendance to kingship was not bloodless—there was resistance from some of the Picts and their nobles. But all future Scottish kings are numbered from MacAlpine. His sons succeeded him, and his family line continued in the kingship—a shift from the ancient Celtic tradition of eligibility extending to the larger kin group. Around A.D. 900 the term Alba started being used to designate the territory originally considered the land of the Picts, reflecting a movement toward national identity. People of Alba became generally known as Scots in the 900s, and the Pictish language and unique symbols disappeared from use.

On the European continent, Gaul was conquered by Caesar in the first century B.C.; by the fifth century A.D. Gaulish language was almost extinct. (Brittany's Gaelic was reintroduced by immigrants from southwest Britain and Wales during the fifth and sixth centuries.)

Christianity was the most significant force of change during this era. It was introduced in Scotland first by Saint Ninian in 396, and again, more extensively, by Saint Columba in 563. By the early tenth century most people were familiar with it. Roman Christianity, introduced in the early eighth century, brought about the biggest consolidations, as the ambitions of the clergy merged with the political aspirations of the nobles. The Church was pro-state, supporting kings and nobles and promoting primogenitor inheritance of kingship rather than the more unpredictable up-for-grabs methods of the Celtic past. Those methods, among other things, had avoided the problem of weak

kings and of minority succession, problems that were to repeatedly
imperil Scottish autonomy. The Church heavily influenced kingship
as well as monopolized literacy. It became a major landowner and
shifted the bonds of social relationship from a tribal, communal orientation to one based on a belief system.

In the course of these changes, which included the activities of
thanes as land administrators expanding royal territory, kings were
no longer considered simply part of the extended family. Saint
Columba, related to Ireland's High King and descended from a warrior aristocracy, replaced the traditional Celtic deities of protection.
Evidence of this can be seen in the use of incantations invoking his
protection and in the stories of his paranormal exploits outshining
those of Druids.

If history makes you drowsy, think of it in personal terms, a family
narrative. It is the story of your people, the path that brought you to
where you now stand, to who you are. Someday you too will be an
ancestor, something of history. What gift from the past do you carry,
and what, in turn, will you offer those who follow? Continuity and
creativity, both, are not random, though may be expressed unconsciously. When awareness is brought to both, creativity can be applied to continuity as an act of regenerative healing; knowing your
people's history is a part of this awareness. Early Celtic history in the
British Isles, especially in Ireland, has a mythological or Dreamtime
quality that frustrates scholars but reflects the fluid basis of Celtic
perspective. In mythohistorical cycles magic, shapeshifting, and de-
scendence from and intermarriage with deitific beings all contributed
to the Celts' understanding of themselves as a people. Ancestors, particularly tribal leaders, were associated with deities and faery people,
and access to ancestors was available through congress with the
Otherworld.

Unlike Romanized continental Europe, there were no towns in
early Ireland and Scotland (invading Vikings established Ireland's
first towns) and no coinage. Cattle and other livestock were the primary measure and medium of wealth. The basic communal unit was
the extended family, which included everyone with blood ties hark-
ing back four generations. In Scotland this became the clan basis, existing as early as the sixth century, and formalized through surnames
and land relationship by 1057. Most clan names appeared in the tenth,

eleventh, and twelfth centuries and were traced back to Koarn and the other sons of Erc, Irish brothers establishing the kingdom of Dal Riada. Some of the claimed clan origins, like that of the Campbells, seem fictitious to historians; others hark to Norse ties (such as the MacLeods) or Norman beginnings. The clans were a corollary of the Irish *tuatha*, basic Celtic groupings encompassing social, territorial, and economic alliances, centered on kinship ties.

The geographies of Ireland and Scotland were naturally conducive to small communal arrangements; the terrains were not well suited for grandiose endeavors. Ireland was organized, physically and metaphysically, into "four fifths," now known as Ulster, Connacht, Munster, and Leinster, with Meath the center. Old Scotland divided into seven tribal provinces—Fife, Strathearn, Angus, Mar, Moray, Ross, and Caithness—corresponding to the original Pictish districts (which corresponded to the seven sons of Cruithan, the first Pictish king). Each Scottish province contributed territory to form a central district for the king, or *ri*. The provinces were ruled by *mormaors* (subkings) who appointed the High King. In the Norman period mormaors became earls, with three additional earldoms (Buchan, Monteith, and Lennox) added to the original seven provinces. These provinces were all north of the Forth and Clyde. Scotland later expanded to the southern Pictish kingdoms.

Within the clan system fairness was emphasized. In the Hebrides during the old days, for instance, fishing lines were required to be of equal length so no one had unfair advantage over anyone else. Each clan had a chief who governed the clan. Next in succession to the chief was the tanist, the chosen heir, whose duty was to hold clan lands in trust for the people. Chieftains (distinct from chiefs) were heads of houses into which the clan was divided, and the oldest chieftain had a post of honor during warfare and commanded the clan in the chief's absence. By the sixteenth and seventeenth centuries, the heir to chiefship was almost always the first son, though in previous times any suitable male in the extended family was eligible for succession, and there were often female lines of descent. Clan heirs had to prove their valor before becoming acceptable successors. The ceremony of investiture for a new chief involved building a rock cairn on which the heir stood, friends and followers circled about him. An orator (a Druid in the old days) stood beside the cairn and eulogized the heir's ancestry and deeds, making particular note of the family's acts of generosity. The heir was handed his father's sword and a white rod of authority (an ancient

Celtic symbol). A more recent rite of passage, performed by MacLeod clan chiefs beginning with Ruaraidh Mor in the 1500s, involves a huge drinking horn holding a bottle-and-a-half worth of claret. The chief-to-be must drain the horn in one draft "without setting down or falling down." The current chief performed this feat in under two minutes, maintaining family reputation.

Traditional Celtic government was not autocratic or political: the Celts were not empire builders. Historian Ward Rutherford observes that:

> Despite its essentially hierarchic nature, Celtic society did not possess the pyramidal structure of inter-connected allegiances to be found in feudal ones, where each class stood on utter dependence upon the next one above it. Here the social bond was the custom of *celsine* or cliency. . . . No sacrifice of rights or liberties was involved and the *cele* or client could freely withdraw from the arrangement. It is also significant that land tenure was by *fine* (family) and not by individual so that each family with its holding represented a lesser domain within the larger one of the *tuatha*. (It is of course the reason why clan areas are to be found in Scotland and Ireland). Because of this the extent of tribal territory would also be decided by the number of *celes* constituting it, each of whom was basically an independent unit. As a grouping of at least theoretically free entities, mutual agreement in all decisions would be essential and there are good reasons for thinking that this was far from being a pure formality. Everyone in Celtic society was not only conscious of, but exercised his rights and freedoms. . . . Indeed, it is as a result of this that the Celtic regions proved so resistant to feudalism and in many instances avoided it altogether.

In early Scotland, royalty, and aristocrats having many clients, reinforced their presences and spread out household consumer needs by traveling often to visit clients. This was also part of the Celtic tradition of hospitality. There were organized mechanisms within this social-economic system whereby tribute and taxes were collected and distributed, agriculture regulated, and specialized activities and production of prestige goods were supported by surplus resources. These goods were used to create and build upon social alliances and position. At the top of Celtic society were the chiefs and their families; next came Druids, bards, skilled artisans, and warriors, followed by freemen (mostly farmers), then bondsmen (and slaves). Individual position in the hierarchy was not fixed; Druids, artists, warriors, and so on conceivably could originate from lowborn families. Position was often a matter of talent and endeavor—the Celtic roots of the American Dream.

In Ireland, pre-Christian Celtic society maintained an egalitarian system of medical care. Physicians, both female and male, performed such operations as brain surgery, Caesarian section, suturing, and amputation, with only qualified practitioners allowed to give care. These practitioners were required, in Ireland, to train students and to give treatment to whoever was in need. They also had to compensate patients whose conditions worsened because of physician's ignorance or negligence. The physician was only paid if there was a cure. Each Irish territory maintained a hospital situated and operated under strict hygienic guidelines. Irish doctors, beginning hundreds of years before Christ, were renowned healers, many of them coming from family lineages of physicians.

In Celtic families, fosterage was commonly practiced, weaving bonds between clans and encouraging closeness between unrelated individuals, balancing the partisan tendency toward feuding. In Scotland it was said, "Affectionate to a man is a friend, but foster brother is as life blood of his heart."

My own, present-day family is well-mannered and tactful: Crudens don't vent emotions in dispute or violence. Elizabeth Grant (1797–1827), in her autobiography, describes characteristics mirrored in my upbringing. "The Highlanders are fatalists; what is to be, must be; what happens must be borne patiently. . . . They feel keenly too; all their affections are warm and deep; still, they are not paraded. A tranquil manner is part of their breeding, composure under all circumstances essential to the dignity of character common to all the race."

Still, in my family there have been occasions of a quiet type of feuding. Though my grandfather, Percival Graeme Cruden, and one of his brothers, Burgess Alexander, were law partners, my grandfather stopped speaking to his brother Burt because of a moral issue.

Burt fell in love with a dying woman named Isabelle who, on her deathbed, begged Burt to marry her sister, who had inherited syphilis. Burt did so and was good to his wife, but given the circumstances, it wasn't much of a marriage passion-wise. They adopted a son. Burt

fell in love again, however, with a woman I recall from my childhood—Grace MacDonald—and "took up" with her. This was when
my grandfather stopped speaking to his brother and business partner, the silence continuing for years.

But differences are not as important as kinship. Clan is a precinct
for learning and testing loyalty, for conformity and singularity, belonging and becoming. My family, geographically spread around,
stays in touch, accessible but never imposing. Yet there is a ferocious
protective instinct; we were raised to look after one another.

In early Scotland there were perhaps twenty-nine clans, the largest being Campbell, MacKenzie, Duke of Atholl, and MacDonald. In
later years the list of official clans became far lengthier. Border families were sometimes referred to as clans or bracketed with Highlanders in various acts of Parliament; they and other Lowland families
differed from Highlanders in language and ethnic background, though
most Highland clans also had Norse, Flemish, or Norman bloodlines
intermarried with the Celtic. Each Scottish clan had a particular battle
cry and a badge worn on clansmen's wool bonnets. The badges usually depicted a plant or flower totem and the battle cries were often
the name of a landscape feature of the clan's territory. Individual clan
tartans are a modern invention; badges were how clans traditionally
displayed their distinctions.

Clan chiefs had life-and-death power over their clanspeople, but
the Scottish judicial system was administered by *brehons*, or judges,
hereditary posts assisted by councils of twelve to fourteen members.
Arbitration was the primary legal process for civil and criminal disputes, and there was no appeal. It was a system based on reparation
rather than retribution, a basis modern society would do well to ex-
amine. The councils met on hilltops or in level circles surrounded by
higher ground. Remnants of the *moothills* can still be seen in Scotland.
It was the land, the outdoors, that was the literal context and orientation for all aspects of Celtic life: stone cairns or stone footprints were
a traditional element of Celtic coronations; shrieking stones were the
land's vote, legendary in conjunction with Celtic kingship.

Originally in Celtic society, Druids were the judges for all public
and private disputes. They had intertribal jurisdiction—indicative of
basic Celtic solidarity—and operated from a legal system common to
Ireland, Wales, Britain, and Scotland. Irish sources claim that this ancient legal tradition was codified in 714 B.C. The brehons, or *brieves*,
were extensions of that system (which included both male and fe-

male judges). Law was enforced through threat of being ostracized. (Boycotting, a form of ostracizing, originated in Ireland.)

Ritual fasting or hunger strike, *troscad,* was another tool of Celtic justice, used to establish or compel observation of individual rights and often employed by lower ranking people against those of higher rank. The plaintiff usually fasted in front of the defendant's house, thus pressuring the defendant to submit to arbitration. Hunger striking was extensively used by Irish prisoners against the English in more modern times, and has become a worldwide method of non-violent protest.

Because Celtic social systems were deeply entwined with the relationship of individuals to clan, and clan to land, those systems were particularly vulnerable to changes in policy toward land. In the eleventh century, England's saintly Princess Margaret became wife of Scotland's King Malcolm Ceanmore, and influenced him in opposition to the traditional clan system. (She also pushed for a celibate clergy.) As a result, the Gaelic system of relationship to land was modified, a change having profound impact on Scotland's future. Under the new system land passed into the king's possession, to be parceled out as he fancied.

There were two distinct concepts of heritage: one was the prescriptive right to settle in territories over which chiefs customarily provide protection; the other, which was feudal in nature, turned chiefs into gentry by granting land charters from the king—making chiefs landowners instead of clan trustees. The feudal concept was far different from the Celtic clan system, where land belonged to the whole clan and could not be disposed of by the chief, though the chief could be removed by the clan. Much conflict was produced by the attempted merger of those systems, exacerbated by a heavy influx of newcomers during that period, and by the ending, in 1286, of the purely Celtic line of monarchs. Ever after that, as chiefs became landed nobility, often with interests on both sides of the Border, there were clans and families on both sides of all confrontations with England.

It was this creation of elite landowners that eventually undermined attempts to preserve or regain Scottish autonomy from England and its influences on the behavior of nobles and chiefs. In the late 1700s, during the Clearances, the old system of land tenure succumbed completely. John McPhee, in *The Crofter and the Laird,* writes:

After Culloden, the surviving chiefs become landowners—

lairds—in the modern sense. The clan ideas of familial possession and patriarchal responsibility fell away. The clansmen became tenants, and the chiefs, in the course of things,
sold them out. . . . Before long, absentee owners heavily out-
numbered resident lairds. To the new lairds it was clear
enough that their lands were more profitable under sheep
than under people, and so the people had to go. . . . In the late
18th and early 19th centuries, the glens were virtually swept
clean of these people—the residue of the clans—and the lairds,
in removing them, apparently felt no moral encumbrances.
Their factors—general agents, business managers, collectors
of rent—went around to the black houses and gave people
notice of their evictions, and at the appointed times the walls
of the house were pulled down and the thatch and wooden
beams were destroyed by flame. Families sat on hillsides,
often in snow or rain, and watched their homes burn out. For
700 years, torches had called the clans together in time of need,
and now torches cleared the glens. The sheep were brought
in by the hundreds of thousands, and to some of the retreat-
ing population they became known as "the laird's four-footed
clansmen."

The first time I went to Scotland, at age twenty-one, I was alone.
Living for some months in Europe, I endured surgery in a London
hospital and afterward fled north in a rental car—the homing instinct
of the wounded. I drove without map or destination. The landscape
was captivating: hills and lochs, narrow roads, a thrift of intrusion—
no billboards; no arrogant, slovenly sprawl of asphalt and fast food/
used car/shopping marts. The rental car was relinquished in
Inverness. Seeing so much open water and being ignorant of place, I
believed I had reached the top of Scotland. Regardless of this inaccu-
racy, I was in an end-of-the-line mood and Inverness reflected it, grey
and chilly. The tourist shops attracted, then offended, with their willingness to exploit the desire to substantiate heritage, to bear some
small emblem—a tartan scarf, a celtic brooch—affirming and embodying continuity.

Abandoning the search for portable Celtic culture, I turned to the
land, particularly—and predictably—nearby Loch Ness, and visited
the encampment of one of the more tenacious and well-known seekers of the Loch Ness monster. He had been installed at his site a long

time and showed me his purported monster photographs, news articles, research equipment, and other pseudoscientific flimflam. He reminded me of an intense professional special-services officer who has never actually been in the military.

Well, to my mind, of course there was a Loch Ness monster. But scientific investigation seemed undignified and fruitless. A Loch Ness monster is a Celtic entity, which means proof is irrelevant, possibly intrusive. Evidence gives an illusion of knowing, when the only understanding of a Loch Ness monster is in the way imagination relates to an ancient shadowy being. Realizing this, I felt better about giving up on cultural tokens. If kilt pins and bagpipes and lassies doing the Highland fling had become tourist commodities, I would have to reach deeper to touch what went into making me who I am.

Lessons of clan, tribe, or extended family are experiences of interdependence and what it entails. Clan is an ecosystem, an enlargement of self-interest vital to maturation of character and consciousness. Without it, orientation remains egoic, shortsighted, grasping, and small-minded.

Modern nuclear families are stunted versions of clans—parents trying to fulfill too many roles, children having too few resources. They are island habitats. Society malnourishes and insidiously isolates people from one another through stratifying children in schools, marginalizing elders, demeaning women and girls, and separating work from communalness, among other fragmentizing strategies. Two deliberate ways the United States government originally disrupted American Indian tribalism were by removing children from their homes and communities—sending them to boarding schools—and, like Scotland's King Malcolm, promoting greedy concepts of property. It only took one generation for Native culture, like the Gaelic way of life, to irrevocably change.

Tribalism has its pitfalls, certainly, if it becomes a closed system used to exclude, stifle, cause strife, or promote notions of superiority. Examples of these abound—the very word *clannish* has negative connotations. But clan is a step in expanding connections and responsibility to larger context. The Lakota phrase "All our relations" or "We are all relations" is a key reminder of the ultimate clan or tribe that includes everyone.

In the light of both relationship and uniqueness it is dismaying to repeatedly hear generalizing refrains such as "you whites," as though Caucasians have no distinct and various families, tribes, heritages, and ways of life; as though we are a facelessly monolithic, karmically damaged tide of oppressors, brandishing guns in one hand and crosses in the other. Children of all races and ethnicities should be able to grow up knowing and honoring what is particularly good in their heritages, and respecting both the differences and commonalities encountered in the world. Both otherness and lack of distinction can be blindfolds obscuring capacity to really see one another or know ourselves.

Whites in America are so used to both status and isolation as conquerors that it is hard sometimes for people to relate emotionally to a depth of feeling about heritage and ancestral homeland. I used to often encounter a blankness of response when attempting to speak about the sense of relief and gladness experienced whenever I visited Scotland. In America I was aware, not only of being a "white on Native land," but also of the guardedness with which I lived amid a society that marginalizes beliefs and values I cherished.

Chopping cedar kindling outside my house on First Thought Mountain on a stunning February day, the sky, a clear, brilliant turquoise, the snow dazzling and pure. The green of fir and pine seemed to flow downslope from the curving ridges above me, into the creek's narrow glen. Looking west over the valley to the mountains beyond, I saw an eagle cruising lone and easy over the river. It was the American West in all its grand, elemental beauty.

What is this yearning for Scotland? I asked myself, as the ax split a cedar round from a tree toppled in a previous winter's storm, releasing the clean, heady scent of the wood. "You whites"—the refrain returned to mind. It has effect, hearing that one's people are intruders. For centuries my ancestors were buried in this ground, but, regardless, forever we are the strangers, the bad guests. Our behavior has indeed not always been admirable, but where is home if not on this mountain that holds me kindly amid its rocks and trees, among its deer and bears and coiling rattlers? Where, if not on land I sweat and bleed upon; on land whose sanctity, endurance, and renewal I cry for, pray for, my own sense of well-being woven into its roots, held in its stone? The ax cleaves the wood, two halves falling, parting ways. For more than twenty years I have lived in the countryside away from towns, usually without electricity, phone, or running water: living with the land.

"Whites," "new-agers" and "hippies" as labels are often backhanded failures at discerning, reconsidering, or allowing clearer identification. Celtic men traditionally wore their hair long, and often braided; Scot chiefs wore eagle feathers; Celts made offerings to trees and sacred waters. Why is it that long hair on a white male now makes him a hippie or a Native wanna-be? How has it been determined that a white person conversing with trees or honoring the spirit in water is a "new-ager"? There is something deadend in appellations that both exclude people from what is indigenous to this land and ignore their connectedness to age-old customs and spirituality from their own pasts.

Celtic Americans going to Ireland, Scotland, Wales, Brittany, and Cornwall to renew or explore ancestral connections sometimes face derision or unwelcome in the very places they have been urged to "go home" to. Celtic Americans, seeming arrogant or presumptuous, are often not embraced as long-lost relatives in those lands. It is difficult for locals to feel much in common with Americans having leisure and money for travel, or with those unconcerned with the virtues and behaviors valued by local people, or who do not know and suffer the particular hardships of Celts left amid the destruction of their old way of life. It doesn't help that wealthy Americans have joined the ranks of rich English, Arabs, Danes, and so on who are buying Scottish islands, estates, and castles, using the Highlands as a private playground.

Jim Hewitson, in *Tam Blake & Co.: The Story of the Scots in America*, says:

> American Scots are tied emotionally—some would say oversentimentally—to Scotland, or more accurately to the rediscovered clan culture. Paradoxically, the majority of resident Scots do not share this clan consciousness, this "Celtomania," and operate in a world of unemployment, urban neglect, and seemingly out-of-touch government. . . . Scotland is a nation still, a complex people with complex aspirations, not a theme park. . . . The Scots descendants need somehow to be bound closer to the practical realities of present-day Scotland so that the country's ambitions may be better transmitted and understood by the country at large. Scotland, for centuries as much a state of mind as a genuine political entity, has been

and remains the spiritual home for countless Americans, and these links—arguably in need of some fine-tuning—are inescapable and important.

It was well after dark when the man delivering firewood to my house chugged up the mountain, his pickup sagging under a pyramid of eight-foot lengths of larch. I went outside, abandoning dinner preparations, knowing the man appreciated presence and small talk while unloading. He muscled heavy logs out of the truck, practiced movements, deft for the weight involved. In the darkness the drag and thud, rasp of breath, and clank of boots on metal truckbed seemed amplified, but there was an ease to it also, and to the spare, amiable talk between us. I stood, hands jammed in pockets, sometimes shifting position to let logs rumble past. The man talked about his job, his back, his truck's broken muffler—had I come across a piece of it in the driveway? He told me about the cougar encountered at a logging site, how he instinctively veered toward it, magnetized, wanting to see how close he could get—and at the same time reviewing how to fight it off with the 40-inch chainsaw he carried, should the cat take offense at his approach. It is typical, this mixture of attraction to and destruction of wildlife. The man had little book-learning but was a keen observer of life, and the conclusions he spoke of were often psychologically sophisticated, regardless of limited vocabulary.

I have been around people like this man most of my adult life: rural people—many of them bigoted, mean, and physically tough; yet also philosophical, with humor both crass and subtle; nit-picky but not quitters; pragmatically helpful. As a rural person I am part of their world, accepted on their terms, given some leeway because I am not, after all, rich, citified, incompetent, or lacking in challenges to which they can relate. These people are simpler to live around than either the middle-class neighbors I grew up among, or members of the counter-culture I later encountered. Why is this? Perhaps because rural people engage in direct relationship with the land. Whatever that relationship's ills, the engagement is not distant or metaphorical. They are people with a sense of place and habitat, a reality rooted in the land, in the power of locality.

I found an even deeper sense of place among people in rural Scotland, and fell into a similar ease of relationship with working-class people there, with whom I could banter and discuss simple everyday concerns as well as philosophical questions. What intrigued me in

Scotland, however, was how interested and well-versed working-class people were in matters of history and culture. An Ayrshire biker who had been kicked out of school waxed eloquent about the nuances of a bagpipe competition and sharply quizzed me about my genealogical relationship to Robert Burns; an ex-cop fluently described intricacies of Celtic clan balances; a hostel owner in the Hebrides enlightened me about elements of Gaelic poetry. Small talk with Scots demanded a degree of thoughtfulness and nimble intellect with which I often was slow to match pace.

Alexander Carmichael, writing in the nineteenth century, had a similar observation:

> The unlettered cottar who knew no language but his own, who came into contact with no one but those of his own class, his neighbor of the peat bog, and who had never been out of his native island, was as polite and well-mannered and courteous as Iain Campbell, the learned barrister, the world-wide traveler, and the honored guest of every court in Europe. Both were at ease and at home with one another, there being neither servility on one side nor condescension on the other.

Anne Ross also recognized this, in *Everyday Life of the Pagan Celts:*

> As a people, the Celts have always had a strong natural feeling for learning and intellectual exercise. . . . One can today carry on a conversation about literature and languages and philosophy with a Gaelic or Irish or Welsh postman or cottar which would put many a university-educated outsider to shame. . . . What we know of the present-day cottar and crofter in the remaining Celtic regions does then suggest very strongly that their similarly placed Celtic ancestors in the pagan Celtic world had a comparable reverence for the mind and the spirit and all their cultural manifestations—a regard which the humble nature of their material circumstances could in no way influence. . . . The buffoon, the empty-headed handsome hero, the lovely but stupid goddess, these could not have been tolerated in Celtic society on any level.

Unposturing conversation nourished me in Scotland, talk that knowledgeably spanned wide-ranging subjects, evidence of a people rooted not only in locality but in a rich depth of indigenous culture, the resonance of which my neighbors in America lacked. "America doesn't have a culture yet, other than consumerism; it's still in the formative process," I said to an islander from Skye. "That's what we think about America too," the Scot replied, "though I wasn't going to say so."

Sometimes I imagine history reversing like a quickly rewinding video: the Lakota zooming backward to North Carolina; the Hopi making lightning-fast migrations; Spaniards reverse speedboating to Europe; Navajo zipping back over the Bering Strait; the Mayflower bounding in fast reverse over the waves, the Cherokee perhaps rocketing back to the Pleiades. Where we all come from seems a complex thing to ponder: Is home a land tenure defined by duration, or by heart? Is it, like clan, something born into—bonds inherited and nurtured over generations—or can it be also like marriage, the matedness of love, affinity's embrace?

I picked up the two halves of the log I had split, a tree divided through its center, rings that were now only half complete. Beautiful land I stood on; beautiful Scotland, my native ground. My son learned Highland dancing in college; at night, by the woodstove, I played Celtic songs on my guitar. Not much was said about heritage in our household when I was growing up, though my grandfather once told my sister that our family is related to Robert the Bruce. Heritage was innately felt, however, the sound of bagpipes stirring each of us the same, an unspoken, fierce welling in the heart, both joy and pain.

In Scotland in 1997, I relied on a sense of resonance when deciding where to spend my months there. As always, the northwest Highlands and islands claimed my heart, but I felt pulled to Perthshire as well, spending weeks in the area around Crieff and Dunkeld, easily absorbed. When I talked to my father he said some of our family once lived there: heritage's language articulated through place.

The romanticizing of heritage is easy to fall prey to: a sentimentality, a nostalgia, or a glorifying pride about ancestors and their ways of life. Even easier, sometimes, is romanticizing cultures not our own that have appealing aspects—real or imagined—missing in modern life. Those images often leave out mundane or distasteful details of reality, or reconfigure reality altogether.

In the late 1800s people in the eastern United States and Europe attended Buffalo Bill Cody's Wild West Show in droves, enamored of Indians in war bonnets, beads, and buckskins, while on western reservations Native language and customs were prohibited. Practicing

Native religion was a punishable crime. In the 1800s Europeans whose forebears massacred the Druids of Anglesey and, later, converted Celtic pagans to Christianity, went through a romantic affair with druidism as well. In *The Highland Clans,* L. G. Pine writes:

> Simultaneously with the removal of the clansmen from their native glens, there began the modern movement to romanticize the Gael, a movement which within a very short time had made Highlander synonymous with Scotsman, and the so-called "garb of Old Gaul" the usual style of dress in which all manner of Scots were depicted. The Highlanders having been got rid of and sent off by shiploads to the colonies, the Highland idea was taken up with enthusiasm but without much thought.

But pride and nostalgia, and even sentimentalized, inflated versions of a cultural past, are not without value. Myths and legends carry powerful teachings and tell stories of our relationship to the cosmos. Likewise, there are important dreams of beauty and honor within cultural idealizations. What we can imagine we sometimes can, and perhaps will, enact. A vision of what was good and what inspired greatness vitalizes the continuity of goodness and inspiration.

Severance from the past, from elders, from the old stories, from wider context, from the deep loam of ancestry, produces ungrounded generations whose orientations are often dreamless and resentful. Indeed, there is tribal warfare, ethnic fighting, all those ugly ills of separation that feed on pride and cultural distinctions. And indeed, many people—perhaps most people—have so many bloodlines woven into their pasts that distinction may be an affectation or arbitrary matter of upbringing or preference. But there is an imperative to nourish a richness of cultural expression. If we cannot do this we endanger our "gene pool" of societal potential in the same way we have already imperiled the earth's essential biological diversity. In *The Indigenous Voice in World Politics,* Franke Wilmer writes:

> What sets worlds in motion is the interplay of differences, their attractions and repulsions. Life is plurality, death is uniformity. By supressing differences and peculiarities, by eliminating different civilisations and cultures, progress weakens life and favors death. The idea of a stable civilisation for

everyone, implicit in the cult of progress and technique, impoverishes and mutilates us. Every view of the world that becomes extinct, every culture that disappears, diminishes a possibility of life.

Global well-being rests on differences; it is a paradox with which we must come to terms.

What are some of the attributes making Celts distinct?

The ancient Celts did not orient to central authority or political leadership. Power abided in individual fitness as part of collective resources of clan. Frank Delaney, in *The Celts,* writes:

> The Celts' great and ceaseless migrations predicated and epitomized physically their political posture: the freedom of all movement, intellectual, social, environmental, artistic, had always been too important to accept any ordered enclosures such as the bureaucratic processes of the Roman Empire. . . . In modern times, and allowing for pretentiousness, the cultural revivals of the 'Celtic Fringe' represents this refusal to participate with the conqueror.

In Ireland, kings could not become or remain kings unless they were strong, just, and without disfigurement. They had to be suitable mates for Ériu, the land that was also Goddess. If a king was cruel, faltering, or capricious, the land declined and the people's welfare suffered. This association of good kings with good harvests remained intrinsic to Celtic consciousness well into modern times. The Celts had little tolerance for leaders lacking qualities considered important: generosity, perspicacity, vigor, courage, fairness. There were sometimes up to a hundred kings at once in old Ireland. It was not monarchy as we tend to think of it; the kings were chiefs of tuatha and not above common law.

When the Sioux moved to the Great Plains of western America, families grouped into hunting bands in order to effectively follow food sources across vast areas. These hunting groups became the tribe's primary communal units and repositories of individual well-being and social bonding. Celtic tuatha and clans provided similar overall stability for the Celts, and fostered a collective rather than personal basis of prosperity and responsibility.

Early Celtic society was pastoral and agricultural. The Celts were mobile though not nomadic. They had great architectural and building skills and were also adept at metalwork, weaving, ceramics, enamel work, and jewelry making.

Their houses were circular—twenty to thirty feet in diameter—and roofed with thatch. Walls were vertical timber planks, dry stone, or wattle and daub. Doors were framed with oak and walls caulked with moss or resin; there were tongue-and-groove panels inside, and joints covered with extra planks for weather-tight quarters.

Storage pits the Celts used for their high-protein, high-yielding strains of grain were tested by modern researchers who found a spoilage rate of less than 2 percent. This rate matched or bettered those found with modern grain-storage systems. The Celts grew oats, barley, wheat, and rye as well as vegetables such as kale, peas, beans, cabbages, and (later) turnips. They utilized wild foods—fungi, nuts, fruits, herbs, and honey—and their cattle, goats, and sheep were raised as much for dairy as for meat. The Celts particularly cherished horses (and horse racing). Rutherford notes that "Wherever they settled, the Celts brought the benefit of improved agriculture and animal husbandry. . . . Almost all words in Latin connected with horses and horse management are Celtic loan words."

But there was no private land ownership; there were no towns or jails, no preoccupation with buildings and material permanence, no written records. Systems of clientship and cattle leasing gave opportunity for some of the poor to improve their standing; though it was far from perfect—life was very hard for the poor—there was both mobility and security through the layers of social structure. The land's resources were held in common; they were not the property of privileged individuals. Brehon law was specific about use of natural resources, protecting future abundance. These ancient law tracts—detailed, exhaustive, but also bequilingly poetic—*precisely* listed what could be taken from forest, loch, and burn. Depredation was not tolerated. The concept of commonality of resource is deeply embedded in Celtic sensibility and has not been uprooted despite the passage of centuries and the impositions of feudalism.

In Celtic society the entire tuath was accountable for any honor price or penalty owed by an individual. Emphasis on collective responsibility, and recognition of an interdependent nature of reality, balanced the flamboyance and touchy willfulness also characteristic of Celts. It was neither a society that subsumed the individual nor one that isolated individuality from collective accountability.

It was the Celts' resistance to authoritarian concepts, however, that allowed the Romans to conquer Britain—though Rome never tackled Ireland or made headway into Highland Scotland. As with the American Indians' struggle with the United States army, Celtic tribes were defeated who might have proven invincible had they banded together. It is an error, however, to think of the Celts as without cohesion. Anne Ross and Don Robins, in *The Life and Death of a Druid Prince*, point out that:

> The unity of Celtic society and its ultimate control rested with the "men of art," the triumvirate of learned men headed everywhere by the Druids, who were more than priests. . . . Caesar asserts that Druid power originated in Britain and that Britain remained the center of druidism. . . . For the Celts the worlds of commerce, craft, warfare, and religion were all interwoven into a dense and inextricable whole. The world of the gods as familiar and acceptable as the mundane activities of barter and battle. . . . The traditional picture of the native Britons as a disorganized and primitive community of woad-painted savages, living in huts and hovels and bowing powerlessly before the Roman advance, is demolished by the uncovering of the [Celtic gold] route, [from Ireland to Anglesey and across the British Midlands], and its druidic masters. We now see why the Romans had no need to threaten the Celt's religion. . . . The real target was the elite core of Druids who held the administrative, political, judicial, and economic keys to Celtic wealth and skill.

In A.D. 60, Romans butchered the Druids of Anglesey and cut down the sacred groves. Jean Markale, in *Women of the Celts*, says:

> The Druids represented an absolute threat to the Roman State, because their science and philosophy dangerously contradicted Roman orthodoxy. The Romans were materialistic, the Druids spiritual. For the Romans the state was a monolithic structure spread over territories deliberately organised into a hierarchy. With the Druids it was a freely consented moral order with an entirely mythical central idea. The Romans based their law on private ownership of land, with property rights entirely vested in the head of the family, whereas the

Druids always considered ownership collective. The Romans looked upon women as bearers of children and objects of pleasure, while Druids included women in their political and religious life.

The Celts left no written historical records, but their art reveals much about their character as a people. John O'Donohue, an Irish writer, says in his book *Anam Cara: A Book of Celtic Wisdom:*

> The Celtic mind was never drawn to the simple line; it avoided ways of seeing and being that seek satisfaction in certainty. The Celtic mind had a wonderful respect for the mystery of the circle and the spiral. . . . The circle never gives itself completely to the eye or to the mind but offers a trusting hospitality to that which is complex and mysterious; it embraces depth and height together. The circle never reduces the mystery to a single direction of preference. Patience with this reserve is one of the profound recognitions of the Celtic mind. . . . When the secret is not respected, the sacred vanishes.

Paul Jacobsthal describes Celtic art as ". . . refined in thought and technique, elaborate and clever, full of paradoxes, restless, puzzlingly ambiguous, rational and irrational . . ." Knot-work designs and other distinctive Celtic creations integrated a complex spiritual subtlety with compelling physical vitality. These qualities were apparent in Celtic myths and sagas as well, transcribed into written form by the first Irish monks. Jeffrey Gantz speaks of early Irish literature as ". . . romantic, idealistic, stylized, and yet vividly, even appallingly concrete." He notes the constant tension between material reality and imagination in tales that are "graphic but also magically bright and achingly beautiful." In today's Ireland, people making a living from the arts are exempt from taxation, something emblematic of Celtic priorities—what society values and encourages. Ross and Robins observe:

> The Gaelic language is one of the most difficult tongues in the world. And it is in its linguistic complexities and subtleties, rather than in its material remains, that Ireland stores the secrets of its druidic past, the lost system of philosophy and beliefs that was likened more than once by classical

observers to that of Pythagoras. Even today, the scholar, the
priest, and the poet still command high respect in Gaelic society. . . . The habit of *thought* and a tendency to favor intellectual rather than worldly pursuits still characterize the Celtic
attitude to life. Diogenes Laertius, who lived in the third century A.D. and wrote a compendium on the lives of the philosophers, comments that philosophy was widely held to be
an invention of the barbarians.

The image of Celts as philosophic lovers of art and beauty, as a naturalistic, spiritual people who were deeply sensitive, eloquent, fair, and
idealistic, seems to clash with the Celtic reputation for being fear-
lessly and ferociously inclined to dispute.

In ancient Ireland, the *fianna* was a socially accepted, organized
band of young, usually highborn, warriors, often living apart from
their own tribes. These warriors were an elite; the fianna offered an
arena for testing and honing fighting skills and for acquiring fortitude
and honor. Much of the fighting was ritualistic—single-combat prestige bouts. Delaney notes that "Grace and individualism and panache
were expected, and these, as much as the necessary technical, physical
abilities, counted toward success." Cattle raiding was a traditional activity—and often a rite of passage—carried on well into recent history.
It played a role similar to that of American Indian horse raiding, having both a practical (economic) and status-building basis.

Warfare, for the Celts, was mainly considered an individual art.
Even major battles could be settled by combat between two champions (a practice the Romans thought insane).

Greek historian Diodorus Siculus described the warm-ups to such
combats: "They loudly recite the deeds of valor of their ancestors and
proclaim their own valorous quality, at the same time abusing and
making little of their opponent and generally attempting to rob him
beforehand of his fighting spirit."

Every great family in the Highlands had a chief bard or Druid to
foretell events, decide causes, and recite genealogies and ancestral
deeds. Before battles this orator addressed the warriors, praising ancestral prowess and exhorting present fighters to valorous behavior.
Clan Donald's "Incitement to Battle on the Day of the Battle of Harlaw,
1411" is classic Celticism. Written by Lachlann Mor MacMhuirich, it
is couched entirely in the positive—it is a treatise on how to *be*. Incitement was toward embodying qualities most worthy in a warrior, to-

ward fighting "beautifully." This abides in compelling contrast to in-
doctrinations and incitements of brutal hatred used, for example, in
World War II against Jews and in the Vietnam War against the Viet
Cong.

O Children of Conn, remember
Hardihood in time of battle;
Be watchful, daring,
Be dextrous, winning renown,
Be vigorous, pre-eminent,
Be strong, nursing your wrath,
Be stout, brave,
Be valiant, triumphant,
Be resolute and fierce,
Be forceful and stand your ground,
Be nimble, valourous,
Be well-equipped, handsomely accoutered,
Be dominant, watchful,
Be fervid, pugnacious,
Be dour, inspiring fear,
Be ready for action, warrior-like,
Be prompt, warlike,
Be exceedingly fierce, recklessly daring,
Be prepared, willing,
Be numerous, giving battle,
Be fiery, fully ready,
Be strong, dealing swift blows,
Be spirited, inflicting great wounds,
Be stout-hearted, martial,
Be venomous, implacable,
Be warrior-like, fearless,
Be swift, performing great deeds,
Be glorious, nobly powerful,
Be rapid in movement, very quick,
Be valiant, princely,
Be active, exceedingly bold,
Be ready, fresh and comely,
Be exceedingly fierce, king-like,
Be eager, successful,
Be unflurried, striking excellent blows,

Be compact [in your ranks], elated,
Be vigorous, nimble-footed,
In winning the battle
Against your enemies.
O Children of Conn of the Hundred Battles,
Now is the time for you to win recognition,
O raging whelps,
O sturdy heroes,
O most sprightly lions,
O battle-loving warriors,
O brave, heroic firebrands,
The Children of Conn of the Hundred Battles,
O Children of Conn, remember
Hardihood in time of battle.

Edmund Spenser, in his "View of the Present State of Ireland," says, "I have heard some greate warriors say, that in all the services which they have seen abroad in forrayne countreys, they never saw a more comely horseman than the Irish man, nor that cometh on more bravely in his charge . . . they are very valiant and hardye, for the most part great endurours of cold, labour, hunger and all hardiness, very active and stronge of hand, very swift of foote, very vigilante and circumspect in theyre enterprises, very present in perrils, very great scorners of death."

Celtic warriors in ancient times often fought naked except for their *torcs* (metal neck bands) which had religious as well as decorative significance, and sandals. They roused themselves for battle—chanting, shouting, clattering their weapons, making a din non-Celtic foes found unnerving, and charging at their enemies in a state of sexual excitation and berserk abandon. Heat, both physical and supernatural, is often referred to in relation to Celtic warriors. Battle fire seems intrinsic to an awesome metamorphic process associated with the devastating qualities warriors invoked.

During more recent times, Scots accompanied battle advances with the terrifying skirl of bagpipes. (After 1745, playing pipes was declared by the British government an act of treason. The Scottish Court of Justice, even before that, ruled that a man carrying bagpipes was a man carrying a weapon.) Enemies of the Scots called the kilted warriors "the ladies from hell." But Pine reports that "[The Highlanders'] extreme ferocity in warfare was not paralleled in private, where the best qualities of a soldier—gentleness in peace and extreme bravery in war—were exemplified."

Ancient Celts believed in an afterlife, and probably in reincarnation; death being one of life's vagaries, not its ending. In Ross and Robins' words, "The Celts had no fear of death. This was not due to carelessness of life, nor to reckless bravado; it arose from deep and ancient inherited beliefs, taught by the Druids through countless generations . . . belief in the interweaving of the spiritual and mundane worlds so that the two could hardly be separated. . . ." Celts reportedly even accepted promissory notes from one another to be repaid in the afterlife. Dying in this world meant birth into the Otherworld just as death in the Otherworld meant birth into this one. Rolleston discusses the Celtic attitude toward rebirth:

> Thus the Irish chieftain, Mongan, who is a historical personage, and whose death is recorded about A.D. 625, is said to have made a wager as to the place of death of a king named Fothad, slain in a battle with the mythical hero Finn MacCumhal in the third century. He proves his case by summoning to his aid a *revenant* from the Other-world, Keelta, who was the actual slayer of Fothad, and who describes correctly where the tomb is to be found and what were its contents. He begins his tale by saying to Mongan, "We were with thee," and then, turning to the assembly, he continues: "We were with Finn, coming from Alba. . . ." "Hush," says Mongan, "it is wrong of thee to reveal a secret." The secret was, of course, that Mongan was a reincarnation of Finn.
>
> But the evidence on the whole shows that the Celts did not hold this doctrine at all in the same way as Pythagoras and the Orientals did. Transmigration was not, with them, part of the order of things. It might happen, but in general it did not; the new body assumed by the dead clothed them in another, not in this world, and so far as we can learn from any ancient authority, there does not appear to have been any idea of moral retribution connected with this form of the future life. It was not so much an article of faith as an idea which haunted the imagination, and which, as Mongan's caution indicates, ought not to be brought into clear light.

The head was seen by Celts as the seat of the soul. Celtic warriors liked to take the heads of their opponents; it was not unheard of, in the old days, for heads of particularly powerful enemies to be kept, preserved in cedar or walnut oil, or positioned on posts or stones or in niches, even to be fastened over doorways. Sometimes severed heads were worn around waists or secured to chariots during battle.

Heads played a significant role in Celtic myths, sometimes offering prophecy, conversation, wisdom, or advice. They were considered threshold guardians. Celtic reverence for heads and what they signify was further seen in the profusion of wood and stone carved heads used in shrines and as religious offerings.

My mother, Barbara, and my son and I spent two weeks in 1988 driving around Scotland, tenting in mown, pasturelike caravan parks, examining the faces of chiefs in portraits hung inside castle walls, and hiking through remnants of the great Caledonian pine forest. In Scotland my mother found a human context in which she felt at ease— people who liked to walk and watch birds. They were courteous in a gallant but practical way; observant, rigorous, astute.

Emerging from Gatwick Airport on arrival from the United States, blinking in the morning sun after the dulling hibernation and disorienting time-zone shuffle of transatlantic flight, I suddenly realized my mother and son were looking to me, the experienced traveler, for leadership. It was like a jab in the ribs—"Hey you, what now?" I had become the fulcrum amid three generations; our travels were referent to this balance, unlike the end-of-the-line feeling I had journeying alone to Scotland fifteen years earlier.

I drove; Barbara was tucked in the backseat with our biscuits, cornflakes, strawberries, and other provisions, keeping a journal of adventures and impressions and remarking on salient features of scenery. She has an eye, both technical and artistic, for pattern, detail, and significance. Because of her, we saw and considered things that would otherwise be missed. Beside me, in the passenger seat, rode Gabriel, tall at thirteen, stag slender, eager for castles and Scottish landscapes, an indefatigable companion.

We detoured to Stonehenge, Glastonbury, and Tintagel. Each of us found something of resonance in those over-touristed but still enigmatic places where history and imagination abide together. There is an ancient dignity that endures despite attempts at either demystification or exploitation. In Celtic Cornwall I wrote a poem:

My Son at Tintagel

Sits as he does, a wildflower
stem between his fingers,
*   looking down the coast*
*   as waves surge and clouds move*
inland in migrating herds.
He sits in windy sunlight
*   on cliffs whose quartz veins*
*   watch tirelessly white*
the patterns of gulls between
cliff and ruined castle walls,
*   one birthed from the other*
*   in times when sons*
wore swords. He sits
as he does, fine-boned
*   as a prince, and the rocks*
*   seem to know the weight*
of him pacing the echoes,
setting forth and always
*   returning.*

Barbara, at my birth, wanted to name me after the Isle of Skye. My father objected, saying, "You can't saddle a child with a name like that." In 1952 Americans gave their girl children names like Nancy, Deborah, and Lynn—not Skye. (The island is reputedly named after Scothach, the legendary woman warrior and seer). A generation later saw kids answering to Sunshine, Cheyenne, Shakti; my mother has always been behind or ahead of the times.

On Skye, Barbara, Gabriel, and I tented in a quiet, weedy field with a few other campers. I went for a walk, looking for a water spigot at which to fill a jug. A wiry local lad about seven years old dogged my heels, pushing his bike as he kept me company with a steady stream of chatter. His volubility was startling—the most words I had ever heard at once from a Scot. I was grateful for his friendliness and wanted to reciprocate, but the problem was, though he was surely speaking English, I could understand hardly a word. He may as well have been speaking Gaelic (and possibly could). It seemed that he was carrying on about a favorite television program, thinking I should be familiar with it. Maybe it was an American show. It struck me that, on one hand, though I was so remote from Highland accents and Scots' vernacular, because of my lifestyle I was also quite removed from America's cultural medium, the TV.

We visited Dunvegan, Clan MacLeod's castle on Skye, continuously occupied by a succession of MacLeod chiefs for over seven hundred years, though the current chief (it is muttered) spends much of his year in London. In the castle basement was a stone carved with esoteric Pictish symbols, very old. The plaque beside it said that the meaning of the symbols is unknown, though significance appeared disconcertingly plain to me. The stone looked lonely in the basement—especially with that plaque beside it. I tracked down Gabriel and showed him the engraved stone, which seemed to perk up under our attention. I did too, feeling less isolated from the past.

Customs of hospitality were absolutely adhered to during the clan era. Hospitality, and marriage and fosterage alliances, kept the clan system from degrading into endlessly spiraling feuds. Laws of hospitality necessarily held for even bitter enemies; these were sacred tenets of conduct and honorable relationship, the bedrock of society, of society's consensus and order. One of the blackest events in Celtic memory was the betrayal of hospitality by a member of Clan Campbell who, as a guest, led the murdering of thirty-eight slumbering MacDonald men, women, and children as a favor to King William. A piper still plays in the pass of Glencoe, the Glen of Weeping, every day as a memorial of this event. In the Highlands, even in the poorest home, there was and is no hesitation in offering hospitality and sharing whatever food or drink can be produced. The traditional custom of holding aside a portion of the meal "for the man on the hill" (the chance guest) underlines the important role hospitality played in Celtic life. I found this hospitality present in modern day Scotland. Hiking on the Isle of Eigg with a man who had grown up there, my friend Robin and I were advised not to bother packing a lunch. Indeed, during numerous stops along the road to chat with local folk, we were plied with snacks and drink, along with wry bits of island gossip.

Three gray-haired women I met from Aberdeenshire, while on Skye, warmly insisted I come visit them during my next pilgrimage to Cruden Bay. "If I'm not home just come in and make yourself some tea," one of these women told me, and I could see she meant it. Hospitality is not to be shrugged off. I was with friends visiting Scotland one year when we dropped in on the rehearsal of a local Gaelic choir on Skye. During the choir's break, tea and biscuits were swiftly conjured and my friends and I invited to partake. It was late in the evening, nearing bedtime. In consideration of our bladders we declined refreshments. The choir members were dismayed, cast into baffled anxiety; we had committed a great social error. Rescue came in the form of an elderly woman who solved the problem by simply handing us cups of tea and plates of biscuits, which we repentently consumed.

The Irish, back in their mythohistory, gave one of their kings the pink slip (by way of satire) for his bad manners. It was said that he "left their knives ungreased"—meat being the food with which hosts properly treated their guests. This king was replaced with someone better representing Celtic values. Power and noble bloodlines were not in themselves sufficient qualifications for Celtic leadership.

The Romans described Celts as boastful but demonic in battle; childlike; fond of jewelry, color, feasting, and hunting; remarkable in their bardic poetry, cordial in their hospitality, and unexpectedly sophisticated in their artistic skills. (They were superior in this to the Romans.) All this sounds similar both in particulars and in condescending overtone to how American Indians were perceived by many colonials. Observations like those made by colonizers seldom give pause for consideration of what comparisons form the basis of impressions of people who seem different from ourselves. That pause for consideration may yield insight into both the observer's culture and the observed's, beyond pigeonholing descriptions that prove ultimately dismissive—a dismissiveness that exclaims, "What a strangely gorgeous flower," as the flower is crushed underfoot.

There is a story in an old Irish text about a visit one of the *sidhe* (magical Otherworldly folk) made to Saint Columcille. In this story, the Christian leader drew the sidhe fellow aside, out of hearing of the other monks, to question the sidhe about the mysteries of heaven and earth. Afterward the sidhe vanished, and though the monks begged to know what Columcille had learned, he would only say it was not proper that men be told. Proinsias MacCana, when relating this story, comments, "And as for those heavenly and earthly mysteries which were revealed to the saint, one wonders whether they may not indeed have some bearing upon the origin and final destiny of the world." The foot descends: the blossom is crushed. It continues today, to many indigenous cultures and all they hold.

From historian Delaney:

The Celts, tribal and traveling, could never have established a political entity. They fought too frequently among themselves; in a kindred system too intensive and introverted, the collective personality remained too individual, too undisciplined, too lacking in organization, to permit the global ambition necessary to found an empire. . . . The Norman system of feudalism, with a central power deriving from the kingship and government, dealt the final blow to a society which had been founded on the triumph of the individual. Where the Roman Empire had been a machine which cut deep into the civilization, changing the face of great tracts of it. And where the Norse invaders had been a series of detonations which fundamentally altered the sites where they exploded, the Normans moved straight and smooth through all existing structures. . . . In Wales, the alliances formed with Alfred the Great weakened the chances of any future resistance of England, or movement towards monarchical or political independence. . . . In Scotland, from the eleventh century onwards, a centralized kingship pushed such Celts as then remained farther and farther from the centre of power. . . . Any lingering Celtic aspiration or influence ended with "The 45". . . . The Welsh were eventually conquered and assimilated. On Man, the last native speaker of Manx Gaelic—bilingual with English—died in 1974.

While poring over old books and letters in Portree's Regional Council Library on Skye, I overheard two academics discussing traditional culture's demise in Scotland, and what little is being done to preserve it. They talked of English people, English gardens, English culture filling the Highlands (one-sixth of Skye's current population was born in England); of commercialized, romanticized remnants of Scottish culture; and of international influences, particularly American. Because of cinema and newspapers, by the 1920s Americanization became a bigger threat than Anglicization. I heard many Scots still expressing concern over this.

The academic in the library complained that elderly Highlanders talked and talked about the old days and old ways, but as soon as a tape recorder was brought out they clammed up. I wanted to say to him that Celtic tradition is oral, it lives in the vital relationship between speaker and listener. Scottish poet Sorley MacLean writes of ". . . the humanity / that the ocean could not break / that a thousand years has not / severed." "Loss is inevitable," the academic whose job is preservation said to me, when I finally butted into his conversation. Is it? Perhaps only change is inevitable, though maybe change and loss amount to the same thing if choices are not made giving priority to what is valuable.

Despite unemployment and the draining away of native Highlanders, particularly its youth, population in the Highlands is projected to increase by 10,000, to 218,000 within fifteen years, and to rise to 225,000 within twenty-five years. However, many of those people will not be Highlanders—or even Scottish. James Hunter, in *On the Other Side of Sorrow: Nature and People in the Scottish Highlands*, asks:

> Can those of us living today in the Scottish Highlands—those of us who came here last week, as it were, as well as those of us who could, in principle at least, trace our descent from the Gaelic-speaking folk who came from Ireland to Argyll some fifteen centuries ago—shape our own cultural identity . . . ? Can we define the term "Highlander" in such a way that the issue of a person's ancestry becomes of much less importance than the fact that such a person lives in, works in, is committed to, this quite amazing tract of territory? And can we do all these things while still ensuring that Gaelic does not quickly join the list of many hundreds, even thousands, of languages which have become, or about to become, extinct?

As it stands, 84 percent of Scottish land is owned by 7 percent of the people. Feudalism still lives in the United Kingdom. Pinched between this reality on one hand and Americanization on the other, Scotland seems to exist in several epochs at once, a not un-Celtic state out of which the future is not easily predicted.

Much revolves around the survival of Gaelic. Culture is encoded and communicated in language. What is said in Gaelic cannot be directly and truly translated into English. A man on the Isle of Lewis in the Outer Hebrides told me he could express himself by writing a song in Gaelic in a half hour, but would struggle for days trying to compose those feelings in English. Particularly for an oral culture where words hold great power, specificity, and intricacies of communication, loss of language is loss of heritage. It is cultural amnesia. It is loss of spirit. John O'Donohue says, "When you steal a people's language, you leave their soul bewildered."

In 1997 there were only fifty-two Gaelic-speaking educational units in Scotland, where 1,578 small children carried the language's future. Twenty-five hundred children attended Gaelic playgroups. I was told that French is the language schoolchildren are encouraged to learn, particularly in secondary school. Angus Peter Campbell, in an article written for the *West Highland Free Press,* points out that:

> There are still no Gaelic primary schools in Scotland. Gaelic-medium education in secondary schools remains a joke. . . . There is still no Gaelic newspaper. . . . There is still no full Gaelic radio service. . . . What little development there exists is, one feels, increasingly geared toward learners. To be a native speaker today is to be an increasingly marginalised minority within a deprived minority, an exile within one's own community. . . . For whatever reason—and I have little doubt that most of it is the emotional consequence of having been told for generations that our language and culture was inferior—the overwhelming majority of us still fail to pass our language on to our children. There are many who are so ashamed of it that it would be like passing v.d. on to their children. . . . The future of the language has, mysteriously, been placed into the hands of the largely middle-aged men who sit on committees. The simple idea that language survives because it is spoken, mother to daughter, father to son, has been forgotten.

The only place I heard Gaelic spoken in Scotland was on the outer isles, and one day as I walked past a primary school on Skye where the staff and children use Gaelic during recess periods. It is a beautiful language with no hard, jarring sounds—I have often heard it sung—a language that softly skims, passionate and evocative. A man from Caithness in the northern Highlands told me that his parents were beaten, his mother's toes broken by schoolmasters, for speaking Gaelic. A college student from the mainland near Skye said her friends used to refer to Gaelic broadcasts as "Radio Poland" because none of them could understand what was said; only sixty-five thousand people in Scotland speak Gaelic.

But at Sabhal Mor Ostaig, the Gaelic business college on Skye, enrollment is increasing, though from only a modest fifty students to seventy. Their full-time vocational courses are augmented by a variety of short courses, concerts, and Gaelic performances available to the public during the summer. Internationally renowned bands like Capercallie and Runrig have sparked interest in Gaelic language and music, most importantly among the young. The annual *feisean* (Gaelic tuitional festivals for learning as well as performing) and the *mòd* (Gaelic competition festival) draw hundreds of musicians. When I asked a Highland Council member if he thought Gaelic would disappear from Scotland, he replied that, because of all the tremendously beautiful and appealing traditional music, the language would never completely be lost. Music is the Celtic language of survival, the strand of life through which Celtic spirit freely flows.

When I visited the northern Highlands in 1997 I found the most popular music by far was country music. This is not surprising—American country and bluegrass music originated from descendants of Scots immigrants, as did the dancing that accompanies that music. Now the direction is mirrored back to the Highlands, and many traditional musicians are collaborating with counterparts in Nashville. *Ceilidh* dancing (Scottish country dancing) was on an upsurge of popularity in 1997 as well, particularly among the young. A Glasgow girl recited to me the names of new ceilidh pubs in the city, where "You have to arrive by nine or it's too crowded to get in." (Ceilidhs are Celtic-style evenings of music and conviviality.) I imagined this city girl with her nose ring, punky hair, and languid manner doing "Gay Gordon" at a ceilidh. "We used to think that stuff was just for the old folks and our parents," she said. "Now all my friends go."

My friend Robin and I went to a ceilidh too, at the sixteenth annual Highland Traditional Music Festival, part of which we had attended the previous year. It is a small enough festival that the man taking tickets at the door of Dingwall's National Hotel remembered me from the year before. "No," I protested, "you can't really remember me." He smiled. "Oh yes I do. You were only here for Friday night last year." He was right. "Maybe I'll ask you to dance later," he said.

The music never stopped all weekend; concerts and dances at night were bridged by music in the streets and pubs during the day: pipers, pennywhistlers, acapella singers, bodhran and fiddle players, accordionists. I soaked it up with every cell, experiencing the vital nourishment such music is, and the distinct communal atmosphere it creates and expresses. People we met at the festival unhesitatingly adopted us as friends—greeting us on the street, sharing their restaurant tables, buying us drinks, swinging us around the dance floor. While we were cooling off outside during a break at one of the concerts, one of these friends towed the evening's headline performer out to meet us.

Musicians in Scotland are distinctly unpretentious. They dress as unfashionably and plainly as everyone else. They banter with audiences and hang out with them after performances. Musicians who sell out large city venues are also often found playing in remote village pubs. Celtic music is the people's—the land's—music, but it is no longer insular: I heard bluegrass bagpipes, Celtic rock, Celtic reggae, Celtic salsa, Celtic jazz, Celtic blues, something called "acid croft," and Celtic country music, as well as traditional and folk music.

On the festival's final night we danced past midnight, then were persuaded to stay after the band packed up, sitting with our Highland friends, drinking whiskey, passing a guitar around, sharing songs and the warm lively conversation Scots refer to as "crack." One man hauled out bagpipes and gave us a tune. With a 6:30 A.M. wake-up time looming ahead of us, Robin and I finally tore ourselves away from this congenial circle. Our hands were shaken (and in one case gallantly kissed), invitations extended, and we left with the hard reluctance inevitable to all partings in Scotland, where patterns of leaving and lament cut deep into the heart of experience, and memory is insufficient consolation.

Clan is an intimacy—like reaching out to steady and orient oneself by touching familiar objects. If relationship is too confining it strangles natural growth and exploration. If it is too loose, individuals suffer disconnection and harm. There needs to be healthy interdependence. When I left my parents' house after high school I stayed with my brother Alex. It followed a period of crisis and Alex offered what seemed like effortless acceptance. Never would I find an easier adult with whom to share a house. Afterward, when I went to Europe, he wrote as he used to when I was in summer camp; letters that calmed— they were humorous and thoughtful. Years later, Alex and his wife put my son Gabriel through college.

Twice my sister Leigh and her husband provided me with vehicles; Alex gave me his old car to drive when I was a midwife. After my son's car accident my sister bailed us out of financial disaster, sending her savings; Leigh has always been someone I can turn to for emotional support.

Stuart, my younger brother, was one of the few people I confided in during teenhood's isolation. Close in age, we tried to help each other—sometimes helping each other into trouble. Sometimes one giving the other perspective; sometimes there was the help of simply sharing similar contexts of experience. I trust all my siblings.

George, my father, became a friend when I crucially needed him, doing what he could to let me know he cared. He parted with his beloved VW bug when I left home. He took me fishing, passing on the mysteries of the outboard. When my husband and I looked for land out west, George and his wife, Louise, invited us to live at their place for a year.

My mom, Barbara, was a staunch friend also. Living frugally on a small income, still she sent money. Twice we were land partners, and occasionally we were traveling companions. During eight years of midwifery she was the one who watched over Gabriel while I dashed off to deliver babies at three o'clock in the morning. My first husband, my son, and I camped in her cabin's living room for several weeks after our place burned to the ground. She didn't say a word about the loss of her uninsured antiques and family jewelry, stored with us and destroyed.

Clan is a reality of support that demonstrates how to live rightly by acts of love and constancy of acceptance. Clan is relationship that nourishes a capacity to recognize and respond to connection, giving mutual strength.

In modern life, people often replace or augment a clan of blood relationship with a clan of friends. Within friendship is sometimes found opportunity for a second family. Wounds and negative patterns from childhood may find venue for healing amid a compassionate circle of friends. These clans of affinity can be supportive alliances and mirrors of perspective and challenge, much as can be family. But there are attributes unique to each kind of kinship; they are not altogether interchangeable, though many of the ways in which they function are similar. One of the primary differences is that family love and acceptance is (or should be) a given, not predicated on understanding, liking, or like-mindedness.

It is clear, whether buying flour at the co-op or gathering tomatoes from the garden, that well-being depends on the earth's gifts and on wise relationship with its web of life. There is nothing making existence possible or good that is not an aspect of habitat, inner and outer. It is clear, also, that life is directly upheld by the generosity of people—family and friends. Even in solitude—especially in solitude—there is keen and grateful awareness of an interdependent environment. Learning to receive, as well as to give, is a path of healing. Feelings of isolation because of unconventionality become entrenched in silence, pride, and stoicism. I have lived my adult life close to the bone. It is painful when someone hands me money I have not earned, unless I remember that it honors what is important: love, interrelationship, the valuing of spiritual priority. It is both personal and impersonal.

T. W. Rolleston tells us that "The Celt has always been a rebel against any unspiritual and purely external form of domination. It is too true that he has been over-eager to enjoy the fine fruits of life without the long and patient preparations for the harvest, but he has done and will still do infinite service to the modern world insisting that the true fruit of life is a spiritual reality, never without pain or loss to be obscured or forgotten amid the vast mechanism of a material civilization."

The castle ruins of Old Wick, a fortress on the North Sea coast, are windswept and bleak even in July. The stones are skeletal remains of what was a lonely Highland outpost. The sea churns below, seabirds wheel, long grasses flatten in the wind. It is not a much-visited place— Gabriel, Barbara, and I had it to ourselves; it took a hike to reach the ruins from the road.

We explored following individual whims, standing within the blocky foundations, wandering along the narrow arm of land extending into the sea, gray waves battering the shelving rock as they had for millennia. Each of us, in silence, imagined what it was like for the men stationed there, twelve or fourteen at a time with nothing to do but scrutinize the horizon, listen to the gulls, shiver in the wind, wait.

Gabriel sat, the grass tall around him. I located a nook amid foundation stones where the wind was diverted. Barbara found a knoll a little ways off and sat on a rock, a white gull-feather in her hand as she gazed over the North Sea. Wind, sky, stones and waves, the keening gulls; it made us silent, inward, empty. Wildflowers dipped and fluttered in the breeze. I sensed what clan meant to people living amid wilderness, amid starkness and mysterious complexity where most of what abides spoke an elemental language sometimes awful, sometimes strangely and deeply moving to the human heart.

In Michigan, when Gabriel was young, I lived on the edge of a forest with my mother as neighbor and land partner. At 3:00 one morning I woke—something was scratching at the back door. Half-asleep, thinking it was the cat, I quietly padded through the kitchen and opened the door. A porcupine obligingly trundled in.

I was dazed by the incongruity of its presence in my kitchen, and my mind couldn't seem to proceed past this point. The porcupine seemed befuddled also, as if suddenly realizing its predicament, but I couldn't get it to go back out the door. The porcupine lumbered to a corner of the room and stood like a recalcitrant child presenting its back to me, a formidable, bristling display poignantly undermined by the spreading yellow puddle around its paws; the porcupine was so scared it was piddling.

We were at an impasse. I telephoned my mother, sure she would know what to do. Ten minutes later, my front door swung open. "I am dressed for porcupine!" Barbara announced with a grand flourish of the broom she carried. She had donned protective raincoat and rubber boots over her pajamas. I felt the relief of the rescued. Barbara herded the porcupine out the door, gently whacking it with her broom.

It is a simple but needful thing, the leaning we are able to do on each other at 3:00 A.M. in a forested world. Without the leaning or the forest we are severed from both comfort and mystery, the necessary extensions of individual experience.

Modern western individualism, the guiding mythic paradigm of our era, uses technology as its primary resource. The extreme result of this has become the potential of a single person to destroy the world, a stunning thought to consider. The primary resource of clan, however, is the power derived from wholeness being greater than the sum of parts. That check on egoic dominance is appallingly lacking in the modern paradigm. Both the unchecked individualism and the infatuation with and addiction to irresponsible technology has inflated ego, distorting sensible discernment of priorities and ignoring communal and ecological balances. The personal myth is the Hero myth, but who does the Hero serve? This is what has been forgotten.

A surprise birthday party was engineered when Gabriel turned eighteen. It was actually his first birthday party ever, and its planning took months of surreptitious maneuvers. We lived one hundred miles from an airport, twenty-five miles from any motel, and most of the party guests were from out of state. My family rarely meets en masse.

On this occasion everyone was able to come except Stuart and his son, Dillon.

Barbara flew in from Michigan; the following day Alex and his wife, Dedria, arrived by plane also, renting a car and driving my mother north with them to the celebration on the mountain. Leigh and Bill, my sister and her husband, motored eleven hours from Oregon, though Leigh had recently endured back surgery and the ride was agony for her. Two friends made their way across the state, another came from California, and two arrived from Canada. My father and Louise, like Leigh and Bill, drove up from Oregon. Our land partner and her daughter had the least distance to cover. It was an extraordinary convergence—a clan gathering—all unbeknownst to Gabriel. The surprise was a success.

Each person brought a favorite memory of Gabriel's childhood to share, and a bit of perspective or counsel to offer for his future. Crowded into our little house, perched on desk, woodbox, window sill, whatever sufficed as seating, with Gabriel in our midst, one by one the memories of family and friends were unfolded, the counsels bespoken. Much of it made us laugh, but much of it also made us cry, something Crudens usually do, if at all, only privately. The words were offered as poems, letters, or pithy essays; afterward Gabriel put them in a scrapbook, something cherished. The gathering was like the launching of a boat carrying the best of our dreams, heritage, hopes, and most of all, love. We were Gabriel's safe harbor.

During one of our visits to George and Louise in Oregon, Gabriel came into the house out of breath, his eyes shining—he was about eight years old. "An eagle swooped down over me—I looked right into its eyes!"

My sister nodded confirmation. "I saw it from the window," she said. "A golden."

Gabriel was alight with excitement. "It *spoke* to me," he said. "It gave a cry, then flew away."

I looked at him as if seeing from afar this radiant child—as though the faeries had taken him, his spirit eagle-touched. As a teenager, he wrote this prayer:

Light of the morning
Love in our hearts

Freedom to fly
Joy touching all

A beginning, an ending
The power and strength
Growing and changing
In yourself, happiness

Light of the morning
A beginning, an ending
Love in our hearts
The power and strength
Freedom to fly
Growing and changing
Joy touching all
In yourself, happiness.

The Celts became hostages and exiles, remaining in lands con-trolled by conquerors (whether the lands were lost through battle or politics) or driven to emigrate. The outlook of hostages is resentful, apathetic, or complying. The exile's consciousness becomes divided in itself, an inner mirroring of outward separation.

This excerpt from a poem by Ruaraidh MacThòmais of the Isle of Lewis, written after his emigration to North America, was translated from the Gaelic:

Madness! The foolish heart
lapping along these ancient rocks
as though there were no sea-journeys in the world
but that one.
The heart tied to a tethering post, round upon round of
the rope
til it grows short
and the mind free.
I bought its freedom dearly.

Historian Delaney writes:

The Bretons in France fight for independence, speak the lan-guage, wheedle, force or cajole grants-in-aid out of the central

government in Paris. And all in order to distinguish themselves from France and the French by holding on to their in-
tensely Celtic traditions. . . . The Welsh have perfected this
device: their language is frequently operated, manipulated,
as a true border—the speaking of Welsh in a public place ac-
cumulates and takes on greater significance if "strangers" are
present. The Scots display more sense and realism; language
and poetry, as spoken and practiced particularly in the western islands, keep the sound alive, and some of the spirit intact.
. . . The Celtic credentials of Ireland, which politically, cultur-
ally, and linguistically remained vivid up to the seventeenth
century, have been eroded, surviving only in the fabric, in the
collective unconscious—emerging unselfconsciously in the
music, the speech, the imagination. . . . Ireland had experienced centuries of the worst kind of oppression. After the genocide intended by Elizabeth I, and the unbridled murderous-
ness of Oliver Cromwell, and the life-denying, vastly unjust
Plantations of the sixteenth and seventeenth centuries, which
threw long-incumbent families out and installed lesser British
citizens, Celtic Ireland lay ragged. . . . Thus, the confluence of
ancient mythology and imagistic Catholicism formed the new
Irish identity but diluted the true Celtic spirit.

Canadian novelist Hugh MacLennan said of the places from which
his Scottish ancestors had been driven: "Above the sixtieth parallel in
Canada you feel that nobody but God has ever been there before you,
but in a deserted Highland glen you feel that everyone who ever
mattered is dead and gone."

Culture that changes due to imposition, loss, oppression, and severance instead of evolutionary process or an organic transformation
is a culture irreflective of its people's hearts. I think of Gabriel's prayer:
"Joy touching all / In yourself, happiness." The sage's definition of
joy and happiness is that joy is what a person in the desert feels in
finding the oasis and happiness is the experience of drinking its waters. These things are blighted for those driven from the oasis or barred
from drinking its waters. The solution, for individuals and tribes, often must take a transcendent course. Delaney goes on to say:

As the Celts necessarily mutated, forced from grandeur into
vassaldom, reduced from membership of the king's extended

family into abject and insecure tenantship often of an absentee landlord—how could their poets reflect gold when the people needed bread? To look, therefore, for the same wondrous style of the flagons or weaponry or illuminations among later Celts is to look in vain. But another part of the spirit survived—the ability to wring art from the life on the ground. The poets had always spoken their verses or sung them. The Bards—in the true sense of the word "bard" not the hopelessly romantic, pseudo-antiquarian nineteenth century notion—may have made poems for kings but they also made them for people, and now necessarily so.

Scotland's Dougie MacLean could be considered a modern-day bard, his songs articulating both Celtic continuity and its evolution. In facing what is lost MacLean also names and nurtures what can flower. His songs—proud, ironic, honestly romantic, cleanly beautiful—ignite rather than sentimentalize; they say, "We are still alive but not unchanged." The lyrics to "It Belongs to Us," which refers to Scotland's Stone of Destiny, removed from Scotland by England's King Edward, typify the challenge to creatively move forward without losing what grounds us.

It stands within a time of dreams
Engraven stone on which it seems
Ten thousand naked hands have drawn an endless line
Where man and earth were more than one
With fire, water, moon and sun
We touch it and were centered in this place and time

They try and tear it all away
O but turning heads can't hear what heavy hearts must say
It belongs to us, it belongs to us
It's our sacred rock you hold
And it's our destiny that you have thrown away
It's our sacred rock you hold

These canyons where our ancients sleep
They rise above our heads and keep
Connection with the winds on which our seeds have come
And it's there we lay and rest our dead

It's there the last goodbyes are said
We see it and we know that we will all be one

They try and tear it all away
O but turning heads can't hear what heavy hearts must say
It belongs to us, it belongs to us
It's our sacred rock you hold
And it's our destiny that you have thrown away
It's our sacred rock you hold

You may think it's worthless
You may think it small and for that we have no need
But reality is bigger than the lies you have grown from your
Spiritless greed

There is a deep and distant force
That knows the way and holds the course
We've traveled so uncertainly from year to year
And it strengthens as we pass it on
Our children growing graceful strong
We feel it and we're certain that our way is clear

They try and tear it all away
O but turning heads can't hear what heavy hearts must say
It belongs to us, it belongs to us
It's our sacred rock you hold
And it's our destiny that you have thrown away
It's our sacred rock you hold

Reality is not fixed, and need not be defined by suffering, but neither is oppression something to which the spirit adapts—not truly. Hostaged or exiled Celts had—and have—to seek positive direction rather than lock into modes of despair or vengeance: "Give their roofs to the flame and their flesh to the eagles" is not a mindset that resolves suffering (though, as the IRA knows, it may avert apathy and complicity).

Renewing cultural integrity is a task simultaneous with that of family and individual integrity, and inseparable from the honoring of ecological integrity. These are concentric circles within wholeness. Even in these times of fragmentation and unraveled strands, we are not without adequate inner and outer resources with which to engage the challenge. Dissolution gives opportunity for creation. It is a task for everyone—for life itself: "Joy touching all / In yourself, happiness." Dougie MacLean tells concert audiences about the ceilidhs in his neighborhood. He speaks of a particular evening when he was playing the fiddle as a close-packed crowd of dancers—estate owners, crofters, kids, grandparents, teens, rich and poor, wise and ignorant—surged together in joyful, heated harmony: a vision of what the world could be. "You should come to our ceilidhs," he told the concert audience, and I could see that everybody wanted to.

In Scotland, after Celticism's defeat at Culloden and the draining of Highland vitality through the Clearances, Celtic culture gave a false impression of abiding only in the form of impotent nostalgia. Victorian literature featured spectral and romantic Scottish landscapes; by the 1920s and 1930s, lack of Scottish reality in writings about Scotland was almost a prerequisite to that literature's popularity. Scots poet Hugh MacDiarmid, born in 1892, typified Highland reaction to what MacDiarmid called "The bunkum of the Celtic Twilight," saying, "There is nothing more detestable, perhaps, than this Tibetization of the Hebrides—this myth that represents the islanders as all some sort of spiritual sportsmen, specializing in weird and wonderful soul states."

This Victorian tendency is echoed in some of the New Age and neopagan literature about the Celts—fantasizing that misrepresents truths still vital to living Celtic people. Modern poet William Neil remarks that, "I have read a great deal of poetry in the Celtic tongue. Formal stanzas, clear images, and lack of obscurity are the characteristics of its best exemplars; Celtic mistiness is an invention of non-Celts and bad romantic novelists." In a like vein, Kenneth Jackson, translator of ancient Gaelic poetry, says, "The Celtic literatures are about as little given to mysticism or sentimentality as it is possible to be; their most outstanding characteristic is rather their astonishing power of imagination." John Prebble explains that:

> At the moment when the example set by [Robert] Burns might have been followed by others, the language he had used was crushed by the monumental work of his admirer, Walter Scott. Though this unique and tormented man had an accurate ear for the common speech of the Scottish people, he could not or would not use it in verse or narrative prose. His novels are

rich and diverse, teeming with imagination and subtle invention, but they are English literature. The best of them express Scott's romantic and nostalgic pride in his country's
past, and may have helped anesthetize the pain of its surrender to the present. Consciously or unconsciously, they appeal for England's respect and admiration.

Murray Pittock, in *The Invention of Scotland: The Stuart Myth and
the Scottish Identity, 1638 to the Present,* notes that, "[Sir Walter] Scott
often changed the unsuccessful gestures of the past into futile ones.
In doing so he intensified their romance while depoliticizing them."
Pittock prefaces this by saying: "Between 1820 and 1860, Jacobitism
was turned into a tourist industry, a heritage trail into extinct history,
the virtues of which could be patronized and the vices forgotten. *Yet
the radical edge remained . . .* though in an altered form"(italics mine).
Pittock goes on to say that, despite "sham Celticism, the radical un-
dertow continued to exist. . . . Burns had shown that Jacobitism and
radicalism could meet. . . . It is interesting to note how much genuine
commitment remained amid the tinsel and boom of an imperial British version of the Scottish past."

The Jacobites were supporters of restoration of the traditional
Gaelic way of life protected by an autonomous Stuart monarchy,
usurped by England. In medieval Europe Scotland was considered
among the most conceptually advanced (and oldest) kingdoms in its
view of sovereignty and nationhood. Those ideologies developed
during the twelfth and thirteenth centuries, when Scotland was in
crisis after Alexander III died and the country was temporarily
kingless. The conclusion to the Declaration of Arbroath (written in
1320) says in part, "For as long as one hundred of us shall remain
alive we shall never in any wise consent to submit to the rule of the
English, for it is not for glory we fight, for riches, or for honours, but
for freedom alone, which no good man loses but with his life."

In modern America we take this kind of "Give me liberty or give
me death" statement for granted, complacently congratulating ourselves on being a "free nation," but in the European context of the
1300s, the words of the Declaration of Arbroach were radical, astound-
ing, and profoundly Celtic.

Pittock observes that, "Enthusiasts for the traditional past had to
differentiate themselves from those for whom the past was merely a
sentimental construct of defeats. Nationalist or pro-crofter action made

this differentiation public, visible and resented." The William Wallace Monument on Abbey Craig went up in 1856, and reaction to it in the English press showed obvious affront. The English were offended by this focal manifestation of an animate Scottish nationalism, one not safely extinct or "quaintified" after all. *The Times* labeled Wallace the "merest myth," and scoffed at the "Scotchmen [who] seem to do nothing but masquerade in the garments of their grandfathers." The Monument and other expressions of renewed cultural identity were then, and now, denigrated by English under the label of provincialism, with the implication that Scotland should prove it is not provincial by submissively melding its identity with England's. Scots, however, continued to decry misuse of the name "England" to describe Great Britain.

In 1901, Theodore Napier specified the aims of Scottish autonomy in his newspaper, *The Fiery Cross*, the title of which referred to the traditional method used to raise the clans.

Napier's twelve articles were:

1. Restoration of the Stuarts
2. Restoration of Parliament
3. Restoration of the Mint
4. Restoration of [the] Privy Council
5. Restoration of [the] Court of Admiralty
6. Restoration of [the] Stone of Destiny (briefly done in 1950 and finally achieved in 1996)
7. Restoration of Royal Arms in Scottish quarters in Scotland
8. Deletion of Saint George and the Dragon from British coinage
9. [The name] England not to be used in an Imperial sense
10. Restoration of the clan system and of the people to the land
11. Multiple voting
12. Opposition to "jingo imperialism" and "militarism"*

In these articles it was once again apparent that, for Scots, there was a Celtic conflation of conservative and radical elements of Jacobitism in contemporary politics. But political bodies of modern-day

---

*Article twelve is a reminder of the disproportionate, appalling loss of life suffered by Scots serving in Britain's armed forces. England was fixed on colonizing, and spendthrift with Scottish soldiers, many of whom, like Blacks in America, were in military service due to lack of economic or social opportunity elsewhere. Article eleven refers to franchise reforms.

Scotland proved seriously lacking when it came to cultural priorities. MacDiarmid stated that "there can be no minimizing the high significance of a Cause (however romantic and unreal it may seem to those 'practical people' who have brought us to so sorry a pass) which retains such unexhaustive evolutionary momentum as to appear with renewed vitality after being suppressed for a couple centuries of unparalleled change."

MacDiarmid saw Scottish nationalism as fostering cooperative democracy that would provide a catalyst for the creative arts, where the past is an "evolutionary momentum" celebrating Scottish potentialities. This perspective was similar to that of William Yeats toward Ireland. Pittock points out that "MacDiarmid saw the classless Scottish spirit as deriving from the clan structures iconically opposed by the Jacobites to the class-based structure of the British state."

The Calvinist Reformation in Scotland, moreover, was seen by many as having been not only divisive, but inimical to the arts (which the Stuart monarchs consistently promoted). A group of Scottish schoolteachers I spoke with on Skye related childhood memories about Calvinist strictness that prohibited them from even clipping fingernails on the Sabbath. Swingsets were tied to prevent children from playing. In the old days, fiddles and pipes were burned, joy was silenced. "John Knox has a lot to answer for," one of the schoolteachers said at last, in the contemplative quiet following discussion. "He bled the color from Scotland, turned it grey."

An alternate perspective is offered by J. D. Mackie:

> Those who denounce the narrowness and the disregard for beauty of the early reformers should remember that the Kirk [the church] they produced trained up a people strong in faith, patient of discipline, ready to venture, and even to die, for their beliefs. If the loftiness of the idea led sometimes to disillusionment and sometimes to hypocrisy, it led also to achievement.

And in a provocative statement echoing the integrated outlook of the Celts: "It did not occur to the philosophers of the time that economics could be separated from morality."

Religious matters have never been separate from state and political matters in Celtic countries. From Druidism to the arrival of Roman Christianity, through the Reformation, and beyond, religion has been a force of primary influence on Celtic destiny. It is conspicuous in the complexity of their history and in relationships, informing decisions, alliances, the rise and fall of kings and queens, and the experience and fate of the people. John Knox was effective because the Catholic Church had degenerated into the kind of bureaucratic, hierarchical, hypocritical corruption inimical to Celtic social and spiritual sensibilities. The Reformation offered to clear away what obstructed the common person's access to God, and cleanse governmental and religious institutions of parasites draining society's lifeblood. But, in essence, one kind of oppression was traded for another; the Reformation may have returned God and church to common access, but it split the people, prevented political cohesion when it was urgently needed, and set itself against what was most beautiful in Celtic culture and spirit. During the time of the Clearances, the disruption of the Calvinist church, in which ministers and congregations broke away to form the Free Church, included the reaction to the established church being used as a tool of the sheep lairds. Once again it was a matter of common people trying to reclaim the directness and honesty of relationship with religion intrinsic to Celtic consciousness. In its very name the Free Church was an assertion of the Celts' essential need for collective independence. But it, too, in trying to prove itself more Calvinist than the established church, became grimly oppressive. Today the established and Free churches are reunited, though factionalism perpetuates in the form of the Wee Frees and other ideological enclaves.

Dougie MacLean tells a story that seems to me an instance of the common Celt once again acting in accordance with ancestral spiritual directive. There is an ancient Pictish healing well on the hill above Dougie's house. One night, after a few whiskeys, Dougie and two friends climbed the hill to wash their faces in the healing waters. While there they came to the conclusion that the large stone, carved with a cross, which Christians long ago placed within the pagan well in an attempt to Christianize its reputation, should be removed. Dougie and his accomplices felt it was time to liberate the well. With difficulty the heavy stone was hauled forth and loaded into Dougie's car, then stashed in the shed beside the MacLean house, where a neighbor discovered it one day while borrowing a ladder. The neighbor was horrified. "Ye must put it back," he entreated Dougie. "People've been lookin' everywhere for it, greatly disturbed. Ye must put it back or I'll have to tell."

Having only one accomplice this time, and not daring to use his car, Dougie smuggled the stone back up the hill in a pram, and was thereby responsible for the Christian miracle of the stone's return to the well. The story's moral may be interpreted according to personal perspective, but liberation's impulse continues to move Celts to acts expressing spiritual alignment.

Division between Protestants and Catholics is no longer the violent matter in Scotland that it continues to be in Northern Ireland. Irish and Scottish histories diverged with the founding of Dal Riada and again with the Reformation, but ties remain intimate. The hostel I lived in in southern Skye also housed two men from Northern Ireland—one Catholic, one Protestant—who were on Skye working on Sleat's electrical lines. Arthur, the Protestant, lost his job in Northern Ireland upon being arrested for acts of terrorism; it is not often a Protestant is charged with such crimes. After a thirteen-month trial at which he was found innocent, Arthur nonetheless couldn't get his job—a good one in electrical engineering—back, and his life was shattered by the whole affair. Not only that, but he was now a target for militants on either side of the political fence. He said the BBC planned to do a story on him and perhaps this would aid his plight; in the meantime he was in Scotland doing lineman's work, for which he was absurdly overqualified.

Arthur's bunkmate, Chris, was from Catholic Donegal. The two men, who had met on the job in Sleat, were buddies off the job as well. One night at the pub, where Peter MacDonald and my friend Robin and I sat having a bit of "crack" with the Irishmen, talk turned to "the Troubles." Chris and Arthur both held that violence had become an end in itself to a small, mainly young, group of Irish militants who would always find political excuse to feed the stimulating habit of bloodshed. The pain of conflict has become so ingrained into the daily lives of Northern Irish that the people—the majority—wanting peaceful settlement react with resignation rather than the kind of shock that would say "No more!" to the killings.

Peter's reaction to this perspective was so vehement I thought violence would certainly erupt right there at our pub table. "You Northern Irish are a DISGRACE to the Celtic nation!" he shouted. "You're a bloody DISGRACE to the Celts!" But the Irishmen, schooled to patience, patience, patience, were unangered by this fierce condemnation. Their voices remained gentle; more drinks were bought. They talked about how they thought Northern Ireland would suffer economically if reunited with Ireland. Peter, still seething, said the rest of Ireland didn't want Northern Ireland anyway. It was an eye-opening interchange.

Most Scots I spoke with seemed cautious in discussing the Irish Troubles, especially if English people were present. Some expressed the opinion that Northern Ireland's most peaceful course would be to join with an independent Scotland. Ulster's Protestantism originally came from transplanted Scots. No one felt that any English government, ever, had acted with the intention of resolving the problems in Northern Ireland. I met a man from Liverpool whose father had been from Donegal. The man remembered that, though his father never talked about his Irish heritage, in their house in England were momentos of the Irish Republican cause. All these disappeared from view at one point. When his father lay dying in the hospital and Matti was an adult, he asked his father why the Irish memorabilia had been removed. "I didn't want to offend our neighbors," the old man said. Matti resolved to go to Donegal, to see the town in which his father had grown up, and to honor his Irishness. "And did you?" I asked. "Yeah I did, but not until after my dad died, and I'll always regret that."

In Scotland, where many English own summer homes and estates—some Highland villages now have as many English as Scots inhabitants—the English always describe their nationality as "British" in hostel registers, whereas Scots invariably designate themselves as "Scots." Feelings still run high and the English do little to make themselves loved in the rest of the UK. My roommate in one of the hostels was an English hillclimber who said if Northern Ireland and Scotland wanted independence that was fine with him: good riddance, though he conceded that Ireland does more for its people in terms of social service than does Britain. He hoped the Highlands would remain a rural paradise for hillclimbers—he thought England would someday be "one big city." He ended our conversation by saying he knew nothing whatsoever about Celtic history and could not imagine why I would write about it.

In June of 1997, Mary Robinson, Ireland's president, spoke at Sabhal Mor Ostaig. She [talked] movingly of links between Ireland and Scotland, and of Celtic culture's future.

> Despite the divergence of our histories and despite the passage of turbulent centuries, we can still recognize a shared inheritance. And it is on the islands off the coasts of Ireland

and Scotland that this legacy is most strongly preserved, in language, in storytelling, and in music. . . . The plantation of Ulster settlers from Scotland defined the character and religion of that part of Ireland. A pattern of migrant labour was established between Scotland and the west of Ireland . . . which has lasted up to current times.

When I became president of Ireland I spoke of a province of our imagination, a common ground in which we could come together and celebrate what we share. . . . I am particularly conscious that this may enable people in Northern Ireland to reclaim parts of their inheritance which have been denied them.

Too often, in an Irish [not Scottish] context, Celtic or Gaelic culture has been identified with Catholicism and nationalism, which has the effect of inhibiting those of the Protestant and Unionist tradition from claiming part of their inheritance. John Montague writes:

The whole landscape a
manuscript
we had lost the skill to read
A part of our past disinherited. . . .

Seamus Heaney, in "Station Island," says:

You lose more of yourself than you
redeem
doing the decent thing, keep at a
tangent.
When they make the circle wide,
it's time to swim

out on your own and fill the
element
with signatures of your own
frequency,
echo soundings, searches, probes,
allurements

elven-gleams in the dark of the whole sea. . . .

In the past, it seems to me, there was a dichotomy between those who saw modernity as a threat to the preservation of traditional values and culture, on one hand, and those, on the other, who regarded tradition as inhibiting and parochial. We now are offered a liberating resolution to this dilemma, whereby tradition is enhanced by a modern idiom.

I see evidence of this liberation in every sphere of Irish life, a new mood of self-confidence which is invigorating and refreshing. I see young people who are at home in traditional and in modern idioms and who refuse to deny the validity of either. I see a cross-fertilization of styles, whether in dance or in music, which has found a new popularity not only in Ireland but also around the world. I read writers who are versed in traditional learning but who are equally immersed in an emerging global culture and find no contradiction in this. . . . I remain profoundly optimistic about the survival of Gaelic culture in Ireland. Not only have official attitudes changed but so have public attitudes. There is evidence, for example, in the number of schoolchildren now attending Irish-speaking schools and in the way in which modern means of communication are being used to promote and preserve the language.

For the future, Ireland and Scotland have much to learn from each other and to share. There are no two countries in western Europe which are as close; not only in a shared past but also in what we have in common today.

In Scotland, the association between Lowland Presbyterian and commercial as well as religious interests in the Union of 1707 remains an issue to Nationalists and neo-Jacobites. Economic exile, starting with the Clearances but continuing well beyond it (630,000 Scots emigrated between 1911 and 1921; many thousands more were killed in World War I) emphasized the sense of loss attending the exiled Stuart monarchy and the failure at attempts to restore it. Cultural continuity remains alive, nonetheless, and beyond a mere presence as relic. Pittock asserts:

Unless the Jacobite analysis posed a continuing question about Scotland and its future, there would have been no need to sentimentalize and diminish it. It was patronized because it was still potentially powerful. . . . The fact that Scotland's separate history is clearly not over has been one recognized increasingly in this century; and part of the continuing development of Scottish thought and understanding has come from those who are inheritors of the questions posed by the Jacobite analysis.

Scotland's John McGrath, in the preface to his play, *The Cheviot, the Stag and the Black, Black Oil,* in 1974 wrote:

> One thing I insisted on was that we broke out of the "Lament" syndrome. Ever since Culloden, Gaelic culture has been one of lament—for exile, for death, for the past, even for the future. Beautiful, haunting lament. And in telling the story of the Highlands since 1745, there are many defeats, much sadness to relate. But I resolved that in the play, for every defeat, we would also celebrate a victory. . . . At the end, the audience left knowing they must choose . . . they must have confidence in their ability to unite and win.

Orientations such as McGrath's and Mary Robinson's suggest ways of addressing challenges of cultural renewal in the quest to reaffirm and cultivate integrity. In Britain's 1997 national elections, not a single Tory retained or won a parliamentary seat in Scotland or Wales. Not one. For the first time in eighteen years Great Britain had a Labour government, with Tony Blair at the helm. The conservatives were out. The most momentous follow-up for Scotland brought about by these election results was the successful referendum for constitutional change, voted on in September, 1997, to bring back into existence a separate Scottish Parliament with tax-varying powers. Seventy-one percent of the Scottish voters polled at the time of the referendum expressed the opinion that a separate Scottish parliament is effectively a step toward ultimate Scottish independence.

Scotland, with nine percent of the UK's population and one-third of its land mass, holds the bulk of its oil and natural gas reserves, as well as 30 percent of the European Union's fish stocks. But Scotlands' battered self-respect is vulnerable to whispers predicting failure and inadequacy, though that vulnerability lessens as direction is clarified and confidence grows.

Celts have a passion for social cohesion and social justice. When I asked a man from Caithness, in the far northern Highlands, what was distinct about Scots, he said it was their concern for the common good. A man on Skye defined it as their egalitarianism. A shopkeeper in Edinburgh spontaneously volunteered a great deal of perspective as I poked through piles of sweaters: "Scotland, despite what's happened in our history, is a gentle, caring society—a social democracy," she declared. "Our legal and educational systems are unique and fair—my daughter is studying to be a lawyer. We Celtic women are strong women; the men don't rule the roost here. We care about people's problems—we're a sensitive society."

I asked her about what the politicians were doing for Scotland. "Those lying gets; they don't do anything for us," she snapped. "The youth are disillusioned with politics but they're interested in heritage. My son will get his kilt when he turns eighteen. We're Mac-Donalds on my mother's side; the whole family gathered for her seventieth birthday—the mother's clan is important. My mother sat in the midst of us and told stories. I hate computers. Celts have an oral culture and computers are destroying that."

The shopkeeper's remarks about computers mirrored my own concerns, three in particular, relative to Celtic culture: imperilment of memory, connection, and actuality of experience.

Cultivation and exercise of memory languishes around computers. Memorization's disciplines also develop acuity of observation, listening, consideration, and associative linking—vital aspects of thinking and relating. Memory is not just an organic storage system harmlessly replaced by a machine's storage system. Memory in oral cultures is developed to phenomenal degrees and so, naturally, are its accompanying capacities. What happens when we discard these skills? When we abdicate humanly carrying our stories, our past, the richness of our culture, the power of spoken, face-to-face communication and interaction? What happens to social realities and relationships?

The degree to which a person is engaged with computers already has been acknowledged as a degree to which that person is lacking or losing social skills and connection to social responsibility. And what of a computer society's severence from natural habitat and natural rhythms—its disconnection from truly knowing the Earth?

Knowledge is multilayered, interrelated, and requires a foundation of associative understanding. Knowledge to become wisdom, to become genuine in its personal and social dimensions, requires experience. Reading about something is not the same as doing it. Viewing sex, or war, or poverty, or a mountain lion in a video is not the same as direct experience. But a convincing illusion of knowing is offered by simulated realities and cascades of information available by pushing buttons. The result is not only loss of humility and of paths of wisdom and character depth; the result is also a false knowing with little relationship to source or consequence, to meaning or implication: detached and rootless.

What the shopkeeper said about Scottish gentleness has much to do with interactive, interpersonal wisdom. I found that Scottish people from cops to taxi drivers lacked the edge, the common adversarial nature, I have often found in other societies. Scots gossip; their humor is wicked, but there is a kindness that makes village—even most city—streets safe at night. Street-corner groups mainly mind their own businesses; they are not preditory. Interactions have an astute element, leaving everyone's dignity possible—people treat each other like people, they mix and are authentic. Role playing and image projection are minimized. The ego dance is minimized. Rural Scots are perhaps the most unfashionably dressed Europeans I have ever seen. Scottish cuisine is unpretentious. Yet their arts, their minds, their sense of how to make functionality graceful, express brilliance.

Peter MacDonald, on Skye, said, "We have imagination. It doesn't work to always be methodical like the Germans—though I admire the Germans." A history book mentioned that it was to the Scots' advantage that they were so tolerant of the ways of others; their egalitarianism helping them assimilate into North American society when many emigrated. Murray Pittock asserts that a divided Scotland mainly was referent to the seventeenth and eighteenth centuries, when political and religious divisions were caused by a succession of governmental policies. Jacobite tradition views all Scotland—Lowlands and Highlands—as fundamentally Celtic, and Celts are fundamentally tolerant. It is worth pondering, however, that both the Ku Klux Klan and the antislavery movement in the southern United States were founded by Scots descendants: equality and freedom—and their distorting shadow.

"Maybe she's French," the woman whispers to her husband.

"Pardonne," she says to me.

"Maybe she's Italian," the husband suggests.

Before his wife can say, "Scusé," I jerk my head out of the backseat of the car, having suddenly become aware of being addressed. Actually the couple has been speaking to me for some moments, trying one language after another in hopes of getting me to allow them access to their car, snugged close to ours in the castle's parking lot. I have been rearranging supplies in our backseat (a compulsive and absorbing organizational task), and paying no attention to nearby voices.

"Oh, dear!" I exclaim apologetically in my best American English. "I'm not French *or* Italian—I'm just oblivious!" It is amazing that they have not nudged me out of their way, or at very least, lost patience. I wonder how many more languages they know or how many they have already tried in efforts to get some response.

The metaphor of their patience is striking—recognition of a need for many tools of communication, and a courteous perseverance in searching for which of those tools will be effective in a given situation. This couple is trying to get into their own car, in their own country, but are quite willing to try to discover my language—whatever it is—and give all the personal space I seem to require.

When my books started being published friends and family said, "We're proud of you." Even the postmistress said it. This seems the most valuable kind of pride—that which we can have in each other. It is a communal sense of mutual support, a clan consciousness. Bette Midler laments, "The hardest part of success is trying to find someone who is glad for you." Separation's wounds are inflicted by envy, by desperate competition. "I'm proud of you" warms speaker and hearer in its forging of positive, encouraging links of identity. In Celtic society, oaths were considered sacred, hospitality was inviolable, loyalty to one's chief was taken seriously, and marriage bonds were respected. All these underpinned a way of life based on the valuing of honorable communalness rather than on a fearful church morality.

Gregory Cajete, in *Look to the Mountain,* lists Native American aspects of education that develop "people with a heart, a face, and a visionary foundation," identifying these as: guidance, kinship, diversity, ethical modeling, role clarity, distinct customs and practices, recognition of accomplishment, community work, special regard of children, intimate connection to environment and place, and spirit. These could apply to Celtic clans as well as Native American tribes; they could be attributes nurtured in modern societies as well. It is plain what is missing in today's versions of community. Gangs are aberrant degradations of fiannas; everywhere people gravitate toward clubs, support groups, neighborhoods, needing to experience affiliation and communal identity, to be among. At worst, klans, gangs, militia, modern society's manifestations of tribal impulse are horrifying. At best they are poignant ghosts of what was or could be: the '60s hippies, the Rainbow Tribe, the remnants of Native traditional culture.

On my recent trip to Scotland I spent a great deal of time on public transportation, mainly buses. At first the kindness and good humor of bus drivers was disconcerting because it was unexpected; the job is, after all, a stressful one. Well into a journey from Skye to Inverness an elderly Scotswoman realized she had gotten on the wrong bus—she was trying to get to Glasgow, in the opposite direction. The driver stopped the bus, helped the woman off, unloaded her luggage, and carried it—the woman leaning on the driver's arm—to a bus stop down the road. We sat and waited. After ten minutes the Glasgow bus pulled up to where the driver stood with the elderly lady and he helped her board, explaining her predicament to the Glasgow driver, then walked back to his own bus and off we continued toward Inverness. A woman near the front of the bus piped up to say, "You'll be rewarded in heaven," and the driver just smiled.

Another bus driver once forgot to let me off at my stop. I lurched up the aisle under my heavy backpack and said, "Wasn't that my stop back there?" It was a hostel I had never stayed at before, but I had seen the sign for it flash past. "Ach! I clean forgot!" he said, immediately halting the bus and climbing off with me in tow. He left his bus sitting in the lane of travel—there being no way to pull off the road—and stood in the opposing lane to flag down an oncoming bus. He hustled me aboard it, breathlessly instructing the driver to convey me back to the hostel entrance.

The second driver imperturbably remarked, "You must've dazzled him," then proceeded to find out my surname and land of origin, and to assure me that the hostel accommodations were quite well thought of locally, all during the quarter mile we traveled before I was graciously dropped off.

When I was not riding buses I was walking. Usually there was a distance of two to six miles between hostels I lodged at and food shops where I obtained groceries. One rainy day I was carrying a week's worth of food home. Part of the walk took me through a long stretch of road-repair work. The construction men each greeted me as I passed:

"Mornin'."

"Mornin'."

"Mornin'." This went on for a half mile or so—lots of gruff, civil, sly greetings. One rough fellow ventured to ask if I was enjoying my walk. "Well, not particularly," I answered. "I've a packful of groceries."

Fifty yards farther down the road I heard a vehicle approach. The construction worker stopped his truck beside me. "Want a lift?" I hopped in and we drove in silence for a bit, then the man asked, "Might I ask why it is you're carryin' a rucksack full of horseshoes?"

Horseshoes? "Horseshoes?" I asked, then understanding dawned. He had misheard me; Scots don't especially use the term *groceries*, and my accent is indeed North American. No wonder he had felt sorry for me, and curious enough to come offer a lift home.

On the Isle of Skye I was trudging between food shop and hostel along the shore where the Sound of Sleat separates mainland from isle. Weary, I paused to rest on a low stone wall edging the road. I relieved my shoulders of the pack and gazed out over the water, then took some offering tobacco from the pack's zipper pocket and held it as I made prayers of gratitude for the endurance of the land's beauty and the people's spirit. As I was finishing these prayers a work truck pulled up nearby; a man got out and began putting a road sign in place. "Resting?" he asked. I nodded.

"Where are ye headed?"

I gestured toward the direction opposite the one the worker had been headed in. "Kilmore—about two more miles."

"Ach—that's nae far; ye could *joomp* that," he scoffed, which made me laugh.

"The last two miles are the hardest," I said, and stood to shoulder my pack and continue home.

A few minutes later, as I was plodding along, still smiling at the notion of "joomping" to Kilmore, the truck roared to a stop beside me and the workman waited for me to climb in. "Don't ye have nice places to walk in yer own country?" he asked, trying to comprehend tourist mentality.

"Sure," I said.

"Daft—it's daft," he muttered, but took me all the way to the hostel door. Rain began pelting as I passed inside.

Susan Watson, the young Highland woman who ran the hostel I stayed at in Perthshire, was another example of humor and kindness. She grew up on estates where her parents worked—her father was a gamekeeper and deer stalker. She said her home village in the

Highlands now has more English than Scots living in it, and the estates bordering the one on which her father works are owned by Arabs. "The Highland villages shut down in winter," she told me. "Even most of the pubs shut down; there are not enough year-round people to sustain them. The tourists and estate owners are resented but they're where most of the jobs come from, so feelings are mixed."

Much of my stay in Perthshire was pre-tourist season—the hostel was often quiet, almost empty. Susan and I watched TV and talked. She loaned me ordinance maps for my hikes and tried to make sure no one else bunked in "my" room. She said that during periods when I was away she continued thinking of it as my room and was absurdly reluctant to book other visitors into it. When her mother came to see Susan I was introduced as "part of the family here," which warmed me greatly in those months of being a stranger. I was often surprised at being remembered by hostel managers who recognized my voice, face, or name weeks after a first encounter. I always hoped recollections of me were not due to bad manners. Americans are notorious for being pushy, ignorant, crass, and self-centered. Australian and Japanese tourists in Scotland have not endeared themselves either. It has to do with courtesy and not putting oneself forward, reminding me of American Indian attitudes I had encountered.

When Highlanders landed in New York in the 1750s it was reported that Indians flocked to receive them as brothers. It was not difficult for eighteenth-century Scots to adapt to Indian lifestyles. Scots were both assimilated by and fought the American Natives. Particularly in the southeastern United States, the cultural structures of the Indians and the Celts were quite similar. John Ross, Cherokee chief, had a grandfather born in Inverness and he raised his descendants like Scots, even to the wearing of Highland clothes.

Alexander McGillivray, born in 1759, was the son of a Scots trader and a Native woman; he became the leader of 45,000 Creek, Chickasaw, and Seminole Indians and was a renowned statesman. The son of William MacIntosh, captain in the colonial army, and a Creek woman, became a powerful chief of the Creeks in southern Georgia, leading them against the British in 1812. MacIntosh codified the Creek laws. Highland Scots were asked to act as shields for the British colonists in the southeast, buffering against both the Indians and the Spanish. Chief MacIntosh's great grandson, Chief Waldo Emerson MacIntosh, used to attend Scottish festivals in an Indian headdress and tartan plaid. Clan MacIntosh had an Apache branch created by Archie MacIntosh, son of a Chippewa mother and Scots father. Archie married an Apache woman and become an army scout and Indian fighter. Many Scots married Indians; some were kidnapped by them.

Alexander Arbuthnot, who was a Scottish trader in Florida during the early 1800s, became concerned about the plight of Indians who were being cheated by Americans and abused by English. He wrote a series of letters at the Creek's behest and was hanged for his sympathies. Famed also, for opposite reasons, were Scots descendants like Davy Crockett and Daniel Boone. Scottish connection to North America runs deeply through both the Native and non-Native populations and their stories. In 1997, in the outer Hebrides, a Scotsman I talked to compared his people's situation to that of the American Indians. There is a resonance that continues to surface.

There is a bond between Scots and immigrant descendants of Scots, and also among immigrant descendants, that persists beyond pretensions and confusions, beyond mere sentimentality. It is worthwhile to find the core of what is carried, the resource and reality of continuity: gifts for our lives, our children, and our nation of immigrants.

At nineteen I had not thought much about heritage. Hitchhiking in Rhode Island, heading home to my brother's house, I was picked up by an elderly, irascible fellow, his crankiness intimidating. He wanted to know where my ancestors were from, but before I could reply he launched into a rant about what was wrong with a long list of possibilities.

In a dismaying display of bigotry, he gave capsuled negative summations of Italians, Jews, Poles, Asians, Africans, Germans, French, Hispanics, Dutch, Russians, Arabs, and even the English. This topic obviously was an obsession. "Well," he demanded, abruptly reaching the end of his list. "So, what are you?"

"Scots." I said nervously.

He grunted, hunched over his steering wheel, trying to find the right slot for this catalyst. Finally, grudgingly, he said, "I can't think right off of anything bad about Scots."

A relief, though when I got out of the car and started walking homeward I wished he had dared insult the Scots so I could have defended my heritage. Then I was ashamed of not trying to abort his rant about everybody else's ancestry; I wondered where the old man's family was from. Partisanship is different from hatred. The right hand does not despise the left. Heritage is about knowing your ground and, within that, nourishing seeds that will bless the world and its future, bless the common good. Knowing where you are from is a gift toward healing, not a burden, or a basis for superiority. It is a resource not only for connection, but for extension, and a creativity that knows, and acknowledges, what has made the moment possible.

Scotland's wars of independence under William Wallace and Robert the Bruce were also wars of freedom for small landholders and, in John Prebble's words, "Gave the Scots commonality a robust self-respect, a contempt for arrogant chivalry. The French who were sent to Scotland to fight for it against England were shocked by the impudence of Lowland country folk. When they protested against the outrageous prices they were charged for meal and forage, they were told it was small repayment for the fields destroyed by their knightly games." There's a saying about people from the Outer Isles that is applicable to most Scots: "You can lead a Lewisman with a hair but you can't drag him with a cable."

In 1304 Scots defended Stirling Castle against England for "the Lion"—the Scottish symbol of kingship—though at the time Scotland had no king. It was not politics that guided the people then, nor politics that guides them now. In the interwar years of the twentieth century it was Scottish culture—and its low rather than high culture—that maintained the distinct national identity abandoned by Scottish governmental institutions.

Americans who watch *Rob Roy* and *Braveheart* think they thereby know Scottish history. Scots love *Braveheart*, too (I watched it in Scotland with a Scot and an Englishman—"the millionth showing," the hostel manager wryly announced), though Scots are quietly annoyed at the movie's historical inaccuracies and inventions, especially those regarding Robert the Bruce. But to understand even the heroics of Wallace or the choices of Rob Roy, the vast context of Celtic history must at least be modestly explored. Connection with Scots heritage has little resource to offer if its only basis is a family tartan and pride at being of the same race as Braveheart.

Wallace was a Celtic Lowlander (historians doubt that he wore a kilt or spoke Gaelic), but he lived at a time when there was little conscious distinction between Highlander and Lowlander. In the thirteenth century, royal power reached into the remote Highlands through both military force and the creation of a dependent elite—Gaelic and Anglo-Norman feudal landowners, many of whom were clan chiefs. After Robert the Bruce's death in 1329, that system collapsed into factionalism out of which arose the power of the MacDonald Lordship of the Isles.

MacDonald chiefs pretty much ignored kings and governments and were a kingdom unto themselves—one that included not only the western isles but also significant portions of the western mainland. For 150 years the MacDonald lordship stabilized that region of Scotland and promoted a Gaelic cultural age in which the arts flourished, and schools operated by artists, bards, and so on were open to lay people. In the late fifteenth century, the lordship of the isles was destroyed by the ambitious maneuverings of MacDonald chiefs and a period of upheaval followed, lasting until early in the seventeenth century. This violent period marked Highlanders as lawless and wicked in the minds of Lowlanders—a hard image to shake. In the northeast, meanwhile, collapse of royal authority and the dying out of the senior male lines of the powerful alliance of Earls of Moray, Earls of Ross, and Murrays in the late fourteenth century caused factionalism in that region also. This was the era of the Wolf of Badenoch, and such fearful disorder added to Lowland perception of Highland barbarism.

The feudalism that infiltrated Scotland from the south co-opted clanship's social structures, designed for defense and security. The clanship system was exploited, clansmen used as private armies in power struggles between nobles. The traditional concept of clan lands became empty of legal or actual truth, though it was not until the eighteenth century that social arrangements became wholly contractual. These changes paved the way for the Clearances.

Several of the larger clans—MacKenzies, MacDonalds, and notably, Campbells—became imperialistic; no longer was clan truly a matter of blood ties. Clan branches were formed to control various land areas, and weaker groups allied with stronger in volatile shifts of power. There were often groups following a chief whose lineage had little to do with their own bloodlines. Surnames did not become common until the seventeenth century. There were feuds, expansionism, forfeitures, and annexing by the Crown. In 1724, twenty-six chiefs could call out 18,890 warriors. Cattle raids were often a proving ground for martial prowess, especially for young heirs needing to show their valor.

The Church and burgh that stabilized Lowland life had far less influence in the Highlands, where the situation grew increasingly militaristic. Highland cohesion was sustained mainly by traditions of bardship, feasting, and the enduring belief of the clanspeople in *duthas* (collective heritage). Land was still viewed by them as communal. James Hunter notes that, "What was most striking about the Highlands in the seventeenth century, and even in the early eighteenth century, was the extent to which the region's clan-based society continued stubbornly to resist the many attempts made to disconnect it from its past."

The government policies of James VI and other Stuart kings were aimed at colonizing and "pacifying" the Highlands. Particular targets were the southern branch of Clan Donald, the MacLeods of Lewis, the MacLeans, and the MacGregors. The king would periodically lure chiefs of recalcitrant clans to meetings and then throw them into prison—even execute a few. The son of a MacDonald chief, on release from prison in 1427, promptly burned Inverness in rage over his confinement. The chiefs were not overly humble. Statutes against the clans were attempts to impose Lowland values on the Highlands and create more elitism. They included the suppression of beggars, control of alcohol, strengthening of the reformed church, Lowland education for Highland heirs, prohibition of arms for clansmen, and limitations on chiefs' retinues. (That retinue usually consisted of a chief steward and his men, a bard, a *sennachie*, a harper and his gillie, a piper and his gillie, a keeper of the sporran, a flag bearer, a cupbearer, a huntsman, a watcher, a ford man, a debater, a luggage man, an immediate body man, a big youth, and a clown.)

Massive indebtedness was incurred by lairds in the seventeenth and eighteenth centuries due to government actions, absenteeism, and consumption. Traditions of hospitality declined, but the 1692 massacre of the MacDonalds at Glencoe was all the more shocking to people because by then chaotic violence had become less common. This made the banditry of the MacGregors seem even more barbaric, also. Most Highlanders who fought in the Jacobite rebellions of the 1700s had never before been to war.

In 1996 and 1997, talking to people in Scotland, I asked whether there was still any sense of clan in Scotland, and if names still mattered. "Ach, no. That's all gone," people would say, then contradict the statement with others, clearly showing how much kinship and name *do*

still matter in Scotland. Local people do not notice it in their lives because it so permeates the culture that it is taken for granted, ingrained in context.

"How could you hire a Campbell?" I heard a Highland woman ask a hostel manager.

"I'm a MacKenzie—enemy of the MacPhersons," an old man disconcertingly replied to my friend Robin's inquiry about whether the man knew any local Gillises, relatives of the MacPherson clan. His statement, like most referring to clan differences, was made in an ambiguously half-joking, half-serious manner. But clan pride and clan rivalries have not been forgotten. "MacLeods! MacLeods! They're not even Celtic—they originated from Norsemen!" This from a descendent of the (half-Norse) MacDonald Lords of the Isles: MacDonalds and MacLeods mightily feuded.

Almost always when I glanced up from my research work in Scottish libraries and museums I would find a local person across the table engaged in genealogical work. It is a national pastime. Traveling through villages and cities I was struck by how many businesses carried family names, rather than being called Acme Furniture or Speedy Print or some such designation. Almost every Scot I met asked what my surname was, and when I answered, often nodded and said, "Ah, Cruden, from Aberdeenshire." The asking, the recognition, and the answer pleased and amazed me—it gave a sense of belonging, a sense of home never experienced in America. People continue to associate family names with geographical regions, the ancient clan relationship with locality. Sleat, in southern Skye, is still home for thirty-five MacDonald families and thirty-six families of MacKinnons.

One of those MacDonalds, when a visitor remarked that she had heard he was a descendant of the famed Flora MacDonald, coolly replied that, actually, Flora was more *his* descendant—not the other way around—since he was linked directly with the Lords of the Isles and Flora's family was simply an offshoot. It was extraordinary, the way this man sat—in his torn crofter's work clothes, several of his teeth missing, shirttail half out—and declared his superior pedigree. "It doesn't hurt that my name's MacDonald," he said, when I asked if traditional clan relationships still mattered in his region.

We were riding together to Portree, Skye's largest town. I ventured to tell him about my convoluted family ties to Robert Burns, and how my immigrant great aunts used to take my grandfather to a park every Sunday afternoon and there recite Burns' poems and songs.

"My grandfather was very proud of his heritage," I said. MacDonald nodded.

"And well he should be," he replied, as we drove along in a timeless moment of Celtic accord.

At Portree, a wedding finished as we pulled into the village square. The stone steps of the church were thronged with kilted men and ladies in their finest dresses. In that square on another occasion I stood in calm evening light listening to the Skye Pipe Band. They marched in their elaborate regalia—pipers and drummers, the young men and the old, their brave wild music filling the summer air—and I felt the goodness of it; it was not the Celts of long ago, but it was good.

From 1603 to 1747 the Highland clans were the main force the Stuart monarchs could rely on, despite the harsh and often underhanded treatment Highlanders received from Stuart kings James I, IV, V, and VI. It was mainly the faith of the common people, not the side-changing, opportunistic nobility, that kept alive the Scottish passion for autonomy. It took the famine of the 1690s and its attendant economic disasters (including the tragedy of Darien) to open the way for Scottish Parliamentary Union with England in 1707. Even then Scots commoners— both Lowlanders and Highlanders—were vehement in resistance. David Daiches, in *The Last Stuart: The Life and Times of Bonnie Prince Charles* writes:

> The most astonishing reaction, and the strongest proof of the unpopularity of the Articles of Union, was that of the Cameronians, those extreme Calvinist Covenanters of the south-west, who hated with equal ferocity Popery, Episcopacy, and Jacobitism. They actually talked of joining the Jacobites to restore the exiled James Francis Edward, the Catholic Stuart whose immediate forebears had so persecuted them. There were fierce demonstrations in the streets of Edinburgh and Glasgow, and elsewhere. . . . But too many members of the Scottish Parliament had been persuaded that it was in their interests to vote for the Articles of Union, and though the debate was often fierce and sometimes splendid, the conclusion was not really in doubt. . . .

Whig statesmen in power in England feared a Stuart restoration, especially of James, a Catholic. To pressure Scotland toward union, the 1705 Aliens Act deliberately placed Scotland in the category of "Alien," disastrous for trading purposes, unless Scots agreed to a Hanoverian succession to Queen Anne. To further ensure passage of the Articles of Union, the Whigs in Scottish Parliament, notably the Campbell Duke of Argyll, were well rewarded for the task of persuading other Scots legislators to accept union.

The parliaments were thus combined, but with Scotland allowed only sixteen representative peers and forty-five members of the House of Commons (compared to more than five-hundred English members), Scots public opinion was hostile and disorderly, sometimes violent in its opposition to this legislative sellout. But to no avail.

Prebble describes how "England's lack of sympathy for Scotland's particular needs seemed sometimes perverse and malicious, the triumph of a small boy who is winning a game he has himself devised. . . . This was not a union of equal peoples. . . . The English had inherited four centuries of contempt for Scotland, and saw no reason to change their minds because their most exclusive club had just admitted forty-five new members." J. D. Mackie notes that, "though in theory after 1 May, 1707 there was no English Parliament, but a wholly new 'British' legislature, in practice the English Parliament simply absorbed the Scottish one."

Three of Scotland's key institutions—educational, religious, and legal—remained intact after union, law becoming a draw for many sons of the gentry. Scottish political affairs were largely left in Scottish hands because they were "too difficult and convoluted for London to understand."

In the Lowlands the business class had a fluidity wherein, in accordance with tradition, there was no stigma attached to the landed elite also being merchants. Christopher Harvie, in *Strangers Within the Realm*, writes that, "They became noted for creative improvisation in trade and developed great efficiencies in the use of capital resources in trade, credit, and general commercial transactions."

But what of the wild Celts of the Highlands? After, as well as before, union with England, the Highlands were regarded as a frontier zone, its inhabitants uncouth, bloody barbarians. Clan histories are indeed violent, confusing dances of alliance and feud, each clan with its glories and disgraces, heroes and villains. It is often strictly a matter of partisanship who one concludes to be hero, and who villain. Especially confronting is the frequency of division within clans and families, brother fighting brother and son opposing father. But a pragmatic matter of survival was often an underlying basis for those divisions: the hope of at least some of the family being on a winning side to sustain clan lineage and holdings, something vital to Celts. The MacGregor clan was proscribed—relentlessly hunted and killed, a capital crime to even bear the name—for two periods totaling nearly two hundred years, yet when proscription was lifted, 825 persons came forward to reclaim the MacGregor name: tenacious survivors.

Into this framework came Bonnie Prince Charlie, last of the Stuarts to attempt to regain the throne. The Jacobite movement was named after Charlie's grandfather, the James (Jacobus) ousted by William of Orange, James' son-in-law. Charlie's father, another James, was a brave but melancholy man whose temperament was quite unlike the ardent, unruly, and gaily charming prince's. The second Jacobite uprising, attempted by Charlie's father in 1715, was mainly due to dissatisfaction with the parliamentary union, religious dissent, and sympathetic (though inadequate) support from Catholic Spain, France, Austria, and Italy. There was also the desire from some quarters to rein in the Campbells. Prebbles points out that "The strong core of the Jacobite army came from those clans whose hatred of Argyll (the Campbells) was fiercer than their loyalty to the Stuarts." The Jacobite rebellions were all complex affairs.

Only in the Highlands of Scotland could a military force be so swiftly mobilized, and this was due to the mechanisms of clanship, something that would later be exploited time after time by Britain in its imperialistic wars. Prince Charlie, born in Rome, ill-preparedly but determinedly sailed to his homeland at age twenty-four in hopes of fulfilling the royal dream of restoration in 1745. His father, James, having experienced repeated misfortune and defeat, did not give Charlie much encouragement, but admired his grit. The French, on whose "auld alliance" with Scotland Charlie depended for support, gave only token help. And the Highland chiefs, when Charlie arrived, bid the prince to go home. "I am home," he said, and loyal chiefs bowed to the task.

Why did they follow him? Partly because he was rightful Chief of chiefs, and their last hope for an autonomous Gaelic future. The Stuart mythos was something Scots reflexively responded to. And in Pittock's words, "The Stuart myth was no accretion of sentimental Jacobitism; it was contemporaneous with Stuart rule, not merely nostalgic." The myth of the Stuarts was Celtic. The oak was an early symbol for Stuart kings, bringing to mind druidism of old. There was also the recurring association of Stuart kings with the renewal of the land's strength and fertility, a concept directly connected to Celtic pagan belief. One hundred thousand Scots died in the famine years of Dutch William of Orange's reign, in a country that still related good harvests with good kings.

But the prince's army rarely exceeded 8000 men—at maximum he had 5710 Highlanders, 4220 Lowlanders, and 1200 assorted English, French, and Irish fighters. He mainly had to be content with a group of about 5500, and 4500 were clansmen out of a Highland potential of 32,000 fighters. The clans of the far north supported the government, and others, like MacDonald of Sleat and Macleod of Dunvegan, simply held aloof. Little was heard from the Welsh, and only 300 English Jacobites joined the cause.

Between one-fourth and one-third of the government's 30,000 soldiers opposing Charlie were Scots. The prince's Catholicism was a primary reason for lack of support for Charlie in the Lowlands and, to some extent, in the Highlands as well. But even with a £30,000 bounty on his head—a fortune in those days—no Scot turned in the prince, before or after Culloden.

Charlie's venture seems foolhardy, but strategists still debate whether the prince might have won through sheer Celtic panache had he continued, as he sorely wanted to, from Derby to London— where the city was in panic over the prince's advance.

The "barbarian" clansmen, during their battle campaign, gave cash for supplies acquired on the march and behaved remarkably well. "Yet instead of commentators and observers recognizing its merit, it was merely noted as astonishing conduct on the part of savages and banditti. . . . It was commonly believed in England that the Highlanders were cannibals." (Pine)

One of the prince's main problems, and not a new one for commanders of Highland troops, was keeping his army intact. Clansmen traditionally fought for economic reasons or for feuds, not for love of war or politics. Even famous leaders had trouble keeping Highland armies together, particularly if the fighting moved out of the Highland region itself. Like American Indian warriors, Highlanders seemed to become dispirited and homesick away from their families and lands. After victorious battles they tended to take the immediate booty and go home; and in defeat or retreat, to simply go home. So, on top of all else, Charlie and his lieutenant commander, the able but conservative

George Murray (who was at constant odds with the impetuous prince) had to deal with the effect of continual troop desertions even when they were winning.

Historian Daiches tells us:

> The Highland army was a volunteer army, at least as far as the chiefs were concerned. The chiefs themselves felt free to come and go as they wished, and even those of their humble clansmen whom they had forced from their routine labours to join them had no scruple in slipping away when they had some booty to take home or some domestic problem to attend to. It is difficult for the modern mind to comprehend the precise mixture of unquestioned loyalty to the chief, deep sense of blood kinship with other members of the clan, and individual feelings of pride and independence that co-existed in the mind of the ordinary clansman. Charles discovered that the loyalty of those Highlanders who had pledged themselves to him was both passionate and devoted and at the same time hedged around with a touchy sense of their own dignity. He learned by experience to take from the chiefs what he would never have taken from any subject elsewhere. He found himself involved in concepts of honour that had long been lost in the rest of civilized Europe, and he had to play it by ear. The paradoxes—the apparent mixture of impertinence and devotion, of obstinacy and high courtesy, of absolutism and individualism, of graspingness and generosity, even of prudent timidity and extravagant courage—fascinated Lowlanders throughout the eighteenth century.

Leading the government forces in the final battle was the Duke of Cumberland, younger son of King George II and cousin to Prince Charlie; a professional soldier four months younger than the prince. (Both Stuarts and Hanoverians gained thrones through female lines.) Moray McLaren, in *Bonnie Prince Charlie,* describes the final battle:

> The Prince's soldiers had neither time to eat, nor dally over positions in line of battle. . . . The men were mustered with the aid of pipes, drums and the occasional boot. Officers ran about on all sides to rouse them . . . some were quite exhausted and not able to crawl. . . . All nine thousand of [Cumberland's]

troops were fed and fit. . . . Colonel Belford gave an order for the government artillery to open fire. . . . Belford's gunners poured cannonballs into the clan formation with a continuous roaring that was itself terrifying. The effect was devastating. Great holes were cut in the Highland lines within the space of a few minutes. Desperately the chiefs shouted to their men to close ranks. The men, in turn, begged for the order to charge; they were expected to stand and be killed for no reason except that someone had not given the command that could stop the carnage. Most of those who died in the battle were killed at this time, their limbs parted from them and hurled among their fellows. For nearly half an hour Belford's guns thundered, destroying a third of the Highland army before Clan Chattan broke line and charged. . . . Before the clansmen could negotiate their own dead, the government infantry began their musket roll. Of twenty-one officers who had run forward with Clan Chatten, only three survived the first volleys. . . . The MacDonalds had to run for more than half a mile, in the face of unwavering fire, before they could respond to the Duke of Perth's futile cries of "Claymore, claymore!" . . . The Scots paid dearly for their devotion to Prince Charles and the House of Stuart. . . . Cumberland's aim all along had been the pacification of the Highlands, and with this he now proceeded by systematically destroying the economy of the region and the society upon which the army of clans was founded. The brutality which followed the fight on 16 April remains inexcusable.

The massacre of the clans at Culloden was so excessive it earned Cumberland his appellation, "the Butcher." Charlie escaped but most of the loyal clansmen and their families did not. Blanket oppression and cultural proscription ensured no future uprising. The clans and their Gaelic way of life, a seven-hundred-year continuity, were smashed. In Prebble's words:

This time the policy of repression was inexorable. It began immediately with an order for the extermination of the wounded who still lay on the field. It was continued by the harsh imposition of martial law, the shooting and hanging of fugitives, the driving of stock, the burning of house and cottage. . . . The prisoners taken were tried in England, lest Scot juries be too fainthearted. . . . The carrying of arms was forbidden under penalty of death. The wearing of tartan, kilt, or plaid was banned. . . . When the proscription on Highland dress was lifted in 1782, few common people accepted it. It became the affectation of the Anglicized lairds, the fancy dress of the Lowlanders, and the uniform of the King's Gaelic soldiers.

The military occupation lasted nearly one hundred years, and such measures as sterilization of Jacobite women and destitution of seed corn and farm implements were considered by Parliament. James Hunter starkly points out that the Highlander's "failure to qualify as 'civilized' [rendered] them liable to treatment of a kind that eighteenth century Britain would never have considered meting out to any of the several European nations with which the country was so frequently at war."

From 1782–1820 and 1840–1854, the Highland Clearances, which were mainly the work of Highland chiefs and ducal landlords, brought shameful conclusion to the honorable, long-abiding relationship between clanspeople and chiefs. No chief after Culloden had much left of his traditional authority, and, legally, had no obligations to clanspeople. The one right the chiefs clung to was that of treating tenants and subtenants as a military resource, now at the disposal of imperial Britain. Those recruits who refused to serve were often turned out of their farms. Even those who went into the king's regiments often returned to find their homes burned, their families scattered. As Prebble said of the chiefs: "A glen that had once supported five townships of his children, giving him little more than their affection and loyalty, could make him richer than many Englishmen if he replaced them with four shepherds, six dogs, and three thousand lowing clansmen of the True Mountain Breed."

The Clearances generated massive emigration, both forced and voluntary. Sheep, and deer for sport hunting, replaced Highland families, and the people were reduced, in a historian's words, to "utter insignificance." Pine comments that "The strangest feature of the Clearances was that the men made hardly any resistance, astonishing indeed from a race whose ancestors had been so martial. Women, aided by boys, opposed the sheriff's men, the police, and in some cases the soldiers who were sent to evict them."

Pittock observes that:

The replacement of people by sheep, and the abolition of the ancient system of land tenure, together with the resultant experiences of hardship and exile, are issues which remain emotive. . . . Culloden and the Clearances go together because the latter even clarified and intensified the effects of the former. . . . The clan system's privileges and powers had been rendered insecure by the laws passed after Culloden. In the circumstances, what could be more likely than that the leadership of the old system, their positions undermined, would seek some measure of *rapprochement* or integration with the victorious structures of government? . . . By the end of the eighteenth century, up to a tenth of the population may have been lost through emigration.

None of the chiefs (except the Grants of Glen Urquhart and Glen Moriston) who kept their lands or had them restored after Culloden were innocent of evicting their clanspeople. More than one-third of Scotland's population lived in the Highlands in 1750—today only 5 percent do so, and many are not Highlanders. Pittock states, "Such stark depopulation, matched only in Ireland, is to be attributed to economic pressure and economic tyranny. In 1811, there were 250,000 sheep in the Highlands; in the 1840's close on a million. The space for them was bought at the cost of human suffering."

Some of the Clearances were carried out not for sheep economy, but for the making of a deer-hunting paradise for the well-to-do, again mainly on arable land previously inhabited. Why didn't clansmen resist the Clearances? Memory of Culloden's aftermath was still strong; the working class was held in economic subjugation and under threat of transport to such places as Botany Bay. The people were isolated—they had no resources or support, and communication was difficult. The Church served (and was well rewarded by) the sheep lairds, and the clansmen had a wretched reluctance to break from traditional loyalties; they blamed the middlemen but not the chiefs. Self-respect was crushed.

R. Hago's poem, published in *Making Certain It Goes On: Collected Poems*, says,

Lord it took no more than a wave of the glove,
a nod of the head over tea. People were torn from their crofts
and herded aboard, their land turned over to sheep.

They sailed, they wept.
The sea said nothing and said I'll get even
Their last look at Skye lasted one hour. Then fog.
Think of their fear . . .
Think of loss that goes stormy knots beyond bitter
and think of some absentee landlord home in his tower
signing the order and waving off a third ale.

Some of the clanspeople had to be chained and bound to be put aboard the ships, others went willingly as immigration became a collective rejection of the punishing social and economic structures of the day.

Lowlanders in this period meanwhile grappled with assimilation in the larger world. In the 1700s, "The Scots, especially in London, enjoyed the dubious distinction of being marginally more unpopular than the Jews" (Bailyn and Morgan). Gradually, ostracism was overcome, only to be repeated overseas where the "extrovert energy" of the Scots and their successes in the Atlantic system were so remarkable as to cause Samuel Johnson to accuse the Scots of exploiting the English!

Generally Scots in America, except the Ulster Scots, supported George III in the Revolution, gaining them more animosity, though back in Britain Scots received positive notice not only for their contributions to philosophy and science—appreciated in Europe for some time prior to union—but also for other gifts. In 1757, David Hume wrote:

> Is it not strange that, at a time when we have lost our Princes, our Parliaments, our independent Government, even the Presence of our chief Nobility, are unhappy in our Accent and Pronounciation, speak a corrupt Dialect of the Tongue which we make use of; is it not strange, I say, that, in these Circumstances, we shou'd really be the People most distinguish'd for Literature in Europe?

The Highlanders, however, with their poverty, isolation, and profound rural conservatism, alienated from their lands and chiefs, remained resistant to assimilation, refusing to cooperate with impositions made upon them and protesting outrageous rent increases and other abuses. The government language of improvement was condescending, a vocabulary of colonization that treated the proud High-landers as backward, at best as "noble aborigines," in contrast to the Lowlanders and their vigorous participation in newfound opportunity. The only realm in which Highlanders of this time distinguished themselves in the eyes of the conquerors was in that of service to England in foreign wars, from which, the English noted with relief, "few will come back."

In our own ways, some of us do come back. Roaming the hills above Newtonmore, my friend Robin, a descendant of Clearance immigrants, said, "This journey has given me back my heritage." Connection steadies and strengthens us as individuals, as parents, and as participants in community. Connection defeats the resourcelessness that shadows isolation, giving us something to call upon, whether amid society or in solitude, making us less alienated from ourselves and each other.

The restless dreams taking us soaring and blundering into raw experience again and again find maturation in locality, in commitment to the land. The return is not just to heritage, but to what can flower from those roots. We are the current outcome of our ancestors' prayers, choices, responses; descendants of a fractured but not vanished culture. We are its far-flung shards, seeking a new cohesion in the truth of a people's vision.

Every Beauty

Day's sensitivity—evening
when soul hears itself single
as a mistle thrush
on the gaunt March moor;
blue-hushed as Hebridean
twilight, endless June;
like prints pathing tide-cleaned shores;
the bend of grass, forever streams
of wind smoothing the braes;
repetitious and unconforming
as sea waves, green translucent poise,
froth curling, skirts cast upon stone;
the sheerness of cliffs, of peregrine's
fall; conjured silver loch of moonlight
quivering upon the Cuillin Sound;
every beauty perilous.

PART II

SPIRIT

"H"AVE NOT ALL RACES HAD THEIR FIRST UNITY from a polytheism that marries them to rock and hill?" asked Willie Yeats, quoted by Maud Gonne in "Yeats and Ireland."

Marriage to rock and hill is perhaps the most enduring cornerstone of Celtic spirituality, despite overlays of Catholicism or Protestantism. Land sense remains primary, in both subtle and concrete forms. Thus, Celtic spirituality is most easily understood if considered within the environmental context of Celtic lands: Ireland, Britain, Scotland, Brittany, Wales, the Isle of Man.

These are places of mists and standing stones, of vivid green luminosity, of wind-haunted moors, treacherous bogs, and sea-battered islands. In this environment it is clear why Celtic reality is a fluid, transmutable affair. The Otherworld is not only an afterlife domain; it is an alternative reality coexistent with the mundane world, ever present. Burial mounds, the ocean, sacred wells, and sidhe mounds are portals to Otherworld reality. In Anne Ross's words, "The everyday life of the Celts included the supernatural equally with the natural, the divine with the mundane; for them the Otherworld was as real as the tangible physical world and as everpresent." John O'Donohue says, "The Celts had an intuitive spirituality informed by mindful and reverent attention to landscape. It was an outdoor spirituality impassioned by the erotic charge of the earth."

I climbed down a sea cliff to explore the shore's caves and rocks on a remote peninsula of the Highlands one grey spring day. As I clambered over kelp-slick boulders and peered into the crevices of sea stacks a fine, misty rain began falling, swirled by breeze. I found a snug nook inside one of the caves, putting my wool gloves beneath me to lessen the stone's cold, writing in my journal until my pen ran out of ink. I packed up papers and headed up the cliff; the footing had not improved, and I was not dressed for rain. The climb was long and tiring. Rain increased. High above the shore I paused to rest on a rock and suddenly realized I had left my gloves in the cave below. "Damn!" I thought. Then I thought about the lovely stones in my backpack taken from the beach and about the offering tobacco sitting in my hostel room, and about lessons I teach and sometimes forget in my own living of a spiritual life. The issue was not whether the gloves stayed or were retrieved. It was the practice of integrity.

Abruptly I knew I had to go back for the gloves. I slid down the precipitous slope, fast and risky. The tide was coming in. I picked up the gloves and left an offering, then doggedly mounted the cliff again as rain flattened the ocean swell. About three-quarters of the way up I angled toward a rock overhang and wedged myself beneath it. At my back was a deep narrow crack in the stone from which wafted a draught of cavelike chill air, a subterranean exhalation. Braced there, rain dripping off the eave and down the rugged face of the stone, rain dripping from my saturated hair and clothes, I gazed out at the swaying sea, at the mists shrouding the outer isles, the land at the edge of the world. Behind me, a sudden sound distinctly like the slamming of a door came from deep in the black cleft I leaned against, and the cold stream of air ceased. It was at the same time eerie and ordinary seeming. In a museum archives, weeks later, I came across references to the Gille Dubh of Loch aDruing, the region's most famous faery of more modern times. In the 1700s a party of gentry unsuccessfully rode out to try and shoot the faery (though he was a beneficent faery if ever there was one). The Gille Dubh lived about two miles from Rudha Reidh, where I was hiking that day on the sea cliff. I like to imagine I was not far from his threshold, and that he perhaps accepted my offering.

Fluidity was expressed through many avenues of Celtic conscious-ness. Knot-work designs—indeed, much of Celtic art—flowed, fig-ures rising out of abstraction, transforming into other shapes, then back into abstraction: strange and complex. Many Celtic deities were triple-aspected, the number three and its multiples being considered mystically significant. The soul was seen as a triple spiral, or as a butterfly, moth, or ball of light. Its name in Gaelic, *anan*, related to *anal* (breath), signifying a mobile life force having no predestination but reliant on integrity of heart, mind, and soul. Anan abided in the head and hair but moved in blood and breath and could travel into animal or other shape. (Ingesting someone's blood created kinship bonds.) Also triple were the "releases" of grief, joy, and repose that restored the soul; these were often embodied in Celtic stories by three harp notes or three bird songs.

Fire, used to avert ill, was carried sunwise around people, dwell-ings, or objects three times as a blessing. In the Highlands it was cus-tomary to welcome or bless people by circling them three times and wishing them happiness and well-being. The new moon—preferably caught sight of outdoors and not through window glass—was bowed to three times in greeting. A prayer collected by Alexander Carmichael in the Highlands expresses Celtic relationship to nature: "Hail to you, the Moon of my love. I am bending to you my knee, I am offering to you my love, I am giving to you my hand, I am lifting to you my eye. You joyful maiden of my love, I am bowing to you my head."

Fluidity of Celtic spiritual perspective carries through in the rela-tionships between humans and deities; there was much intercourse (of all kinds), and it was sometimes hard to distinguish between mor-tals and immortals. Gods and goddesses were ancestors, not creators, of the Celts. Prophecy was sought through sleeping on the grave mounds of ancestors—these mounds gave access to realms in which ancestors and the sidhe abided. Grave mounds, except those of plague victims, had doors included in their constructions. The future was learned from the past; it was a fluid knot-work of transmigrating, shifting continuity.

Traveling one year in Scotland with my friends Catherine and Robin and Robin's daughter, Gia, we stopped at a number of Pictish stone circles and cairns. Northeast Scotland has hundreds of these circles, most of them three to five thousand years old. At Loanhead was a complex of stone rings with cairns in their centers for cremated remains. I had a compelling urge to spend the night there—an urge

that made sense when I later learned this was a traditional Celtic practice. At Cullerie, another burial and ceremonial site, farmworkers next
door were noisily wrapping hay bales in plastic with a machine, trac-
tors roaring, but none of it particularly disturbed the atmosphere of
the cairns.

We sat against the stones; the atmosphere of the place was more
enclosed than at expansive Loanhead, more focused toward center,
with both a feeling of loss and of sustaining power. Images of ashes
and spirals arose in my consciousness amid a circulation of awareness and vitality. A third site, Tomnaverie, was reached by opening
and shutting a cattle gate, climbing a rough hill, and walking through
a loitering herd of cows to a rock-shouldered promontory where the
stone circle—small but striking—stood in the center of a 360-degree
panoramic view. The countryside there was gracious—big stone farms
and estates nested into valleys and hillsides; there were green meadows and graceful hills, spreading trees and sparkling rivers.

In windy sunlight we sat with the stones, sensing the linking of
those hundreds of circles, ourselves part of their pattern that day.
Tomnaverie seemed weighty despite its airy venue—an atmosphere
of endings and passings, but also one of strong regeneration, sexuality: bull medicine. I had an impulse to lie down as I had at other
circles with "recumbent" stones. Catherine did lay down, her consciousness sinking into another realm. When we rose to leave, I felt
the distinct physical sensation of something dropping away from me,
something long carried. My life turned a corner—so simply—but
everything changed.

Ritual and daily life merged for the ancient Celts, with no segregation of place of worship from the land. Both spirituality and life were
naturalistic. The priests—Druids—were not peasantry but were nonetheless oriented to the land, not to cities or ostentatious cathedrals.
Celts worshiped in groves and at holy lakes, wells, and springs, and
what shrines they built were simple, transitory structures or banked
earthen enclosures. Ross tells us that "Religion and superstition . . .
played a fundamental and profound role in the *everyday* life of the
Celts. . . . Perhaps even more than other ancient people, the Celts
were so completely engrossed with, and preoccupied by, their religion and its expression that it was constantly and positively to the
forefront of their lives." There is an old Celtic saying that translates

thus: "The land of eternal youth is behind the house, a beautiful land fluent within itself." The Gaelic phrase *fighte fuaighte,* which means "woven into and through each other," describes this fusion of ordinary and Otherworld realities.

Ancient Celts practiced magic. T. W. Rolleston says, "The fundamental conception of magic is that of the spiritual vitality of all nature. This spirituality was not, as in polytheism, conceived as separated from nature in distinctive divine personalities. It was implicit and immanent in nature." This is an important clarification to understand. Celtic spirituality was perhaps more akin to the religions of ancient Egypt and the Middle East than to those of Rome and Greece.

Until the eighteenth century, astronomy and astrology were the same science, and part of Druidic knowledge. Rites of prophecy were another branch of practice, involving various kinds of divination: interpreting the flights of birds; the movements of clouds; the patterns of entrails; the casting of inscribed hazel wands *(coelbreni);* dreams and visions; and the answers given by the spinning *peithynen* with its wheel-like staves of carved wood. Precognitive dreams were obtained by sleeping in conducive places, such as ancestral mounds or on certain animal skins, or in particular positions, all augmented by ceremonial preparation. The *filidh* (learned laypeople) in Ireland used *teinm laegda,* "illumination of song," a technique involving visionary or trance poetry and chanting combined with psychometry. Other of their oracular methods included *dichetal do chennaib* (inspired incantations) and *imbas forosna* (kindling of poetic frenzy), often using myths and stories as pathways to the Otherworld. The Druids were known to be capable of raising mists and storms, bringing slumber upon people, and performing other feats of magic.

Among Scottish Highlanders, even into modern times, the gift (though many regarded it more as a burden) of second sight was well evidenced. Like skill at piping, it was considered a bestowal of the faeries. There were many kinds of second sight, as evidenced by the various words used to describe them: *bruadar* meant "visionary dream"; *taibhsear* meant "spectre-haunted"; *fioschd* was augury and *fiosaiche* was knowing the future; those with *tannasg* saw apparitions of those already dead and those with tamhasg saw specters of those about to die. The inclusive term for all these was *dá-shealladh,* literally, "two-sighted." Another gift was the power to work the *sian* spell, an incantation for making objects invisible, often for seven-year intervals, after which the object rematerialized. Some people were multiply gifted with the sian, second sight, and other visionary abilities. Most instances of second sight occurred in ordinary folk with no desire for or cultivation of magical skills.

To the ancient Celts the land had spiritual orientation. Anu (or Danu) was a source goddess; Aine was life's sparkle and vitality; Grian, her sister, was goddess of the sun. Ross describes Celtic goddesses as controlling the land and seasons, and notes that "they were sexually potent and maternally inclined." The Celts made pilgrimages to land formations that were significant in their relationship with the sacred—those places were circled clockwise (sunwise) and prayers and offerings made, sometimes represented by cloth ties (similar to some American Indian forms of offering). Before knowing of the traditional sunwise circling, when I visited sacred sites in Scotland, I spontaneously circumambulated them several times before entering their precincts.

Movement in those historic places of ceremony often can still be guided by implicit patterns created by centuries of use, even if that use has been in abeyance for a long time. If a modern person is perceptive and willing to be guided, much can be discerned, making possible the participation in an evolution of Celtic spiritual practice.

The vitality of Britain was considered to be guarded by dragons abiding in the Welsh mountains of Snowdonia, the land's spiritual heart. In Ireland, the country was seen in terms of the four directions and center (the "four fifths"), with Knowledge in the west, Battle in the north, Prosperity in the east, Music in the south, and Kingship in the center. *The Yellow Book of Lecan,* a Middle Irish text, describes an ancestral view of Ireland's realms:

> *West:* Her learning, her foundation, her teaching, her alliance, her judgment, her chronicles, her counsels, her stories, her histories, her science, her comeliness, her eloquence, her beauty, her modesty, her bounty, her abundance, her wealth.
> *North:* Her contentions, her hardihood, her rough places, her strifes, her haughtiness, her unprofitableness, her pride, her captures, her assaults, her hardness, her wars, her conflicts.
> *East:* Her prosperity, her supplies, her beehives, her contests, her feats of arms, her householders, her nobles, her wonders, her good custom, her good manners, her splendor, her abundance, her dignity, her strength, her wealth, her householding, her many arts, her accoutrements, her many

treasures, her satin, her serge, her silks, her cloths, her green spotted cloth, her hospitality.

South: Her waterfalls, her fairs, her nobles, her reavers, her knowledge, her subtlety, her musicianship, her melody, her minstrelsy, her wisdom, her honour, her music, her learning, her teaching, her warriorship, her fidchell playing, her vehemence, her fierceness, her poetical arts, her advocacy, her modesty, her code, her retinue, her fertility.

Center: Her kings, her stewards, her dignity, her primacy, her stability, her establishments, her supports, her destructions, her warriorship, her charioteership, her soldiery, her principality, her high-kingship, her oilaveship, her mead, her bounty, her ale, her renown, her great fame, her prosperity.

In Scotland, directions were orientations of wind: there were twelve winds, each with its own color and particular influence. The north wind was black and unfortunate; the south wind was white, bringing good luck and long life. Dun was the color of the west wind, on which death was carried; and most sacred was the east wind, purple, from which no ill ever came. (East was the orientation for most Celtic enclosures, including doorways to houses.) A number of Celtic magical rites were associated with influencing or controlling the wind. In ancient Ireland the winds or *airts* were commanded by Cu Roi, a very interesting king of Munster; the winds were also used in druidic curses. In the Highlands it was considered important to turn away from the north direction while harvesting: "my back to the airt of the north and my face to the fair sun of power." (Carmichael)

It is intriguing to compare Celtic directional correspondences with those of American Indian medicine wheels. The correspondences represented by the winds related to physical experience with weather, tidal effect, and agricultural concerns, as well as with metaphysical influences. Gaelic has numerous terms for different kinds of wind (and rain). *Gobag* is "the biter," the mother of January (wolftime) storms, for instance; and *teadag* is "the whistler" of spring, and *squabag* "the sweeper" of the final three days of spring. In Gaelic, *beither* denotes weather full of lightning and thunder, but the word also means "serpent": *goath na beithreach* is the serpent wind, considered nature's most devastating force.

MacCana describes the Dreamtime perspective of the Irish, their relationship to spirit through sacred geography:

Every river and lake and well, every plain and hill and mountain has its own name, and each name evokes its explanatory legend. These legends constitute a distinct branch of native tradition known as *dinnshenchas,* "the lore of prominent places," which was an important part of the repertoire of the *fili,* the expert in native learning, and which, not surprisingly, became a staple element of literary creation. . . . The *dinnshenchas* is thus a kind of comprehensive topography, a legendary guide to the Irish landscape, and it is for that reason significant that it assigns a conspicuous, even a dominant, role to the female divinities, for it is these, as avatars, or manifestations, of the earth goddess, who are primarily associated with the land in all its various aspects; its fertility, its sovereignty, its embodiment of the powers of death as well as of life, and so on.

More evidence of the Celt's multidimensional perspective is seen in how the sidhe, the magical people of the Otherworld, were characterized by powers of transformation and invisibility, not by invincibility or moral authority, an important departure from many other religions. Celtic spirituality was not paternalistic, hierarchical, or needful of absolutism; and it did not engage itself with sin and redemption or the realizing of ethical behavior through divine policing. Historian Ward Rutherford states that druidic doctrine did not "accept the duality of Good and Evil, but understood their own lives and the universe itself as being guided by a single internal movement. There was, in consequence, no concept of reward or punishment in an afterlife." Irish writer and theologen John O'Donohue agrees with this view of Celtic spirituality when he states that:

The Celtic mind was not burdened by dualism. It did not separate what belongs together. The Celtic imagination articulates the inner friendship that embraces Nature, divinity, underworld, and human world as one. The dualism that separates the visible from the invisible, time from eternity, the human from the divine, was totally alien to them.

Druids were, above all, concerned with truth, which included justice, holiness, and faithfulness, and living in harmony with nature. These were aspects of freedom, wherein lay moral strength. Strabo

called the Druids the "most just of men," and Diodorus Siculus reported that, "They are of much sincerity and integrity, far from the
craft and knavery of men among us (Greeks), contented with homely
fare, strangers to excess and luxury."

Celtic deities were not limited, as were those of the Greeks, Romans, and so on, to certain fixed attributes; they were often paradoxical. There was no tidy pantheon of Celtic gods and goddesses; religion, like the rest of Celtic life, was not dogmatic, centralized, or
political—many deities were localized, like features of landscape.
Anthropologists have collected some three hundred to four hundred
names of Celtic deities from various places, but only a few names
recurred in more than one area: deitific essence recurred but with
variations of expression, as with the variation between an oak and an
ash tree. There were also, notably, no exclusively male cults in Celtic
religion.

An abundance of shapeshifting transpired in Celtic myths and
stories—it was a pervasive element of Celtic perspective. Gods and
goddesses, magical people, even mortals, often took the form of animals; rivers were often goddesses, as was the land itself. Shapeshifting
may be thought of as a movement of power or awareness from realm
to realm based on resonance. It is interesting that the Picts' name in
Gaelic, Cruithni, relates to cruth, meaning shape, form, or aspect;
cruithear means "creator" in Scots Gaelic. (Some translators link the
name Cruithni to "wheat grower.") In many Celtic tales, the spirits
and fates of humans were intertwined with those of animals, trees, or
other beings.

Names—sometimes guarded or withheld—were sacred and significant to Celts, and animals were important aspects of many Celtic
names. Ross and Robins tell us that:

> The Celts have always evinced a strong feeling for and affin-
> ity with animals; it is a fundamental aspect of their culture
> and their character for which there is evidence at all stages of
> their traceable history. . . . Three things are deeply imprinted
> on the Celtic subconscious: the concept of druidism; the pre-
> occupation with naming, and with ancestors; and fundamen-
> tal respect for wild creatures . . . animals, birds, fish, and even
> plants. . . . To say the Celts were animal lovers, to imply that
> they were unusually compassionate toward animals, would
> probably be erroneous. But they felt that other creatures

coexisted with them, both in this world and in the hereafter, that they had their own powers and, especially, their own magic. It was, Celts believed, possible to learn the languages of the animals and birds. It was also possible for other creatures to adopt human shapes and vice versa. In the early Celtic world, there were no barriers between things, all which coexisted and mingled in a timeless existence. Death was but an extension of life, and a living creature could appear in any guise without exciting wonder or incredulity.

In Scotland's Hebrides, certain families were considered, even in fairly recent times, to be descended from seals. One of these families of *sliocha non ron,* was the MacCodrums of North Uist, a family of bardic lineage. The MacCodrums lived in a seal-killing area, but no one bearing the name MacCodrum would kill or eat seals, or use their skins or oil. The MacCodrums lived by the sea and by seal rocks but abstained from profiting from this proximity. Their adherence to this connection with seals lasted beyond the totemism observed by other clans, perhaps due, in some part, to this proximity. A MacCodrum woman used to be seized with violent pains at the time of the annual seal hunts in October.

The MacLeod clan was associated with horses, the MacDonalds with dogs, and the MacIntoshes, MacNichols, MacNeishes, and Clan Chattan with cats. The Hebridean MacCrimmons of Skye and MacPhees of Colonsay claimed seal lineage. The MacKelvies were linked with doves, the MacMasters with pigs, and the MacGregors—at one time themselves hunted down with dogs—were associated with bloodhounds. Animal totemism was prevalent among the Picts also.

Fluidity of perspective and absence of authoritarian dogma made the Celts extraordinarily tolerant of other religions; there was no compulsion to either defend or impose their own beliefs and practices. Ireland may be the only place in the world having no Christian martyrs. The ancient Celts did not conduct religious persecutions; it is unfortunate that, as Christians, this tolerance seems diminished. Still, religious freedom continues to be a Celtic issue and was, for many, reason for emigration. Historian Rutherford questions:

> Why, for example, was the Protestant Reformation so complete in Brittany, Wales, Scotland, Northern Ireland, the Isle of Man and the Channel Islands? In Brittany, it is true, Ca-

tholicism later made good the losses it sustained at the hand of Calvinism, though only by dint of massacre and repression and even then was forced to accept compromise. The Catholicism of Brittany is still acknowledged as possessing an individualism all its own and much the same can be said for that of Southern Ireland. Could it be that something in Druidism, some attitude or cast of mind it developed in its adherents, had lingered to explain this?

Robert Van de Weyer, in *Celtic Fire: An Anthology of Celtic Christian Literature*, in also trying to bridge the perspectives of druidism and modern Celtic religion, says:

The second major influence [Druidism being the first] on Celtic Christianity was the desert fathers of Egypt. . . . The quirky humor of the desert monks, their stubborn individualism, and, above all, their love of nature, appealed to the Celtic spirit, greatly enhancing the attraction of the Christian faith. . . . The third main influence was the doctrine of the great British Heretic, Pelagius. . . . He was repelled by the lavish comforts of the Roman bishops and priests, and by the huge inequalities of wealth in Roman society, which were to him an affront to the simple morality of the gospel. And he hated, too, the fashionable doctrine of original sin, which taught that all men are helpless sinners and can only be saved by the unmerited grace of God. . . . Morever, he urged people to regard Jesus, not as some remote divine figure, but as an intimate friend and brother.

During his lifetime Pelagius was accused of trying to revive druidic philosophy on nature and free will. Saint Brigid's father was a Druid, and his daughter probably was also; just as some aspects of druidism merged with Celtic Christianity, so did some Druids merge into the Christian priesthood and its politics. Druidic influence was still noticeable into the eighth century, and Druids were specifically discriminated against in medieval Irish law codes.

The Druids in ancient times were a social class, not simply a priesthood. Rutherford makes a case for them having links to the Persian Magi, the Hindu Brahmins, and the Babylonian priesthood. Perhaps no other religious order has as little known about it and as much imagined about it as the Druids. If there is a paucity of information available about the ancient Celts, due to their lack of written records and their mobile, diffuse way of life with its disinterest in making a mark through monuments and material culture, there is even scarcer information about the Druids. Yet, in the introduction to Rutherford's *The Druids and Their Heritage,* the author says:

> As guardians of the laws and social customs of Celtic civili-
> sation, the Druids codified the ideals upon which Celtic soci-
> ety was based. Druidic philosophy has been of the utmost
> importance in shaping our western ideals. The virtuous war-
> rior, the notion of the benign non-authoritarian ruler, our basic
> ideas of democracy, egalitarian society and sexual equality,
> our ideals of romantic love—all spring from Druidic religion.

This is a singularly important statement to ponder. But modern re-creations of druidism, as developed in neopaganism, have little in common with the priesthood of old and druidism's encompassing of larger social issues. Where has the real Celticism gone?

Neodruidism, like neoshamanism and neopaganism, is easy to ridicule for its yearnings, its costuming, its flakiness and pretension, its tendency to be urban rather than rural, and its sparsity of effective, genuine basis and practice. A dismissive attitude, however, not only overlooks the presence of adept practitioners, but ignores the positive quest within a yearning toward natural and ancestral forms of spirituality. Neodruids are not perpetrating religious wars and persecutions—a pertinent observation to bear in mind. They tend toward tolerance, the neopagan motto being "And it harm none, do as ye will." As noted in the discussion of heritage, there is something useful in identifying with a continuity of beauty: Whether roots are real or imagined, if they nourish a context for good to manifest, then they serve a pragmatically worthwhile purpose. There certainly are worse partial understandings or illusions than those embraced by neopagans.

This is not to imply support for illusions of tradition, lies about spiritual lineage, gulling of innocent seekers, trivializing of complex practices, or other ills of neopaganism. But if someone wants to call himself a Druid in connection with some form of respectful relationship with nature, this seems laudable in today's rape-and-pillage corporate society. Cynics who demean dreams of spiritual loveliness and magic in turn docilely submit to modern religious absurdities that are often disempowering, lightless versions of spiritual reality. Conventionality, in both its timidity of vision and arrogance of position, has only a squatter's claim to "truth." Neo-Celts lack the training, mindset, and context of their ancestors. In no real sense can neo-Celts become traditional Druids. Druidic traditon's essence however, was the serving of freedom and equality based on integrated concepts of justice. In other words, it was discernment of harmonious function and active participation honoring those balances. This is a tradition toward which neo-Celts can orient and, in doing so, innovate relevant spiritual practices of their own with which to manifest Celticism's living reality.

Druidism of old was well established by the fourth century B.C. or earlier. Aristotle mentions Druids, and even if Celts did not build Stonehenge or Ireland's neolithic passage graves, Druids no doubt made use of those sites. The Druid priests were a highly trained lot; it took seven to ten years for a trainee to attain the level of seer or diviner, and possibly twenty years to become a Druid. Think of it— *twenty years!* Why so long? Remember, the Celts kept few written records, except of the most mundane matters. Everything important was memorized and orally transmitted. Commemorative inscriptions were made in ógham, a cryptic, notched writing on wood or stone markers. There were numerous forms of ógham; in one, each ógham letter correlated to the name of a tree.

Ógham is not believed by many historians to have been used prior to the third or fourth centuries B.C., but Bronze Age ógham was found in New England stone inscriptions dating to 800 B.C. In the first century B.C., many continental Celts were writing in Latin. (Irish became Europe's third language, joining Greek and Latin.) Ógham was mainly seen in inscriptions, some druidic poetry and incantations, and in other sacred contexts. There is controversial evidence of books in Ireland before Christianity, and these were probably druidic texts, though most sacred knowledge was kept strictly in oral form.

Druid historians had to know by heart at least 350 historical and romance tales and be able to recite them at a moment's notice. They had to memorize the prerogatives, rights, duties, restrictions, and tributes of all provincial and petty kings, and had to observe battles in order to give true accounts of all deeds. These historians later become the *seanchas*, the custodians of tradition employed by chieftains to keep family genealogies.

The seanchas in Irish villages customarily told stories each night from Samhain until Beltain, when summer returned. Storytelling was for winter nights—another similarity to the ways of American Indians. It was considered risky to bring Otherworld goings-on into the mundane business of day. Some tales lasted an entire night or were told in serial form. Stories the seanchas of the post-Christian era related were once the province of the filidh, experts in native learning whose repertoires included tales of destructions, cattle raids, battles, deaths, courtships, elopements, feasts, adventures in the Otherworld, and visions. The filidh's art in ancient times was handsomely supported, and fili were immune from criminal prosecution except in cases of murder or treason. The power of breath and word, honed to finest expression, was Brigid's gift, goddess of poetry, smithcraft, and healing. Incantation and poetry were closely aligned: the word *fili* is sometimes translated as "weaver of spells." As told by Cross and Slover in *Ancient Irish Tales*, Amairgen, famed mage accompanying the Milesian Celts invading Ireland around 500 B.C., conjured fish using a creation incantation:

> *Fishful sea—*
> *Fertile land—*
> *Burst of fish—*
> *Fish under wave—*
> *With courses of birds—*
> *Rough sea—*
> *A white wall—*
> *With hundreds of salmon—broad whale—A port song—*
> *A burst of fish.*

Members of the filidh and other seers gained knowledge of the Otherworld through shamanistic practices. One of the most typical of these, witnessed as late as the eighteenth century on the Isle of Skye in Scotland, was that of the seer being ritually wrapped or sewn into a bull's hide. This trance vigil, called *taghairm* in Scotland and *tarbhfeis* in Ireland, was conducted in the dark, and the wrapped seer was often placed in a tree niche, cave, or natural cavity behind a waterfall. This practice invites comparison with the Lakota Yuwipi ceremony involving a tied and blanket-wrapped medicine man.

In the early seventeenth century Irish poets continued the tradition of receiving inspiration and composing in darkness where vision incubates and the mind focuses on the Otherworld. James Hunter reiterates this extraordinary tenacity of Celtic tradition: "The Gaelic bards of the seventeenth-century Highlands performed much the same tasks as their Irish and Gaulish predecessors of some two millennia before. Continuity of this kind was commonplace. It is particularly evident . . . in the relationship between Gaels and their natural environment." As recently as the nineteenth century in Ireland, it is reported that: "Many a winter's night . . . have I heard the old chronicler, lying on his back quietly in the bed beyond the fire, repeat the 'deed of old' to delighted listening ears, but in language so ancient as to be almost unintelligible to most Irish speakers of the modern school." (O'Rahilly)

Bards as well as Druids had magical powers, and not only described and praised what was, but like all true shamans brought what will be into existence.

Bardic schools in Ireland lasted until the Irish intelligentsia was smashed in the seventeenth century. They were one of the few nonreligious educational traditions in Europe, established by A.D. 574. The curricula still contained incantations for divination and satire, suggesting that these bardic schools were continuations of druidic schools.

The Druids were not just priests—religious functionaries. They were walking compendiums of all the knowledge the Celts had. Some of the knowledge, such as astronomy, was sophisticated. The Celts operated on a lunar calendar, counted by nights, not days, and synchronized solar and lunar time by introducing intercalary months in alternation (as opposed to our inserting an extra day every four years). Seasonal festivals were determined, therefore, by the positions of celestial bodies rather than by dates. The Celtic calendar was on a nineteen-year cycle (actually, 19+19+18=56, to bring solar and lunar years into synch), which was also the basis Stonehenge operated from. A Roman historian witnessing a Druid figuring out when an upcoming eclipse would occur—doing this without charts or written figures—reported that the Druid's calculations turned out to be accurate within three minutes.

Astronomy and seasonal cycles were of vital interest to a society that was nature-based in its religion and general way of life. The equinoxes and solstices were significant to the Celts, but the cross-quarters, the four points of the year between solstices and equinoxes, were of greater importance: these defined the seasons.

The festival of Samhain was the Celtic New Year, celebrated at the end of October (now called Halloween). It epitomized reality's fluidity, being the time when the veil between the worlds was most transparent. Samhain was a dissolution of the established order making way for re-creation and, as such, was a transition during which a degree of chaos and destructurizing reigned as realities merged. Samhain was often the time, in Celtic stories, when influential people were conceived, born, or died, or when transfomational events occurred, often involving death (the old order giving way to the new). It was not an appropriate time to be wandering abroad after dark, when the Wild Hunt might swoop by and carry you off, but a good occasion for honoring ancestors, communication between realms of reality, and divination. The Druids employed both vision seeking and shamanic spirit-flight in their work as spiritual mediators, and these skills may have been used most easily at times such as Samhain. Fires were quenched, then relit from the sacred Samhain fire.

In ancient Ireland, Samhain was observed by seven-day provincial assemblies held at sacred sites such as Tara and Tlachtga (both in Meath), and it was the time of year when free-roaming livestock were rounded up preparatory to winter. Pastoral emphasis made the agricultural festivals, like Lughnassad (honoring Lugh, god of light) less crucial than Samhain and Beltain. The May fertility festival, Beltain, was often sited at Uisnech, in Westmeath. Uisnech was considered Ireland's sacred center or "navel," and was where Druidic convocations were held. At Beltain, cattle about to be released into summer pasturage were driven through the smoke of the festival fires to purify and bless them. Juniper smoke was used to smudge cattle, similar to the American Indian use of cedar as a purification. It was a time of great and concerned attention to the promotion of a fertile, successful growing season.

In more recent times, in the Highlands, Beltain marked the time when shieling grazing began, women and children spending that season in the high pastures with livestock, living in huts where the men often visited for courting, singing, and dancing. This was the happiest, most carefree time of the year in the Highlands. The Clearances put a dismal end to shieling grazing. Imbolc, the other cross-quarter celebration, which began in the month of February, marked the arrival of milk for the first birthing lambs of spring. Considered an initiatory period, Imbolc was a fire festival dedicated to the triple goddess, Brigid. Tradition says that a powerful serpent came forth from a hole in the hills on Imbolc—this was the precursor to modern Groundhog Day.

The Celtic assemblies, some of which were annual and others triennial, were great events for a people living scattered about the countryside. In addition to ceremonies, at the assemblies people gathered, old and new laws were recited, poems were aired, sagas were performed, horses were raced, sports competition was lively and fierce, and brisk marketing was accomplished. These seasonal celebrations continued in one form or another into the eighteenth and nineteenth centuries. The angel Michael, associated by Celtic Christians with Lugh, had a holiday of his own on September 29—Michaelmas— which was celebrated until the mid 1800s with clearly pagan overtones. In the outer isles of the Hebrides this festival centered on horses and the sea, both linked with Lugh. Men and women rode horseback to the shore in a cavalcade with no saddles or bridles—only straw ropes to guide the horses—and conducted races. Women competed with the men or against each other; the men wore only short trews and shirts—everyone was barefoot. Horses traditionally could be stolen for the races—it was not considered a crime and the animals were returned to their owners afterward. Then gifts were exchanged between men and women, men giving knives and purses, and women gifting men with fine sets of carrots whose harvest had been accompanied by fertility incantations. Primitive pagan dances were performed and much courtship ensued. It is remarkable how persistent the ancient spirit of Celticism was regardless of what religious guise overlaid it.

Another example of this persistence of pagan beliefs involves a modern clan chief, Sir Reginald MacLeod, who had the most treasured relic of the MacLeods, the Fairy Flag of Dunvegan, mounted in a specially sealed frame. An expert from the Victoria and Albert Museum in London discussed various possible origins of the flag with Sir Reginald, though of course never mentioned anything of a supernatural derivation. The chief listened with Celtic courtesy, then told the expert, with Celtic conviction, "You may believe that, but I know that it was given to my ancestors by the faeries."

In the Celtic world Druids were highly respected as well as highly trained. It was said, for instance, that it was *geiss* (taboo) for the Ulaid —the people of Ulster—to speak before their king; but geiss for the king to speak before the Druids. They had the same honor price as kings. There were various classifications in the priesthood, from seers or diviners to bards—who composed and performed songs, poems, stories, and satires—to Druids, who were often highborn and who conducted ceremonies, presided at sacrifices, interpreted and administered laws, and served as general repositories of knowledge. Druids were invested with authority to settle disputes and even stop battles (they were noncombatants).

Most crimes were dealt with through fines, mainly paid in cattle—a primary unit of measure in Ireland was a *set*, one-half the value of a milk cow. Each person had a worth determined by a common standard, and if a person was wrongly killed, this value (the "honor price") was paid by the tuatha, or clan, of the offender to the tuatha of the deceased. Capital punishment was only used if fines were not paid, and was administered by outcasting the culprit. There were detailed laws of marriage and divorce, laws of sick maintenance, laws of beekeeping, water rights, and much more, all meticulously memorized by the Druids.

The filiad in Ireland were learned laypeople—poets, historians, jurists, seers, and genealogists. They ended up outlasting the Druids, who were targeted by the Romans and the Christians. Until the seventeenth century, the filiad acted as liaisons or co-ecclesiasticals with Christian priests, bridging old and new religious orders. Rutherford notes:

> In the years up to the Roman conquest some dilution of Druidic power must have taken place. . . . Religion was turning into a pure instrument of state under the control of the state's rulers. . . . There is no doubt that Celtic religion, as distinct from Druidism, continued under Roman auspices. . . . As we know, even the legionaries themselves were invoking Celtic gods and not always equating them with those of the Gracco-Roman pantheon. . . . The early Christian missionaries make it clear that Celtic paganism was very much alive at the time of their arrival from about 600 A.D. They refer, specifically, to Druids.

And Van de Weyer asserts that:

> Christianity never took root in Roman Britain. The great majority of Christians were either Roman colonists or Britons that had adopted Roman attitudes and customs, while to the Celtic tribesmen Christianity was despicable as the religion of oppression. . . . Thus when the Roman Empire fell early in

the fifth century, and Angles and Saxons swept across the
south and east of the country, Christianity virtually disappeared. Only a handful of British Christians escaped into the
hills of Wales, where they practiced their religion in secret.

But Christianity reemerged, and did so to the eclipse of Druidism.
Part of what made the Druids so threatening to both the Romans and
the Christians was their mobility. This threatens systems, whether
political or religious, that control through fixity and centralized power.
Mobility, even today, is considered subversive. This is why gypsies,
for example, are so often governmentally and socially persecuted.
Druids were free agents answering to no church, no political authority, no leader. This made them dangerous to those who manipulated
through institutionalized power. The Druids were repositories of
knowledge and law; they were the carriers of tradition. And they were
keys to the Celtic wealth of gold. So, under the Emperor Tiberius, the
Druids were stamped out or absorbed into the Christian priesthood.
The Druids disappeared in Brittany by the sixth century, and were
found in Wales only as a "poetic fraternity" of bards by the 1200s.
Also persecuted were smiths (who in those days were itinerant, and
whose craft was associated with magic) and other wandering people.

Bards were once a powerful order. In Celtic society, words—
spoken, not written—were regarded as an arena of profound influence. Eloquence was highly valued. When considering the bards, one
has to imagine a vastly different world from our own; one where there
was no advertising, no drone of radio and TV, no commercial music;
where the voice was used with artistry and heard with acute attention. Bardic poems and stories were told in consummate presenta-
tions: recitations of sagas made warriors weep, or shout with joy; songs
resonated with depths of feeling consonant with the land's rhythms
and melodies. Irish and Scottish folk tunes are still considered among
the finest in the world.

The introduction to a bard's story was also a reminder of the bard's
power: "Under the Earth I go / On the oak leaf I stand / I ride on the
filly / that was never foaled / and I carry the dead in my hand." In
sharing a story or song the bard aligned listeners with transcendent
awareness: the bard was not just an entertainer but a guide and uni-
fying medium between the worlds, an opener of doors. One of
Ireland's earliest and most legendary bards was Amairgen, son of
Mil, who arrived with the Milesian Celts from Spain. In Amairgen's

most well-known declamation, he greets Ireland with words recognizing an integrated cosmology:

> I am wind on sea,
> I am ocean wave
> I am roar of sea,
> I am bull of seven fights,
> I am vulture on cliff,
> I am dewdrop.
> I am fairest of flowers,
> I am turning in a maze,
> I am boar for boldness,
> I am salmon in pool,
> I am lake on plain,
> I am dispensing power,
> I am word of skill,
> I am grass-blade giving decay to the earth,
> Who else clears the stones of the mountain?
> Who is it who declaims the sun's arising?
> Who is it who tells where the sun sets?
> Who brings cattle from the house of Tethra?
> Upon whom do the cattle of Tethra smile?
> Who is this ox?
> Who is the weaving god who mends the thatch of wounds?
> The incantation of a spear.
> The incantation of the wind.

The power of words was creative but could also be used as a fearful weapon in ritual cursing (called *glamdicín*), or in satires that caused a person to lose reputation, lose honor, or even become outcast—the most dreaded fate in a kinship society. Bards and satirists were feared and, like Druids, had free run of the land; they were immune to tribal hostilities and could travel without fear of being set upon. Celtic curses were savagely inventive and varied, thoroughly covering the terrain of ill-wishing. Blessings were, as might be expected, entirely lovely, being consistent with Celtic relationship to primal energies of nature. The following are two well-known Celtic blessings:

> Deep peace on the running wave to you
> Deep peace on the flowing air to you

Deep peace on the quiet earth to you
Deep peace of the shining stars to you
Deep peace on the gentle night to you
Moon and stars pour their healing light on you
Deep peace to you

Power of Eagle be yours
Power of Raven be yours
Wisdom of Serpent be yours
Voice of Swan be yours
Power of Sea be yours
Goodness of Land be yours

These kinds of blessings were still used in the nineteenth century in Scotland. Alexander Carmichael, in collecting Highland prayers and practices, was told, "The old people had runes they sang to the spirits dwelling in the sea and in the mountains, in the wind and in the whirl-wind, in the lightning and in the thunder, in the sun and in the moon and in the stars of heaven." A crofter told Carmichael that people made these prayers in wild places where no one would see them except "the eye of the Being of Life, the chirpers of the bushes, the fays of the knolls, or the gnomes of the rocks." John O'Donohue says, "In the Celtic world there is always the recognition of the silent and the unknown as the closest companions of the human journey. Encounter and farewell, which framed conversations, were always blessings. . . . Behind Celtic poetry and prayer is the sense that the words have emerged from a deep, reverential silence."

Celtic poetry reveals the affection for and vivid, detailed perception of nature so intrinsic to Celtic life: Kuno Meyer, translator of Gaelic poetry, comments that "In nature poetry the Gaelic muse may vie with that of any other nation. Indeed, these poems occupy a unique position in the literature of the world. To seek out and watch and love nature, in its tiniest phenomenon as in its grandest, was given to no people so early and so fully as to the Celt." James Hunter calls early Gaelic poetry "enormously sympathetic" to nature, and points out the Gaelic poet's "ability thus to merge—indeed identify—with his surroundings," and "his equally striking capacity to evoke these surroundings by means of a wealth of meticulously noted detail."

The keen observation and keen affection for—and identification

with—nature was not mistily sentimental. It was a well-lit relation-
ship, rich in adjectives, spare in exposition, clean and soul-piercing.
As my mother said after reading a poem I sent her by Alexander
MacDonald: "Rousing! What vocabulary! What technique!" To read
Gaelic poetry, both ancient and modern, is to experience the distinct
texture of Celtic spirituality. The continuity is there, from the unnamed
bards of old through MacDonald and MacDiarmid, to Iain Crichton
Smith, Sorley MacLain, Aonghas MacNeacail and others of our time.
One of those bards of old speaks in these stanzas excerpted from *A
Celtic Miscellany*:

> *Little antlered one, little belling one, melodious*
> *little bleater, sweet I think the lowing that you*
> *make in the glen*
>
> *Blackthorn, little thorny one, black little sloebush;*
> *watercress, little green-topped one, on the brink of*
> *the blackbird well*
>
> *Apple-tree, little apple-tree, violently everyone*
> *shakes you; rowan, little berried one, lovely is your*
> *bloom*

In my research I came across mention of women bards, healers,
satirists, prophets, sages, and seers, but in older texts found little or
no specific historical reference to female Druids, other than speculation that Boudicca was a priestess as well as queen. Interestingly, more
recent texts offer assurance that there were indeed female Druids,
and some are mentioned by name. But most of what is known about
Druids, male or female, is based on a patchy, minuscule collection of
facts, anecdotes, and conjectures.

The debate that causes the most consternation is the question of
druidic practices of sacrifice, particularly of humans. (Human sacrifice is more prevalent in accounts about continental Celtic society than
in those about Ireland or Britain, but animal sacrifice, at least, was
practiced wherever there were Druids.) Evidence suggests that human sacrifices, if they occurred, were of three categories: criminals;
war prisoners; and voluntary, probably highborn, victims. The Romans, in their propaganda campaigns, put on a great show of abhor-
rence about druidic sacrifices. Rutherford points out that:

Tacitus, throwing up hands of horror at the Druids' human sacrifices, conveniently overlooked the fact that his own countrymen wantonly massacred infinitely greater numbers with the purely frivolous objective of titillating the mob at the circus than ever the Druids sacrificed. Caesar, in his efforts to curry popularity, was himself responsible for having the Circus Maximus expensively rebuilt and there inaugurating an era of hideously blood-thirsty spectacles. By contrast, the Celts could claim for their activities the serious purpose of sustaining the cycle of existence. . . . In Rome, the practice of human sacrifice had been ended officially only in the early years of the first century B.C.

Other texts place this ban in 657, under the consulate of Cornelius Lentalus Crassus.

Peter Berresford Ellis, who in his book *The Druids* ardently argues the case against there having been any practice, in Ireland anyway, of Druidic human sacrifices, adds, "It can hardly be believed that the Romans, especially during the reigns of such emperors as Caligula and Nero, could be shocked by human sacrifice. . . . When Augustus excluded the Druids from Roman citizenship by forbidding Roman citizens to practice Druidic rites, when Tiberius banned the Druids by a decree of the Roman Senate and when Claudius attempted to 'wholly abolish' them in A.D. 54, it was not, I believe, in disapproval of 'inhuman rites' practiced by the Druids, but to wipe out an intellectual class who could, and did, organize national revolt against Rome."

Dr. P. W. Joyce, in *A Social History of Ancient Ireland*, claims "There is no record of any human sacrifice in connection with the Irish Druids. . . ." And in further support of this says, "The idea of awarding death as a judicial punishment for homicide, even when it amounted to murder, does not seem to ever have taken hold of the public mind in Ireland."

Whatever the policy on sacrifice, trees were certainly venerated by the Celts. There was a time in Ireland when it was a capital crime to cut down an apple tree. In Britain, yew trees were especially honored; in Ireland, the rowan; in Gaul, the oak. Ash trees were held in high esteem, and hazel trees were associated with sacred wells. Divining using hazel rods was performed to detect metallic ore as well as water—the Druids probably used divining rods, in addition, for locating magnetic fields.

Sacred springs and wells were, in later years, pillaged by invaders (and archeologists) for their astonishing wealth of gold and other offerings, indicating Celtic reverence for places considered natural interfaces with spirit. Salmon and trout, living in the sacred medium of water, were thought to have foreknowledge and deitific wisdom. There was little fishing done in Scotland's inland waters during ancient times because of the holy nature of lochs and streams. Islands were especially esteemed for spiritual purposes—Mona (Anglesey) in Wales is a prime example; and there were still Druids on the Isle of Man as late as the fifth or sixth centuries. Remote islands such as the Flannan Isles in the Hebrides were considered inherently sacred; the Isle of Skye was famed for its seers.

Highland sailors and fishermen were known to strictly avoid saying the real names of certain objects and places while at sea, substituting other specific names. This applied during certain nonseafaring occasions and situations as well. The Huichol Indians of Mexico do this same thing during peyote pilgrimages. The Celts, in their nearness to the ocean, had a plethora of superstitions involving boats, and many of their folk cures and healing rituals centered on the use of sacramental water. The Isle of Ewe, in Loch Maree, was considered a faery place, and the waters of the loch were thought to be healing.

White animals with red ears were assumed to be Otherwordly. Picts—who, like the Irish Celts, had Druids—introduced ornithomancy into Ireland; birds figured largely in Celtic spirituality because, like fish, they dwelled in an intermediary realm. Irish poets wore feathered cloaks (as did Siberian shamans). Many gods and goddesses were associated with birds, the Welsh Rhiannon probably the most well-known of these. Lovers often took swan form, indicative of sexuality, benevolence, and purity. Geese were sometimes linked with war, as were ravens and crows (who were also frequently prophetic). Wrens were considered druidic birds. Cranes, often considered sinister and taboo to eat, might turn out to be transformed women and, of course, eagles held perennial appeal for chieftains and warriors. Many waterbirds were linked with the cult of the Sun in its healing aspect. With their love of music, Celts perceived the Otherworld as full of melodious bird song. The shamanic posture of *corrguinecht,* which involved standing on one leg with one eye closed and one arm pointing, was a stance associated with the crane, which like the wren was an important bird to the Druids. Magical bundles were often wrapped in crane skins.

In southern Britain many Celtic deities were concerned with fertility, healing, and agriculture, and many of the gods and goddesses had consorts. In northern Britain the focus was more martial and there seemed to be no consorts. Celtic war goddesses were notable for having both magical and fighting skills.

Brian de Breffny, in *The Irish World,* observes that Irish genius was expressed in spiritual forms—particularly those of poetry, music, and storytelling as a fine art. He summarizes characteristics of the Irish as:

> A respect for the past, an indifference to present time, a sense of the unseen world, intellectual curiosity, the gift of poetic imagination, a cynical sense of humor, a brooding melancholy, a subtle conception of what constitutes truth, an ingenious casuistry and a deviousness which are perhaps related to historical experience, and above all, an inexhaustible interest in words, in people, and in spiritual matters.

Early Irish monks tended to be of the academic sort rather than fanatically religious, though some were extreme in their spartan lifestyles. Many, like the Druids, were married. Later, as Christianity advanced and divided, Irish Catholics and Protestants became estranged. During the famine in 1845 divisiveness between the two boldly widened because of class differences. One effect of the potato disaster was that the peasantry, which was Catholic, turned more heavily toward religion, feeling abandoned by the land's traditional nurturance. Ironically, potatoes were not a traditional crop in Ireland. They were introduced in the sixteenth century and became the staple food of the poor. During the famine, grain was *exported* from Ireland—starvation did not occur because the country lacked food; it was a result of class oppression that prevented the distribution of food.

The Irish poor constricted into fearful conservatism. Arranged marriages—and eschewing marriage—in order to ensure family provision replaced love's spontaneity and sexuality's license. The Catholic Church offered the downtrodden some focus and hope for improvement. Early Irish immigrants to North America were mainly Protestants; the famine immigrants were ragged, starving Catholics. At one point, fares from Dublin to the New World were as low as $12, but many Catholic immigrants perished in the horrifying slave-ship conditions of these passages, and arrivals of the living were not celebrated by North America.

The combination of a religiosity tightened by famine's scourge and a self-esteem battered by years of being spat upon by Protestant English gentry turned Ireland's Catholics into people little resembling their former free-spirited pagan selves. Lost was the linking of erotic and intellectual knowledge with spiritual experience and understanding.

In Scotland, too, Christianity divided and modified the character of the people. Many Lowlanders fiercely embraced John Knox's stern Calvinism that seemed to liberate the people from a degenerate and arrogant Catholic tyranny. Highlanders, some retaining Catholicism, some becoming Protestant, remained mostly indifferent, however, to Lowland religious fervor. But hardship and forced disconnection from the past, occurring in the late 1700s, made religion, whether of Church or Kirk, more of a focus, there being little else to turn toward in endurance of suffering. Religion has always been a mainstay of the Celts.

The larger context of land and circumstances (including ancestral memory) acts upon the genetics of a people, forming particular characteristics. Human commonalties, like plant commonalties, are enrobed in a diversity influenced by conditions of habitat. Even within one form—say, the Irish form of human—there are variations due to environment. The Irish who emigrated to cities of North America adapted to those habitats, becoming more aggressive, fast-paced, and worldly than their kindred in Ireland. But Irishness remained and is recognizable.

Canadian novelist Hugh MacLennan's father, a third generation Canadian, was described by Hugh as "entirely Scotch . . . All the perplexity and doggedness of the race was in him, its loneliness, tenderness, and affection, its deceptive vitality, its quick flashes of violence, its dog-whistle sensitivity to sounds to which Anglo-Saxons are stone deaf, its incapacity to tell its heart to foreigners save in terms which foreigners do not comprehend, its resigned indifference to whether they comprehend or not. *It's not easy being Scotch,* he told me once. To which, I suppose, another Scotchman might say, *It wasn't meant to be.*"

Academics will fretfully sigh at my free application of the word Celt, as though Celts exist as a present people, a distinction. In Great Britain the Picts, Gaels, Angles, Saxons, Norse, Flemish, Danes, Jutes, Normans, and others intermarried and interpenetrated each other's cultures, and yet—and yet—Celts are Celts, as Indians are Indians;

there is a spirit, a particularity in the blood, and I write of a continuity of which I am a part. Many times in Scotland, people would touch my red hair or point to it and say: "Your family must be Celtic; where were they from?"

T. W. Rolleston puts forth that:

> In view of the undeniably mixed character of the population called "Celtic" at the present day, it is often argued that this designation has no real relation to any ethnological fact. The Celts who fought with Caesar in Gaul and with the English in Ireland are, it is said, no more. . . . [But] race-character . . . is not a dead thing, cast in an iron mould, and therefore incapable of change and growth. It is part of the living forces of the world. . . . Of one thing I personally feel convinced—that the problem of the ethical, social, and intellectual development of the people constituting what is called the "Celtic Fringe" in Europe ought to be worked for on Celtic lines; by the maintenance of the Celtic tradition, Celtic literature, Celtic speech—the encouragement, in short, of all those Celtic affinities of which this mixed race is now the sole conscious inheritor and guardian. To these it will respond, by these it can be deeply moved; nor has the harvest ever failed those who with courage and faith have driven their plough into this rich field. On the other hand, if this work is to be done with success, it must be done in no pedantic, narrow, intolerant spirit; there must be no clinging to the outward forms of the past simply because the Celtic spirit once found utterance in them.

Something Celtic permeates my family: my uncle married a Scots McKay and they named their sons Ross and Graeme; my older brother married Dedria, whose mother's ancestry is Irish; my second husband was a Scots McMillen and his mother, an Irish McKay. None of us deliberately sought Celtic mates; perhaps some instinct operated, a natural affinity of heritage. It is no surprise that my land partner is descended from Highlanders on both sides of her family, or that my best friends when growing up were Wendy McGrath, Heather MacFadden, and Ellen MacRae, and my sister's was Mary Stewart, though it is startling now to put the names together and see the pattern.

Anglo-Normans, invading Ireland, were absorbed, becoming "more Irish than the Irish." Land and culture claimed them. They intermarried with Celts and became part of Celtic evolution, its river of becoming, as I am part of it with ancestral shadings of Dutch and English, and as my son is with Sicilian influence from his father's family. Celticism's reality ghosts from between dusty book covers and faraway songs and infiltrates contemporary life. It will not be entombed or homogenized out of existence. Its light shines, though there are also its shadows: Pat Buchanan comparing himself to William Wallace; klans and bigotry.

What happened to the Celts was a spiritual deforestation concurrent with actual deforestation of the land (by invaders and livestock). People and land became foresaken in the violation of an ancient pact. Trees, place of worship, were deitific embodiments for Celts. This is a key point for modern people seeking or claiming a Celtic spirituality to consider. The core perspective of Celtic spirituality was integration and awareness of seen and unseen worlds. I cringed to hear neopagans say, "Well, time to go back to the real world," after an outdoor ritual or a spiritual gathering. Celtic spirituality was not a realm or experience apart from the rest of life, and it was not a pretend realm, but something profoundly ever present and influential. In Celtic and other indigenous oral cultures, there is no distance between an object and its name. To say the word is to invoke the object's presence; to tell the myth is to acknowledge and experience its reality, its ever presence. The modern tendency to compartmentalize is the antithesis of Celticism. Even in contemporary Christian expression, Celtic spirituality is a matter of daily life:

> The Celtic church had steadfastly rejected the authority of Rome, asserting that each individual is answerable directly to God for his actions. . . . The rugged individualism of the Celtic monk, his conviction that each person is free to choose between good and evil, and his insistence that faith must be practical as well as spiritual, remain hallmarks of Christians in Britain. And the British imagination has remained rooted in nature . . . indeed, that peculiar British obsession with gardening is Celtic in origin. Visitors to the British Isles are often shocked at how few people attend church each Sunday. Yet,

> to the Britons, church-goers as absentees, the primary test of
> faith is not religious observance, but daily behavior toward
> our neighbors—and toward our pets, livestock, and plants!
> . . . The Catholic and Protestant traditions are often indiffer-
> ent, even hostile to nature, treating her as irrelevant to our
> spiritual salvation, or even as a source of corruption. . . . But
> in Celtic Christianity we have an entire church which saw
> within every living creature the divine spirit, and so loved
> all creatures for their own sake. Thus the Celts offer a spiritu-
> ality for our time. (Van de Weyer)

Along with integration of seen and unseen worlds, and human integration with nature, was integration of intellect with heart, spirit, and
body. All these are largely lacking in modern conditioning, and their
lack makes questionable the connection between neopagan experience and Celtic spirituality.

Pagan means "country dweller." Paganism arose directly from
primal engagement with the land. There is no mental substitute for
this. Imagination and metaphor cannot create a duplicate experience
having the same reality of impact or power to shape character, understanding, and worldview. Living in physical form, the manifestive,
affective truth of spirit has its greatest reality to us when it carries
through *all* levels of experience. This means that spirituality permeates context, awareness of context, and interaction with context—all
the time.

This is perhaps the most glossed over and yet essential difference
between modern and ancient realizations of spirituality, and the one
most vital to address in terms of ecological survival as well as authentic and useful spiritual practice. There is a propensity toward
mentalizing experience—an infatuation with technology and a vir-
tual rather than explicit reality; something more controllable, less rigorous, less confrontive—and, as a result, less transformative.

Alternative spirituality has become the child of psychology, with
the "Church of Jung" its theological base. This may be the opposite of
what would be most helpful and appropriate—a spirituality encompassing psychology (as well as physics, ethics, and deep ecology) instead of vice versa. Ward Rutherford seems to echo this in part when
he observes:

> But quite apart from the essentially magical character of

Druidism, the abstraction of ethical principles from its only
"statement"—the myths—would have the effect of making
them something other than what, to the eyes of the Celts and
other similar societies, they were. They would then become
religious allegory, and they were nothing of the kind. The
myth exists autonomously. It is not the retelling of events; it
is the programme of the events themselves. . . . Thus there
are not one but many "times" of which the "progressive" one
known to us, that of irreversible change, is only one version.

In 1981, a Potawatomie shaman who became my mentor and friend
invited me to a sweat lodge ceremony. Within that challenging precinct of intense heat and close quarters was found an experience of
spirituality that thoroughly engaged physical integration of religion.
There is no retreat into metaphor inside a sweat lodge. It is elemental
and, as such, affects participants at a core level resonating outward
into complexity. Corbelled sweat houses in northwest Ireland are
traced to the Bronze Age, and were used in Ireland for healing until
the nineteenth century.

Those stone sweat houses, called *teach an alais,* were heated by
prewarmed stones, or by turf fires kindled inside and then removed
when the patient needing healing entered, wrapped in a blanket. After sweating, the patient exited and was plunged into cold water,
rubbed warm, and instructed to meditate in order to achieve a peaceful state of mind.

Vision questing, also cross-cultural, was another practice requiring explicit physical commitment and participation. These ceremonial forms afforded compelling conditions for accessing insight and
healing. Transformation was then apparent and manifestive, not just
a transitory emotional excitement.

Traditional shamans in every culture recognized the importance
of physical effort as an aspect of effective participation. Many of their
practices were arduous, time-consuming, sometimes perilous. They
understood the uses of exhaustive mental, emotional, and physical
states, as well as the resource found in courage and perseverance. It
is for good reason that ceremonies like the Lakota Yuwipi, the sweat
lodge, the Sun Dance, and so on, take considerable preparation and
work. As my mother, upon visiting Stonehenge, noted, modern worship is indeed flabby in comparison. This is as true for neopaganism
and neoshamanism as for mainstream religions.

The ancients did not choose their practices because they could not think of something easier (like a visualization) in the way of spiritual activity. They did not do them because of boredom, deficient imagination, or a need for exercise. Those practices were realized out of the experience of spiritual immanence in earthly context. That meant spirit was accessible—indeed, almost ubiquitous—through embodied expressions of its vitality. Severed from that largeness and pervasiveness of spiritual presence, it is easy to fall into an egoistic isolation that orients awareness and spiritual practice to egoistic concerns, which tend to be fearful, lazy, and ultimately disappointing.

Celtic sympathetic resonance with the land was clear in cultural attention to the fitness of secular leaders—in the conviction that the land's well-being, on which the people's well-being acutely depended, directly reflected a leader's fitness. Land cannot be deceived. It mirrors a truth of our condition as human beings and reveals our mistakes, atrocities, and follies as well as our capacity for good. But today, in the arrogance of shortsighted greed and flippant posturing, many people do not want to look at what the land reveals about our fitness.

In the past I have made special, if not always formal, occasion of equinoxes, solstices, and cross-quarter festival days of Celtic tradition. Because I live intimately with the land, these times are meaningful—their significance real and natural to the rhythm of life. Though not pagan or Christian (or neopagan), I am a country dweller working amid an ancient pattern of seasonal cycles.

One characteristic of those pivotal times of year has been a recurring spontaneous clarity, like a mist dissolving, during which I am aware of a stream of "knowing" about choices and changes to enact in upcoming months. This clarity is not deliberately invoked but frequently occurs at those times, and the guidance derived never proves regrettable.

Lying in a tent in an English campground, trying to get to sleep; it is the eve of Lughnassad, the harvest cross-quarter. But I have lost track of dates so am unaware of the occasion, though kept awake by an overabundance of energy in the air. Relaxing, gradually diffusing my attention, I drift into a twilight strata, neither asleep nor awake, and in that state—which lasts several hours—receive a series of insights and directives about the coming season. Fully waking, very lucid, I think about the guidance received, then abruptly fall asleep. It is worth missing a deliberate honoring of the occasion to realize how deeply attuned to that ancient cycle consciousness is, an alignment neither contrived nor irrelevant.

One morning at my medicine wheel on the mountain I faced east— the direction sometimes associated with air and birds—and prayed aloud. A sharp-shinned hawk flew out of the east, three times slicing a circle in the air above the wheel, then alighted on a sapling directly in front of me. Next I turned south, the direction signifying the warm fires of life, often totemized by the deer. I started to pray, then stopped, enchanted by a doe browsing on the hillside in front of me, due south. In the west, praying in the water direction, I saw the river winding through the valley below; and there in the north, the direction associated with stone, rose the mountain, rocky and steep. Above was the sky, below was the earth; it was all here, clearly expressed. Part of a poem by Native writer Simon Ortiz says:

> We are Existent within knowledge of the land,
> We are Existent within knowledge of the stars,
> All Around and Below and Above,
> East, South, West, and North,
> This is our prayer, this is our knowledge,
> This is our source, this is our existence.

Directness of relationship with the land yields immediacy to spiritual experience and evolution. Immanence is not something forestalled until an afterlife; it is not predicated on merit or priestly credentials. It is a birthright like family or equality or place; spirit is the given— present, illuminating the bird's swift flight, the deer's elegant grace, the river's renewing flow, the mountain's enduring strength. Within experience of the given are keys to transcendent awareness, one opening to, not apart from, the other.

What is most lacking in neoshamanism and neopaganism is what is most powerful and relevant in the potentials of those paths: grounding in the land and integration with other facets of daily life. Celtic Americans, drawn to Native spirituality, often are sidetracked into its cultural forms—thereby annoying Natives, and losing touch with the source of resonance within their own heritage. Those drawn to neopaganism often wander off into its hodgepodge cosmology, ritual theatrics, and fast-track empowerment. Commercialism adds to the circus atmosphere of alternative spirituality. Yet out of the confusion continues to come not only sincerity but healing evolution—despite the hype, the weirdos, the blunders and half-baked understandings.

But to grow, flourish, and bear healthy fruit, there needs to be soil for those spiritual seeds; there needs to develop roots, strong stems, green leaves, beautiful flowers, and these require contact with sun, air, water, in awareness of connection between individuality and habitat. There needs to be a spiritual reality experienced in presentness of place and of thought, action, and interaction; this creates integrity.

Lying on the bed, briefly resting in preparation for a sweat lodge ceremony, my body was positioned heyoka-wise, head at the foot of the bed, providing a different view than usual out the window. I was silently praying, centering in spirit, speaking to Panther totem. In prayer, I turned my head and gazed out the window, then scrambled to my feet; a mountain lion was flowing in powerful surges up the bluff east of the house. It gained the ridgetop and disappeared into the forest, leaving me not so much quietly centered as ecstatically galvanized.

Recurring intersections of intuitive choice with fortuitous experience supports a sense of spiritual immediacy. Celts, with their attention to omen and geiss, to multi-leveled significance within physical patterns and manifestations, recognized the presence of spiritual forces within mundane life. That awareness gives opportunity, in every moment, for enlightened participation.

The Celtic concept of geiss, or personal taboo, was typically paradoxical. On one hand, the *gessa* gave clear and terribly specific prohibitions or compulsions. On the other hand, those taboos inevitably were broken, with fateful consequences. It was a set-up. Heroes, kings, and other central figures in Celtic stories always had at least one geiss (often more) laid upon them, sometimes by themselves or their relatives, but usually by someone with mystical power.

These were not casual directives, especially if one had a whole slew of them to abide by, and the more important the person, the more complicated it was to avoid violation of these taboos. Conare, king of the Ulaid, for instance, had a geiss against three *deirgs* (red men) preceding him into the house of Deirg, which sounds easy to abide by—though of course it turned out to be violated, as did all the other bizarre gessa with which Conare was burdened. More problematic were the gessa dictating that no plundering take place in Ireland during Conare's reign, no single woman be admitted into a house he stayed in after sunset, and so on; a tight and fateful net.

Adhering to *or* breaking gessa were often acts of courage or sacrifice. In other situations, trickery or forgetfulness was involved. Sometimes there was just no getting around violation. Geiss was the seed of change and consequence; it had a karmic quality. It was not really as important what the gessa were (though they were loaded with symbolism) as how a person responded to choices and the crises that occurred when gessa were invoked or broken.

In stories, response to crisis and unfoldment of consequence affected more than the personal. Interconnected karma was discharged, evolution and upheaval occurred; sometimes tribal fate was transcended or transmuted. The geiss was a mechanism by which patterns and change were made explicit and brought to the surface in confrontational moments of truth.

The dismay we feel when seeing the hero (since it seems to predominantly be men who receive gessa) steered into one of those inevitable geiss dilemmas is our wishing for happy endings: for wisdom, security, and escape from dilemmas and their consequences in our own lives. A geiss would seem, with its specificity, to make choices obvious for the hero but, as stories show, this was not always the case, and the hero usually realized that safe, constrictive courses were not ones that would bring about necessary crisis, clearing, or growth.

It is difficult for people looking at the spirituality of the Celts to clearly comprehend Celtic perception if their own mindsets are linear and schooled in Christian doctrine. Even the Romans with their polytheism had little comprehension of the integrated Celtic view of nature, life and death, and their interwoven continuity. The Romans proscribed druidism but not Celtic religion—polytheistic religions tend to be tolerant of other pantheons; what harm can there be, after all, in a few extra gods and goddesses? Devotees of the one true Lord are more likely to flare at the intimation of rival or additional deities. Druidism was crushed by the Romans because it was a cultural and economic linchpin, responsible for the wealth and cohesion of the tribes, not because of the gods and goddesses it served. Its suppression was mainly an imperially political, not religious, strategy.

To understand Celtic religion one must bear in mind a fluid perspective about embodiment. Monotheism usually stratifies humans from the divine, as well as humans from the rest of nature. Thus relationship—both worship, prayer, propitiation, and interaction with the divine; and interaction with nature—operate within static boundaries. Material forms are considered restrictive and, to a large extent, definitive. These boundaries, where a tree is a tree and only a tree, and only according to a particular definition of a tree, did not exist for Celts.

Their sense of the world had much in common with quantum physics. They saw form as transitionally and variously expressive. A tree might also be a goddess, an enchanted human, or an illusion. Treeness, itself, was many things, and what happened to trees was importantly linked to what happened to everything else. Omens and gessa were part of this language of interconnection and multidimensionality. Scientifically, it was a more sophisticated perspective than is the simplistic materialism (and materialism versus spirituality) believed in by many modern people.

It is therefore helpful when considering Celtic deities, and people's relationship with them, to dissolve conditioned assumptions of appearance, immutability, and boundaries. A more fluid mental space encompasses discernment of why, for instance, sacrifice was included in druidic practice.

Sacrifice is commonly conceived of as a bribe offered by a weaker or vulnerably needy party (humans) to a stronger, potentially beneficent or dangerously capricious party (a deity): give the god blood and he will provide a merciful growing season—that sort of transaction. On one level, this is a true enough description. Any sacrifice—whether of life, time, priorities, or needs—is a transaction, qualified by being the giveaway of one, often personal, form of value for the gaining of transcendent, larger, or more selfless good. In basic terms, it is movement and intentional reconfiguration of energy. If static form is not definitive of presence—in other words, if there can be no real loss, only transfer within an interconnected universe of shifting manifestation—then sacrifice takes on more explicable connotations than those of pacifying the appetites of bloodthirsty deities.

A life form is a concentrated system of energies. Released from purposeful cohesion, those energies can be applied elsewhere. Druids were specialists at such releases and reorganizations. In ceremonial contexts, the effectiveness of those acts was amplified by the focus and heightened attention of congregated witnesses. Mutual needs, hopes, and beliefs were enjoined, feeding an intention that was vitalized and guided on its transformational journey.

Celtic deities were not at a remove. A goddess was a river, was a horse, was a field of oats, was one's neighbor's great-grandmother. Sacrificer, sacrificed, and sacrificed-to all trafficked common realms. Like the Hopi bringing rain by dancing, the Celts did not separate spiritual from earthly presence, cause, and effect. Celtic deities were, in secular terms, matrices through which energy was focused and transformed, affecting the land and all facets of manifestive life.

Beltain, May 1, was a time of uncertainty and anxiety as well as celebration for the Celts. Life depended on the goodwill and bounty of the land. The previous harvest had been consumed; the season of potential increase lay ahead. It was a context without supermarkets or significant influxes of imported foods, and the assumptions of security technology evinces. Beltain was thus a Celtic occasion historically associated with sacrifice. The people, led by Druids, endeavored to encourage the land's fertility and the weather's benevolence toward grazing and growth. They invested, through sacrifice and other rituals—including the creative sexual energies of the people's own fertility—in the sacred, essential fruitfulness of the land. They offered life for life's renewal, for transformative continuity.

Energy transfer occurs all the time, naturally and inconspicuously, in organic ecological processes and in conscious and unconscious daily choices made throughout life. Druidic sacrifice is controversial more because it was graphic and in ritual context than because of any singularity as an act. And certainly, the taking of life (whether animal or human) and infliction of pain without consent differs from willing sacrifice.

This topic is shied from by many neopagans, partly because of its association with satanism (which is actually an offshoot of Christianity, not paganism). But efforts to sanitize druidic image ultimately preclude any depth of understanding of druidism, or of Celtic experience and belief. Those efforts also dodge an examination of the life-taking and pain infliction justified in modern life under many guises, and by many who shudder at druidic bloodletting: the sacrifice of millions of soldiers on the altar of war, for instance; or capital punishment; or sport hunting, animals being sacrificed in service of emotional stimulation. And what of daily sacrificing of entire species in the name of the mighty triad Progress, Profit, and Consumerism? Sacrifices that are true losses, and assuredly not made with consent.

Malidoma Patrice Somé, in his book *Of Water and The Spirit*, writes as an African shaman, but his perspective seems as applicable to Celtic or North American spirituality as to African. He says:

> Traditional education consists of three parts: enlargement of one's ability to see, destabilization of the body's habits of being bound to one plane of being, and the ability to voyage transdimensionally and return. Enlarging one's vision and abilities has nothing supernatural about it, rather it is "natural" to be part of nature and to participate in a wider understanding of reality. . . . This kind of education is nothing less than a return to one's true self, that is, to the divine within us.

Somé and others whose educations arose from traditional communities have a direct cultural affiliation nourishing and authenticating their spirituality. They have source and context not only through lineage but through what has been preserved—albeit tenuously—within living communities. Nothing and no one is unscathed by modernization and intrusion from its zealous proponents, but the traditional education of which Somé speaks is still something to which an African, Indian, Aboriginal, or Asian shaman has some access.

What of Celts—white people whose oppressors (also white) submerged and eclipsed Celtic traditions having so much in common with indigenous spirituality? Celtic traditional base now has no village, no elder, no reservation even, to be returned to or drawn upon. Nonetheless, a more subtle base does abide: in Celtic land, permeating it, and in ancestral memory, both of which are accessible, though as references they carry little validity for those relying on more concrete cultural or religious credentials.

When it is heard that a Native shaman was my mentor or that I learned meditation from an East Indian master, my spiritual work suddenly gains legitimacy. On one hand, this is sensible because traditional practices, to be performed effectively and wisely, are well served by being transmitted through traditional practitioners. Knowing my background helps people know what to expect from my work. Valuable as this is, it neglects to take into account or legitimize a larger influential aspect of spirituality's derivation.

After reading Somé's description of traditional education, I put aside the book, staring out the window, pondering how I learned those abilities without being taught them. Even my association with the Potawatomie shaman was not one in which he taught but one in which I was exposed to key experiences that awakened capacity and provided direction and impetus. When he smoked the medicine pipe with me he said, "I could show you the traditional ritual, but that is not what is important; you must be guided by direct connection with the spiritual realm."

There is no credentialing for it, yet direct connection uncovers a basis and continual deepening of practice. My spirituality is empirical, not traditional, though it conjuncts with age-old aspects and esoteric knowledge from many cultures. It comes from a resource of consciousness rather than a process of instruction.

Whites are often accused, understandably, of cultural or religious appropriation—ripping off indigenous ceremonial forms and practices grafting medicine ways and shamanism onto psychology, neopaganism, new age philosophy, and so on. People looking for resource who are from societies that condition them to colonization and grasping are unpracticed at asking, at discerning paths of right relationship, and at looking within the vast, pervasive archives of consciousness. It is believed that using something—adopting something from another culture—is a form of respect and mutuality, a great step toward healing the cultural trampling committed by recent ancestors. People are eager for common ground, not realizing the continued trespass.

This consideration applies to Celtic traditions as well as Native cultures. Peter Berresford Ellis asks, "What price is 'spiritual awareness' with the ancient Celts when we have stood by and allowed their modern descendants to perish? This is the uncomfortable reality for those who would conjure Druids and ancient Celts to their new concepts of 'spiritual enlightenment' while ignoring the plight of the modern Celts." Not only has their plight been ignored; while in Scotland I overheard distress expressed at the presumptuous actions and attitudes of neopagans and new age enthusiasts who made use of Celtic sacred sites in ways offensive to local folk. The behavior generally involved such things as planting crystals in the ground, removing objects, and responding arrogantly to the concerns of caretakers of such sites.

On one hand, there is understandable feeling in Celtic descendants that these sites are part of a heritage they are attempting to reclaim, and, on the other hand, the distress of the locals is entirely justifiable. Development of mutual respect opens the way for development of understanding, but that should necessarily start with visitors respecting what abides locally. Some suggestions in that regard include:

- Asking permission if you want to make use of a site in any way that alters it, even if the alteration is temporary, seems minor, *or seems spiritually guided.*
- Being considerate of the needs and experiences of other visitors. If you want to use the site for a ceremony, consider arranging your activities for a time when other visitors will not be present at the site.
- Being cognizant of and receptive to local feelings, and local relationships to the site.
- Being sensitive to historical patterns of use and to whatever propriety is indicated within interaction with a site. Being aware and responsive, not presuming.

Visiting sacred sites—in any country—with intention to attune to or spiritually interact with what is present might include a process encompassing:

- Preliminary inquiry into traditional uses of the site.
- Personal preparations, such as fasting, ritual cleansing, prayer, clarification of intention, and guidance-seeking or consultation with spiritual allies.
- Willingness to withdraw or adjust behavior in response to what is present at a site.
- Respectfully presenting yourself at the site, and seeking a clear sense of welcome.
- Making an offering.
- Slow, circumspect exploration, paying attention to how you are affected by a site's energies and how you, in turn, influence abiding patterns and balances.

When visiting sacred places, I spend most of my time just sitting, letting my presence attune with place, being peaceful and appreciative. Visiting the same site a number of times deepens relationship with and knowledge of place, perhaps opening the way for more intimate, active intentions to be expressed. Many times, spontaneous directives arise from attunement or from ancestral patterning. It is important to participate with place in terms of what can be offered or returned to it—prayers for the land, gratitude, offering your vitality rather than siphoning power. Reciprocal participation, especially in this era of resource extraction and land abuse, promotes right relationship and a consideration of our responsibilities in heritage's continuity.

Stonehenge is now cordoned off to protect the site from the thousands of people flocking to it each year. Most lesser-known sites are still easily accessed by visitors, and if people treat these places with the same kind of care that has preserved them for thousands of years, the sites will remain a legacy of history and Celtic spirituality for generations to come. Most of those places abide in a natural simplicity of surroundings, and that is part of the beauty and sense of continuity that is present. In the many countries I have visited, Celtic regions have been unique in their seamless integration of those sites into contemporary context, and in lack of vandalizing of those sites.

My friends and I visited the Torhouse Circle in Galloway—a close circle of nineteen boulders around two large and one smaller central boulder. The stones radiated a sense of peace, memory, waiting. We saw sheep in the distance, herded by a dog, the white flock flowing like a foamy river. Stone walls crossed the hills, big clouds scudding above. The circle abided, the people no longer in direct compact with it, but connected nonetheless.

At the Corrimony Cairn southwest of Inverness I found spiritual opaqueness, ringing silence, greyness and cold weight. The stone I leaned against said, "You have come here unprepared," and it was true. Some places ask for more preparation than others, and more wisdom, more specific and appropriate intention, more consent. I withdrew from the cairn.

The Stones of Clava, nearer Inverness, is a place I have visited several times. It is a complex of three major stone circles with cairns in their centers, amid a grove of beautiful beech trees. It is a lovely, peaceful place. On one visit I ventured inside the largest cairn, pausing at its opening, sensing the difference between living and dead, how I could come and go but the dead could not. I later chanced on a small ring of stones off to one side under a guardian tree and sat with eyes closed, feeling the waiting, the long waiting of stones set in a pattern thousands of years old, the stones themselves far older, quietly waiting. I sensed long-ago people and how differently we now move among these stones. Deeper, I felt patience, heating and cooling, seasons upon seasons. "It will bloom again," the rock I sat upon seemed to say, and I wanted to know how soon. Waiting, I felt power rising, suffusing the trees, glowing around me, fountaining through me, joy, and a vitality of activity I had not realized was present until I became still enough to resonate with the fortitude of stone.

During a third visit to the Clava site, with my sister, I again entered the largest cairn to pray and meditate. I felt an ease, a rightness of relationship, and a sense of ongoing familiarity, as though time had not interrupted my dialog with the cairn. My sister, who had never been to Scotland before, intuitively tuned to Clava's patterns, perceptive of subtleties. She slowly circled the stones. After a time she approached the largest cairn, halted at its entrance, and, after a pause, withdrew. Later she told me she had intended to go into the cairn but at its entrance felt a definite, though invisible, barrier.

This willingness to be advised by an immediacy of experience, as well as by intention and knowledge, is an important capacity. As modern people using ancient sites and trying to bridge the gap between what was and what can be, respectful sensitivity is crucial. Awareness is the teacher, and more so these days, perhaps, than at any other time.

Between the terrain of awakening to resources of consciousness and that of appropriation of cultural sacred sites and traditions lies another problematic zone. Modern life lacks societal experiences offering initiation into esoteric awareness and knowledge. There is a habituation to conventions of belief about reality. Even when reaching beyond those, the tendency persists for conditioned modes to interfere with or reconfigure perception. This is visible in much of neopaganism as well as in how people modify, interpret, and apply shamanism. Modern mindset is typically self-centered, noisy, compartmentalized, and fearful, all of which impede expansive states of consciousness. The imperative to both discover one's own path and to be aligned with some rooted continuity often presents dilemmas. Self-knowing is mistaken for a tireless inventorying of personality, to which the accoutrements of heritage—perhaps one's own, perhaps some other—are then attached. But traditional trappings do not recreate ancestral perspective, and egoistic introspection does not yield the alignment or freedom needed for spiritual awareness.

If path and practices are going to be intuitive, particularly for those having no living (or even written) traditional guides with whom to consult, there has to be a thorough depatterning of typical mindset. Rarely is this depatterning seen in contemporary practitioners of shamanism.

Malidoma Somé, who was Western educated as well as traditionally trained, now lives in California. He periodically returns to his village in Africa to be "cleansed" by his elders, a renewal considered necessary for someone living amid the troubling energies of Western civilization. But where, and to whom, do those born of this painful civilization who do not subscribe to its paradigm go for cleansing? Where are our people? Who tends our shrines and maintains our sacred ways?

We do. By living in alignment with the best our heritage has bequeathed us, and with our own clearest awareness of creative response. In consultation with the land, in respectful reconnection with sacred sites; in exploring the symbols and patterns used by our ancestors in their spiritual practices; in, most especially, interface with the primal elements that transform and sustain us. These elements are where we can go for cleansing and renewal. They are in a real and practical sense our wisdom teachers—timeless, ever present, powerful: sea, wind, light, and stone.

There is no return to or re-creation of the Celtic past, and, clearly, that is not what is really needed in today's circumstances. *But what is powerful and good is still present in the land and our potentials of relationship with it, and in the capacity of consciousness to retrieve or to know what needs to be known.* What is really missing for many people is community.

A woman birthing a baby is engaged in a most ancient process. In doing so she is participating, with whatever degree of awareness, in the continuity of women throughout time who have enacted birthing. Yet, even if she squats naked in a meadow for parturition, the modern woman's body is not quite like that of her ancestors, and neither is her mind, nor the land and air around her, much less the society that judges her actions. It is an ancient process, but an experience encompassing what is present in this modern woman's reality.

That is the crux of it: what is encompassed in daily awareness. For it is daily awareness of change as well as of what is intrinsic that gives reference to spiritual realization and belief. Initiation into transformative knowledge comes when passing through resistances of pain and fear, in opening and surrender that releases what is grasped, accepting greater insight. Mindset can indeed change, but the prelude is unlearning, and this is something modern people are most reluctant to do. There is great conceit and attachment regarding knowledge, method, and accomplishment. Society is competitive and constrictive; fluidity is educated out of children. The unknown threatens and mystery is denigrated, romanticized, or confused with illusion.

Somé says:

> When we resist expansion, we foster the unreal, serving that part of our ego that wants to limit growth and experience. . . . The Dagara refrains from asking questions when faced with a riddle, because asking questions and being answered destroys one's chances to learn for oneself. Questions are the mind's way to destroy a mystery. The mind of the village elder has become accustomed to living with questions while his heart dances with the "answer."

The heart's dance is that process of patiently expanding awareness. It is letting go of assumptions, quieting mental agitation, allowing "not knowing" to deepen attention and trustful receptivity, realizing that meaning exists beyond—and is more powerful than—answers and explanations. It's a bit like the Loch Ness monster: proof, disproof— neither has much to do with presence and meaning. That is one of the basic differences between ancient and modern mindsets.

What I practice is not druidism, shamanism, or any other delineated tradition because, regardless of what streams feed the river, the river's water is not that of the springhead's. What I practice is simply the cultivation and application of awareness. Naming gives a sense of identity and connection, but when operating independently from established bodies of knowledge, there is more clarity, if not truth, in leaving things undefined. There was a time when I sought names of things: plants, birds, trees, tracks, stars, clouds, rocks; I learned Latin names of herbs. It was an inquiry within which relationship was strengthened and made specific; observation was sharpened; realms of knowledge intermingled, were explored and applied. But after a certain point a shift occurred and the seeking quieted. Observation and relationship moved to a different plane and there was more silence, living with questions that teach more than answers could.

Learning and unlearning, remembering and releasing, are rhythms like the inhale and exhale of breath and the pulse and rest of the heart.

They are a spiraling dance of consciousness investigating its capacity.

A mailing arrived from a holistic institute describing a summer program of workshops. The teachers' names were familiar—competent people well versed in what they offered; committed practitioners, some of them indigenous. One was the descendent of Celts who "were killed for their beliefs in 1694 on the Isle of Mull in the Hebrides."

Write-ups for the workshops said things like, "Learn new ways of living our fullness while treading more gently on Mother Earth," "Shamanic journeying to communicate with deeply hidden aspects of the self," "Voyaging beyond time and space to experience the healing power of time-absent ecstasy," "Hear the voice of the ancient ones on the wind, heal our past, and summon our destiny." There was frequent mention of trance, visualization, drumming, and transformative shamanistic techniques.

The vocabulary in the brochure has become jargon, words so often used inappropriately in commercialized spiritual hyperbole that their profound meanings have lost impact and depth. Would people attending these workshops actually experience fullness, ecstasy, healing, time-absence, ancient voices? And without preparation, cultural context, developed capacity, or follow-up providing integration and continuity?

Emotions are easily stimulated. Watching a movie can catalyze intense emotional states—grief, terror, anxiety, hilarity, triumph—but these intense feelings are not life changing. People leave theaters affected, but their lives are not transformed. To actually move consciousness to a level deeper than emotional or psychological engagement and free it from egoistic preoccupations may be possible in workshops such as those described in the brochure, but even then—what next? Would participants go home to tread more lightly, live more fully, embrace destinies beyond the mundane, heal and be healed?

Perhaps—always *perhaps:* that is the conviction of workshop presenters—a spark will catch and blossom into light. But most people introduced to shamanism will not experience, understand, or apply it shamanically. How can they without a congruent orientation of consciousness, living as modern westerners do, thinking and believing according to modern conditioning? When discussing spirituality, people may *sound* like shamans; when talk turns to jobs, politics, child rearing, crime, lifestyles, money, personal relationships, conventional mindsets suddenly reemerge, creating question as to whether shamanic mindset was there in spiritual practice either. A practitioner writing about a ceremony he conducted said, "I watch this magick happen, like people going into a dream having these experiences then coming back and blowing them off. People seem interested in a lot of things but one thing they do not seem to be interested in is truth of being." He said this, not to criticize, but in questioning the effectiveness of presenting sacred vision through ceremony for which there is no preparation or continuity of context.

Trying to teach shamanic spirituality may be putting the cart before the horse, dealing with concepts whose meanings have changed. Take, for example, the concept—which is general, not even particular to shamanism—of heroism. Reading about William Wallace, the Lowland Scots patriot, one is struck by his utter commitment and the courage with which he continually conducted himself in actualizing that commitment. He embodied the highest principles he knew, reserving nothing as fallback for personal preservation or advancement. He was a hero, dedicated—unto a hideous death—to his people's freedom.

Recently there was reportage about a US Marine who fell off his ship in the Arabian Sea and was rescued, a day later, by fishermen. The Marine was given a promotion and came home to a hero's parade. Why is he a hero? For surviving? Why was he promoted after falling from a platform he was not even supposed to be standing on? Another young military man was given a medal and presented as a hero for surviving in Bosnia after his plane crashed. This act encompassed many things, but is realization of personal survival heroism?

Is emotional stimulation ecstasy? Is self-analysis shamanism? Is a twenty-minute visualization a vision quest? What happens to engagement with states like courage, transformation, love, vision, or honor when their meanings are diminished? Shamanism, and much of alternative spirituality as practiced by modern people, suffers from that diminishment. Suppose we compare neoshamanism to a person's relationship with a car.

The person drawn to powerful things acquires a car, though she has no real idea of its potential. She sits in the car, polishes and displays it, knows facts and anecdotes about cars, occasionally honks its horn, and derives stimulation from having acquired it. In this instance, the car is an acquisition enhancing ego.

Another person, perhaps a psychologist or someone involved with self-analysis, acquires a car. Its interior fascinates, becoming a place for therapeutic exploration. Everything about the car is symbolic: the circularity of the steering wheel; the upholstery colors; the gearshift—obviously phallic, not to be touched by women; the glovebox and its hidden documents; knobs inscribed with evocative words such as "lights" and "wipers." The speedometer's esoteric numbers, the gauges indicating full or empty, doors to be opened or closed, the presence of a rearview mirror—all are significant. This person may sometimes slide a drumming cassette into the tape deck, leaning back in the seat to let his psyche roam. He may visualize traveling to far-off realms, studying maps and travel guides until those realms seem very present. For this person the car is a symbolically loaded context for self-exploration.

A third person drives the car, perhaps learning to do so from a teacher, perhaps figuring it out herself—incurring a few dents in the process. She uses the car for essential errands, sometimes delivering packages or messages for others. She visits relatives and consultants. The car requires maintenance and fuel; she pays their price and does what is necessary. The car, being nonstandard, can't be insured, so she drives knowing society will not assume responsibility for what happens to her: she might become reckless or inattentive; another driver may act with ill intention toward her; she might even get lost or never return home. This person understands that the car is an actual means for engagement with the universe, a means serving the larger web of community.

This metaphor for shamanism, like the car, can be taken further, but the point is that shamanism is concerned with accessing a pervasive, not just personal, reality, and with mediation between nonordinary and ordinary stratas of that reality for the common good. Shamanism's understandings and applications are literal and concrete as well as representational, engaging both being and doing for purposes expanding relationship to life. But without the larger orientation, reality, like the new version of heroism, remains subjective preoccupation.

In Bear Heart's book, *The Wind Is My Mother: The Life and Teachings of a Native American Shaman*, written with Molly Larken, Bear Heart says:

> I was taught not to fix medicine for myself. I can ask someone to do it for me, but for myself I can't. If I do, that would be about all I could do from then on and I wouldn't be able to

help anyone else. Even though it all comes from the same source, a medicine person goes in one of two directions: either working to help others, or working to help himself.

This teaching seems essentially true in its articulation of a fundamental choosing of orientation for spiritual work and for interrelationship. Moving from midwifery into the practice of spiritual medicine, the perspective of service naturally prevailed in my experience, responding to what was called for, night or day. It did not occur to me to make medicine for myself; maintenance practices were simply part of a context of effective service. Unfortunately, neither did it occur to me to ask for help from other practitioners when needed.

But no conflict of interest exists when service operates within interdependent reality; the best interests of each are included in the good of all. It is with separation from a flow of generosity and receptivity, from mutuality, that needs appear competitive. When I withdrew from community in order to rest and tend to personal challenges, resistance developed toward helping others—constriction engendered by unmet personal needs.

Practitioners must often learn to ask for and open to help from others. This is, perhaps, part of the teaching in Bear Heart's words: practitioner health should abide within balances of healthy community dynamics. Included in this shared health is the circumvention of pitfalls such as power abuse and disproportionate preoccupation with the personal. Where there is no give and receive, people either retreat into defensive urgencies of self-preservation and self-orientation or else enact self-abuse, which can deceptively take on the appearance of altruistic service.

The Celtic key to relationship with community or culture—with life—is participation. To experience being part of something requires participation. This is similar in basis to the axiom "You are what you eat." Celtic society and Celtic spirituality operated through the vitality of active engagement. Celts exercised their rights and freedoms, including lively dispute; arbitrary prerogative has never ruled Celtic thought. No one was out of the picture in society or religion; individual actions affected all else. This awareness can be seen through the mechanisms of gessa; through willing acts of sacrifice; through the telling absence of the apathy, passivity, and frustration endemic in cultures where people feel powerless and faceless amid both society and the larger universe.

Celts participated in the workings of that universe, in the turning of seasons and the continuity of fertile life. They were *partisans*—"part of"—participating in the ripening grain, the rising light, the multiplying cattle. As participants they were superstitious, alert to subtleties that might tip balances; cognizant of the power in words and wishes, and in matters of conduct and relationship. Customs such as first-footing at New Year, the tradition of blessing a house and its occupants as one enters, and of blessing tools as they are passed to coworkers, or the rituals following harvest, all manifested a continuing Celtic recognition of each person's capacity to be a direct agent of blessing or impact in the lives of others. (In *Anam Cara*, O'Donohue says, "In the Celtic tradition, and especially in the Gaelic language, there is a refined sense of the sacredness that the approach to another person should embody. The word *hello* does not exist in Gaelic. The way that you encounter someone is through blessing. . . . Regularly throughout conversation in Gaelic, there is explicit recognition that the divine is present in others.")

As modern people, in what do we participate? For instance most find the concept of individuals having any effect on whether or not propitious conditions attend a growing season absurd. Yet the teachings of physics, in essence, support this concept and others that acknowledge a basic inextricability of eachness from otherness in terms of influence and change.

Even regardless of scientific reality, choices of participation create experience, and experience is, after all, what life is mainly about. Power is both derived from and utilized in participatory experience. People talk about what they are "into," as in, "I'm into computers," or, "I'm into mountain climbing." Being "into" is a modern attempt at being part of, though falling short because of psychological conditioning that quails at boundarilessness. Being "into" is like the undersea explorer in his diving bell rather than the free-swimming selkie who is part of the ocean.

Nonetheless, perspective that comes from choosing to participate empowers experiences of active inclusion in a larger dynamic. If one chooses to participate in meaningful observance of seasonal change, for example, those changes become more significant in relation to life, occupy more awareness, and become an accessible arena for engagement with larger universal forces. Celtic cultural orientation was toward participation in larger cosmic realms as partisans of well-being; they did so through their arts, religion, personal conduct, and general integration of awareness, whether as warriors, farmers, artists, Druids, or kings.

What many of us are looking for are not roots—those are present in spiritual resource and in heritage—but for a place in which belonging can nourish becoming; a place for one's children; nourishment both communal and unique. My generation is full of seekers and drifters looking for admission. Segregation and exclusion change their masks but remain adamant: this door for whites, this door for blacks, this one for Natives, this one for men, this for women, and so on. These doors often lead nowhere we want to go, or into isolated rooms where murmurs of neighbors on the other sides of walls sound sinister or unintelligible.

Modern people of Celtic ancestry of course associate heritage with particular traditions, and many neopagans claiming "fam-trad" lineage in Celtic spirituality also heavily invest in a sense of linkage with the past. As was pointed out in the discussion of clan and Scottish history in part one, the Victorian Age saw the creation of a romantic, misrepresented Celticism whose legacy of individualized clan tartans, the *felie beg,* phony antiquarian literature, and other distortions many Anglo-Celts accept as ancient and authentic tradition.

Like Gardnerian Wicca and other recent inventions hoping to attract luster through claiming antiquarian credentials, much of what passes for Celtic tradition is of fairly recent origin. Some of it, such as the felie beg or "small kilt," is an evolution of older, genuine forms, albeit not always Celtic evolutions; much of it, however, is commercialized or manipulated evolution.

The "discovery" of the purportedly ancient Ossian manuscripts by James Macpherson is an interesting case of paradox. Macpherson was widely concluded to be a fraud and liar, though the Ossian literature, the most well-known being *Fingal* and *Temora,* presented in 1763, were wonderfully spirited sagas. Macpherson's claims for their antiquity were false but, in Murray Pittock's words:

> [This] fails to take cognizance of the special and distressing disadvantages under which Highland society was now laboring. Ossian was a reply to political repression, an assertion by the ancient civilization of the North of the triumph of mind and spirit over the seedy world of Hanoverian commerce and imperialism. Jacobitism was, even before Macpherson, a romantic political movement; it was alienated,

revolutionary, nationalist, and daring and dangerous on a personal level.

Nonetheless, a Scottish national identity that is acceptable to the English must necessarily be suspect. As James Hunter points out,

> Scotland's genuinely historical heroes, such as Robert Bruce or William Wallace, could be cultivated only at the risk of raising questions as to what had happened to the independence for which such men had fought.... Macpherson's mist-enveloped warriors, however, could be celebrated safely. They stood for no cause other than the one of making Scotland out to be a place that was not quite the same as England. James Macpherson, then, began the process of providing modern Scotland, and not least Lowland Scotland, with the slightly bizarre self-image which the country has kept polished ever since.

There are two kinds of romanticism entangled in Celtic tradition. One is the romanticism that is, in itself, intrinsic and intrinsically sustaining to Celtic temperament. The other is a disempowering romanticizing, making Celtic reality discontemporaneous and irrelevant. Traditionality, both genuine and contrived, can serve either of those categories, causing much confusion and dilemma.

The Scots poet Robert Burns was the first to draw together the Jacobite view of Scotland's long struggle for freedom with newer ideas of liberty, and he renewed and contributed to Scotland's oral vernacular tradition. His aim seemed to be not only to revive Scottish culture but to encourage a positive evolution of national identity. Pittock points out that:

> The flaw in this aim was that it could be hijacked by a localized, sentimental version of this identity.... Scotland began to think itself a Celtic country again . . . but it was to be largely a Celticism composed of echoes, the "Tartan Curtain" that divided the new Scottish identity from the realities of both the national struggle of the eighteenth century, and the current tragedy of the Highlands.

Tradition always runs the risk of relegation to quaintness, even when not hijacked for other disempowering purposes. But it is almost always fear that compels hijacking or relegation. When tradition is truly empty—when cultural symbols have no life stirring beneath them—there is no opposing impulse toward dismissal or co-option. Putting Prince Charlie's image on biscuit tins has not changed the looks I see on faces of some of the people slowly walking away from the battlefield monument at Culloden. Out of a dispelling Celtic Twilight may emerge revitalized connection to roots sustaining a distinct cultural subconscious.

Celts were a romantic people, and paradoxical as well, so it is not surprising that romanticizing of Celtic culture presents paradoxes. Nostalgia can be a passivity of defeat or it can be perseverance born of cultural integrity—memory that gives impetus to continuity.

There is something proud and joyous about my son in a kilt, performing the intricacies of the Highland sword dance—the *gille callum*—to the skirl of bagpipes. But the small kilt is an eighteenth-century modification of Highland dress, instigated by an Englishman; and the sword dance was probably created in the seventeenth century, though there is evidence of an ancient form of the gille callum. Even the pipes have only been in Scotland since the fourteenth century. I am glad to know these things—glad Gabriel knows them also. The knowing of history offers grounding, informs evolution, and is a respect offered to ancestry and ancestors, many of whom committed their lives to support contemporaneous cultural truth. Scotland is indeed not what Hunter calls "some sort of cross between a national park and an open-air folk museum." What stirs the hearts of visitors may not be cultural reality or cultural vision for Scotland's modern inhabitants. A similar dichotomy exists in North America in the difference between both urban and reservation Indian life and the versions of traditional Native culture outsiders romantically want and expect.

A Scot in Scotland has an uncontrived identity, part of inherent context. An outsider, though of Scottish descent, has what for identity? Only a Scottish surname, perhaps, or Celtic coloring. It is no surprise that outsiders—descendants of immigrants—are the ones most drawn to externals distinguishing them as Celtic. I watch my red hair turn gray and sometimes it feels like watching heritage slip away; sometimes there is little to hold to—a silent pride, an inheritance of loss and displacement. Like Native Americans of mixed blood-lines (and few Natives are without non-Native antecedents) who view themselves simply as Indians, many Celtic Americans, despite the melting pot of ancestral diversity, identify themselves as Celts. Something in that cultural consciousness, an enduring primary resonance, continues to express itself: pertinent, unfinished, evocative.

When my friend Robin came home from Scotland she visited her parents and described to them her journey. Her dad, a third-generation wheat farmer, pored for a long, silent time over the map of Scotland Robin laid before him. He asked her to label the stones she brought him from the different places in the Highlands she visited.

Something calls across the wide ocean to descendants of exiles and immigrants who, within the gifts and teachings of their new home, still respond to a mother tongue of loch and brae and burn. John Buchan says, "The Scots are the most far-wandering race on earth, but they are eternally homesick." Why is this so? Is it because of something particular to Celtic lands? To Celtic people and Celtic relationship with homeland? Elizabeth Grant, writing in the nineteenth century, said of the Highlander:

> Whig was an appellation of comprehensive reproach. It was used to designate a character made up of negatives; one who has neither ear for music nor taste for poetry, no pride of ancestry; no heart for attachment; no soul for honor. . . . A Whig, in short, was what all Highlanders cordially hated—a cold, selfish, formal character.

Perhaps it is because Celts in general are not cold, selfish, formal characters; that they are people with, as Native Gregory Cajete would say, "a face, a heart, and a visionary foundation," people so unabashedly attuned and attached to the spirit of place—the aware interplay of freedom and union—that there is this enduring homesickness. It is a strong, heartbreaking love within a deep Celtic capacity for love and for lament—beautiful lament—and it is also the interface of mortal love that restlessly yearns, and spiritual love that abides.

She

Women of the sidhe
in stepdancing shoes—
I've seen them;
ones in kindergarten
on the isle of Eigg
weaving futures between
strands of wild-flying hair.
Women of the sidhe,
sober shoes bog-stained,
arrowing through storms,
toting shopping bags on buses,
awakening smoored fires
in the calm fey task of
creating the universe.

PART III

GENDER EQUALITY

AN OBSERVATION CAUGHT MY ATTENTION in the course of research: an anthropologist's note that there was not much phallic representation in Celtic art. Peering through our time telescope at the ancient Celts, we see, in contrast to the Romans, a sexually free-spirited people, their attitudes about sex having a great deal to do with their lack of neuroses about sexuality and with the relative freedom experienced by Celtic women. Relative not because full equality was realized in Celtic society but, because compared to other societies of their time (and since), the Celts were extraordinarily nonsexist.

A Scotswoman replying to a jibe made by Julia Augusta, wife of the Roman Severus, was quoted as saying, "We fulfill the demands of nature in a much better way than do you Roman women; for we consort openly with the best men, whereas you let yourselves be debauched in secret by the vilest."

Sex has long been primary in the restriction of women's freedom and equality, and in casting a shadow over femininity's expression. The paradox of female vulnerability (to rape and other violence) and female power (to gestate, give birth to, and nourish new life) has always been made a fulcrum for control in male-dominated societies. There is often considerable fear of female sexuality in such societies, leading to repressive conditions and denigrative beliefs concerning women.

For ancient Celts, sex had no linkage to notions of sin and was not confined to the institution of marriage. Those two factors made crucial differences in women's—in people's—lives. The Celts were not prudish about sex; it was, as the Caledonian woman puts it, a "demand of nature" responded to with the same frank regard for beauty, enjoyment, and vitality characteristic of other Celtic arts. Women's sexuality was not placed in a tainted category; later imposition of Christian concepts of sexuality's corruption and female culpability in the downfall of "man" did much to undermine the integrity of Celtic culture. When demands of nature become sins, intimacy with nature loses its sacred, ecstatic foundation and human relations perforce suffer.

The Celts' sexual freedom did not result in wholesale promiscuity. People had plenty of things with which to occupy themselves and, though sex was not exclusive to marriage, matrimony was primarily a monogamous precinct. (Polygamy was lawfully practiced only with consent of all wives involved. Brehon law, however, stipulated that any injury sustained by a second wife on the first day of coming into the household of an established first wife was not a convictable offense.) Celtic marriage was a contractual matter, not a religious institution, and its inception was celebrated by feasting, not religious or governmental ceremony. A woman could choose a husband, and a man could choose a wife; either way, there had to be consent. The early Picts were possibly matrilineal, their kings ruling through matrilineal succession. Roman historian Tacitus reported of the Celts: "There is no rule of distinction to exclude the female line from the throne or the command of armies."

There were ten classifications of Celtic marriage, each a specific form of contract, including one that was marriage for "a year and a day," dissolvable (unless children were produced). Some of these classifications were primarily used for making tribal alliances. Divorce in any classification of marriage could be initiated by either husband or wife, and there was equality in divorce settlements—wives did not lose their dowries or increases thereof. Women could personally own livestock herds—Celtic wealth and independence—and, in marriages, household authority generally rested with whoever had the most livestock. Girls could inherit when there were no sons. Women were responsible for their own debts and not those of their husbands, and an outcast husband did not affect his wife's social position.

When sex, marriage, and financial independence are not used as socially, religiously, and politically sanctioned controls of women's freedom, women are then more naturally regarded as equal, significant participants in all aspects of society. In Scotland, women were active in councils and in settling disputes. Women were esteemed, and it was said that "an unfaithful, unkind, or even careless husband is looked upon as a monster" by Highlanders.

In the Celtic world there were prophetesses; women healers, judges, and sages; women bards and satirists; priestesses and women warriors (some of these warriors, in the sagas, trained the men aspiring to be heroes); and an occasional queen or female chief.

Onomoris, a Gaulish chieftainess, commanded the Celtic tribes wandering in Iberia; Credne Coinchend and Estin were Irish women who were warrior champions; Macha Mong Ruadh ruled Ireland from 377–331 B.C.; and Cartimandua headed the Brigantes tribe in Britain from A.D. 43–69. Celtic women were frequently ambassadors, making treaties and participating in assemblies. From A.D. 515–520, Roman bishops protested the Celtic church's inclusion of female authority, and Welsh law drastically reduced women's rights by the tenth century A.D. In A.D. 697, the Christian-influenced Irish Assembly forbade women from being warriors.

Boudicca, of Britian's Iceni tribe, was probably the most historically famous Celtic queen—other than legendary Maeve (Mabh) of Connacht in Ireland. (Maeve was flamboyantly sexual, assertive, reckless but shrewd, and considered more of a leader than her husband, King Ailill.) They say Boudicca was a compelling woman, with her spear and her knee-length red-gold hair. She led her tribe and its allies in revolt against the Romans in Britain after she and her daughters were raped and flogged, and was, for a time, successful in her strategy and leadership.

The advent of Christianity did not, at first, greatly change the status of Celtic women. Celtic Christians, especially in Ireland, were lax about religious rules and hierarchy. Van de Weyer says, "The Druid priesthood included both men and women, enjoying equal status; and this was maintained in the Celtic church, in which, contrary to the practice in the rest of Christendom, women frequently ruled great churches and monasteries. Moreover, like the Druid priestly communities, the Celtic monasteries often contained both men and women, with a woman in charge, such as Kildare under Brigid and Whitby under Hilda." Coed monasteries! And even, it is rumored, an Irish woman acting as bishop. Early Christianity in Celtic countries was an amalgamation of old and new beliefs, attitudes, and practices, much as it was for Native Americans. It took some time for Celts to internalize doctrines turning women into an unclean, lower species on whom men were obliged—for everyone's sake—to keep a tight, punishing rein.

In Elizabeth Grant's memoirs, from 1812, she speaks of the Highland integration of old and new spiritual perspectives:

> There was no very deep religious feeling in the Highlands up to this time. The clergy were reverenced in their capacity of pastors without this respect extending to their persons unless fully merited by propriety of conduct. . . . Our mountains were full of fairy legends, old clan tales, forebodings, prophecies, and other superstitions, quite as much believed in as the Bible. The Shorter Cathechism and the fairy stories were mixed together to form the innermost faith of the Highlander, a much gayer and less metaphysical character than his Saxon-tainted countryman. . . . The old women snuffed . . . and groaned a great deal, to express their mental sufferings . . . Lapses from faith were their grand self-accusation, lapses from virtue were, alas! little commented on; temperance and chastity were not in the Highland code of morality.

There is a Cheyenne saying that the tribe is not truly defeated until its women's hearts are on the ground. Indian women kept the Native heart strong through decade after decade of tragedy and demoralizing cultural loss, not succumbing to paralysis of confusion or despair. They did not lose purpose—their courage endured: women's alignment to continuity. During the Highland Clearances in Scotland it was the women who resisted, actively and despite brutality from police and soldiers, in attempts to protect their homes and ensure their families' survival. The women, who probably had never been as sentimentally attached to their clan chiefs as had the men, seemed to have been less bewildered by or resigned to betrayal by those chiefs. Their courage is unquestionable. John Prebble describes one incident of resistance in the Hebrides:

> MacBean put his men into two divisions and sent them forward against the crowd with their batons. One took the women in the rear, the other on the flank, and drove them

over barley-rigs and dykes, along the deep-pooled shore.
Some of the women fought with the police, calling out to their
men, "Be manly and stand up!" Thus constables and women,
Highlanders both, fought on the wet heather and white sand
for the possession of Lord MacDonald's land, until MacBean's
whistle recalled the officers and the women crawled away to
bathe their bloody heads. . . . On the hill maddened women
were soon shouting "such wishes as that the men might come
down and wash their hands in their enemies' hearts'-blood,
and that the devil and his angels might come and sweep them
out of the land." Cooper was learning that however much he
might belong to the Age of Steam and the Gas Lamp, the
women of Uist were closer to Conn of the Hundred Battles
when roused.

In Ireland during the late 1800s, in the struggle for independence
from England, it was women, also, who kept freedom's flame from
being extinguished. But it was not only with England that the Irishwomen contended; it was also with their own fathers, brothers, husbands, and sons. The bizarre combination of Christianity—which in-
culcated beliefs of female inferiority—and English persecution that
emasculated Irishmen resulted in Irishwomen oppressed by both internal and external sources. Their men insisted that the independence
movement be an exclusively masculine endeavor (despite daily un-
acknowledged dependence on women). Each time the Irish women
organized, forming women's leagues engaging in effective work sustaining the people and furthering the cause of freedom, the men—
their own men—disbanded those leagues. The only time women were
allowed this work was when most of the men were in jail and, just as
women's groups were gathering steam and had gotten the men out
of prison, their leagues were again forced to disband. The men could
not yield this arena in which so much pride and masculine self-
image was invested. They would not yield it; they would not even
share it, though later activists like Bernedette Devlin could not be
sidelined.

Mary Crow Dog, a Lakota woman taking part in the AIM
seventy-one-day occupation of Wounded Knee, justified women's
mainly subservient role, saying, "Once our men [get] their rights and
their balls back, we might start arguing with them about who should
do the dishes. But not before." The trouble with this is few men are

willing to change the gender order of things after they have regained rights and balls. Respect, if not mutually attained and mutually expressed, seldom actualizes.

Being an Irishman became widely synonymous with being a drunk—and often a wife-beating drunk. As with American Indians, alcohol was bravado for the bitter and anesthesia for the despairing— the self-poisoning of a tortured people. Irish who emigrated to North America fared little better in the esteem department than those who remained behind. Common, for those in search of work, were encounters with placards or newspaper ads saying, "Irish need not apply." Being white is not always the admittance key into mainstream America: Jews know this; homosexuals know this; women know this; and so did the Irish in the nineteenth and early twentieth centuries. (It is interesting to note that it was not until 1924 that women and Indians received citizenship in the United States.)

Regarding homosexuality, pre-Christian Celts saw nothing untoward in men admiring one another's physical beauty and engaging comrades in sexual intimacy, though I doubt this same intimacy applied to women of the period. But the Celts seemed almost pansexual in their embrace of natural, ecstatic relationship. They made love, in various ways, with whatever to them embodied divine vitality. Until the end of the twelfth century the kings of Ian Conaill, in Ireland, were inaugurated by publicly copulating with a white mare representing the Goddess, the land. (There is no report on how the mares felt about this practice.) Kingship was an explicit marriage—not a platonic or metaphoric one—with the land. There was cultural recognition of sexuality as something, not only not at odds with spirituality, but a celebrated aspect of creative union.

Women in my family live as rurally as possible. My mother dwells alone on a little lake, in a house she designed and did much of the work on herself. In winter—which in northern Michigan is long and cold—she snowshoes out a three-quarter-mile driveway to reach her truck. An environmental activist, she serves on wildlife commissions and zoning boards, and is someone who not only identifies one kind of bird from another by its call, but discerns variations between individual birds of the same kind.

Leigh, my sister, designed and built a house too, in the high desert of Oregon. Like our mother, she knows her birds, becoming expert during field research for the Forest Service and other employers. Leigh worked for a time at a birds-of-prey rehabilitation center and led nature tours on the Deschutes River. When she could not make a living doing research because she refuses projects that are invasive or harmful to wildlife—which, unfortunately, includes most research—she turned to art, making illustrations of the animals she so fiercely loves.

My mother, sister, and I share an affinity with the wilds that is not exclusive to women, even in our family, but is part of a heritage responding to the land directly and sensitively within daily awareness.

Other patterns besides this are evident in the family tree. One is its number of writers. But another is the tendency toward few offspring even in eras when large families were the norm. Many women, on both my mother's and father's sides of the family, eschewed marriage or, if they wed, had few or no children. This resulted in my having only two cousins, an uncle, and one nephew.

What were these women doing that they did not marry or occupy themselves with childbearing? One of them became a doctor—one of the first women admitted into medical school. Another, Great-Aunt Effie, married but her husband was a fly-by-night who deserted her. Effie sewed to support herself and graduated to running her own business in Chicago (furs); she was successful enough that she bailed Sears & Roebuck out of financial disaster during the Depression. Great-Aunt Effie never remarried; she traveled. I have a set of filigreed rosewood shelves she brought back from some exotic place.

These women in my ancestry seem to have been independent, nervy women who would not settle into what society expected of them. For all our good manners there is something renegade in my family's genetics—some fey attitude spiking reality no matter how sincerely we try to fit in.

In Inverness, Scotland, at twenty-one, I hitchhiked into the countryside, walking, occasionally getting rides. One midday I got a lift from a prosperous man in a BMW who offered to buy lunch. In Scotland on business from London, he said he was bored with his own thoughts and would welcome companionship at his meal. Hungry and nearly broke, I accepted his invitation.

We dined at a restaurant in Inverness, an expensive, clubby sort of place having an abundance of burgundy leather decor and full of businessmen. I saw hardly any women. I was in jeans; my escort was impeccably dressed. He was quite handsome, probably in his early thirties, someone who looked James Bond-ish in a suit. I had misgivings about his motives and was distinctly out of place in the gentrified restaurant, but my escort's manner was relaxed; there was no innuendo or sense of being cornered.

Over lunch we conversed. The man was an engineer. He sketched diagrams on the back of an envelope he fished out of his pocket, trying to explain his project to me, casually patient. His drawings were impressive with their freehand precision of line. He asked about my life—nothing too personal. I was fascinated by the whiteness of his shirt cuffs, remembering being fourteen before my mother let me, a tomboy, wear anything white. Afterward he dropped me at my lodgings without a hint of pressure for a "pay back" for lunch and transportation.

Relieved, grateful, I still somehow felt shamed. There was something geisha-like in the luncheon; there was something about the very fact of being a woman that put me at a disadvantage. It was not just being in the position of accepting a handout of lunch and a ride. That had implications, but that was not, in itself, what was distressing. I still would have been an outsider had I driven myself to that restaurant in my own BMW and paid for lunch with my own wad of cash. In no society in the world can women truly, autonomously relax in public—truly move in a way equal to men. This is not new. There is an old Irish story—almost two thousand years old—that stunningly addresses those issues about women's options for freedom and happiness in a man's world. It is the story of Derdriu's Sorrows.

Derdriu's life was circumscribed even before birth—her destiny foretold. As her pregnant mother, the wife of King Conchubur's storyteller, was wearily going to bed after an evening of serving drink and food to the Ulaid, the child in her womb screamed, a sound terrifying everyone.

Cathub, the Druid, put his hand on the woman's womb and predicted, "A girl, and her name will be Derdriu, and there will be trouble on her account." He declared she would be a woman with twisted yellow hair and beautiful grey-green eyes; a tall, long-haired woman of matchless, faultless form; a woman over whom there would be a "great slaughter among the chariot-warriors of Ulaid."

This upset the warriors. "Let the child be slain," they exclaimed, but King Conchubur had ear only for Cathub's description of how lovely this Derdriu would be. "I will rear her as I see fit, and she will be my companion," he asserted, and so it went.

Derdriu was raised apart from everyone except her foster parents and a woman named Lebarcham who, as a satirist, could not be barred from anywhere she wanted to go. Derdriu grew to be the loveliest woman in Ireland.

Despite Conchubur's precautions, Derdriu one day eluded confinement. It happened that Noísiu, one of the three sons of Uisliu and a young warrior of appreciable attributes, was standing alone on the rampart of Conchubur's stronghold, and he was singing. All three of Uisliu's sons were extraordinary singers; it was said that cows, hearing this music, tripled their milk output, and men grew peaceful. These same three sons were prodigiously skilled fighters as well; it was said that when they stood back to back they could hold off an entire province.

So, of course, Derdriu was attracted and, being a Celtic woman, made her desire clear to Noísiu. At first he resisted, fearing the prophecy shadowing Derdriu, but he yielded to Derdriu's strong feelings. His brothers tried to restrain Noísiu. "What are you doing?" they asked. "The Ulaid will come to blows on your account." But they saw the tenacity of desire between Derdriu and Noísiu, and decided to support an escape from Conchubur. "Evil will come of this," they said. "Even so, you will not be disgraced while we are alive."

They didn't go alone: three fifties of warriors and three fifties of women and three fifties of hounds and three fifties of servants joined this elopement. Derdriu's bid for personal choice did not sever her from societal involvement. Conchubur had them relentlessly pursued. They went from sanctuary to sanctuary among the kings and chieftains of Ireland.

Eventually, Derdriu and the three brothers, without their retinue, were driven to Scotland and there settled in the wilderness. When wild game was scarce they hunted cattle and thus incurred the wrath of local tribesmen. One day men of Scotland gathered to kill them; the fugitives hastened to Scotland's king and were granted his protection.

The three brothers became mercenary warriors for the king. They built a house for Derdriu, secluding her out of sight lest there be violence on her account. The king's steward stole a glimpse of her, however, and kindled his lord's lust with descriptions of Derdriu's beauty. "Until now, we have not found a woman worthy of you," the steward said. "But there is with Noísiu a woman worthy of the king of the western world. Let Noísiu be slain that the woman might sleep with you."

"No," replied the king. Instead, he bade the steward secretly woo Derdriu on his behalf.

Derdriu had no interest in kings and their lusts. She told Noísiu everything the steward said to her. The brothers were constantly sent into terrible battles and the worst dangers, the king hoping to get rid of them this way so as to not reflect dishonor on himself. His ploys were unsuccessful—Uisliu's sons were too skilled as warriors to fall prey to such hazards.

Out of patience, the king decided that outright murder would have to suffice, but Derdriu was warned and the four escaped to an island off Scotland's coast. Derdriu loved the wilderness; she was quite happy to live amid Scotland's rugged beauty with Noísiu and his congenial brothers. She felt no need for anything more than this.

But the men were homesick for Ireland and the good times they remembered as members of the warrior elite. Thus they were receptive when Conchubur sent an offer of leniency. Eager to return home, and despite Derdriu's warnings, they refused to be suspicious, only asking for three trusted guarantors: Fergus, Dubthach, and Conchubur's son, Cormac.

The guarantors arrived and accompanied Derdriu and Uisliu's sons home to Ireland. Conchubur's scheme unfolded: Noísiu and his brothers had extravagantly sworn not to eat until reaching Conchubur's table; Conchubur instructed those hosting them along the way to invite the innocent guarantors, especially Fergus, who was under a geiss not to refuse such offers, to feasts, so Fergus, Dubthach, and Cormac were diverted and ended up trailing the homeward party. Fergus's son, Fílachu, was the only one to stick with Derdriu and her three companions.

A provincial king's son named Éogan had agreed to murder Noísiu and his brothers for Conchubur. The greeting Noísiu received at Conchubur's stronghold was death. Fílachu tried to shield him and they were killed together—Noísiu struck from above through the body of Fergus's son. Noísiu's brothers were slain and Derdriu was taken, bound, to Conchubur.

When news of this reached the dallying guarantors, they rushed to the stronghold and a battle ensued in which three hundred Ulaid warriors died, Dubthach massacred the province's young women(!), and Conchubur's stronghold was set afire. Three thousand outraged followers, in protest of Conchubur's treachery, accompanied the guarantors into self-imposed exile in Connacht, and it was said that, "For sixteen years these people saw that there was weeping and trembling in Ulaid every night."

But what of Derdriu? She had no champion and no way to enforce her own choices. The king, from the first, had determined that she would be a means to his fulfillment no matter how dark that culmination or how unwillingly provided. Derdriu spent a year of misery with Conchubur. She barely ate or slept; she never smiled; she scorned entertainments. In her lament for Noísiu she said, in part:

> *I loved the modest, mighty warrior,*
> *loved his fitting, firm desire,*
> *loved him at daybreak as he dressed*
> *by the margin of the forest.*
> *Those blue eyes that melted women,*
> *and menaced enemies, I loved*
> *then, with our forest journey done,*
> *his chanting through the dark woods.*

When Conchubur tried to tempt her with dazzling gifts, she repudiated him, saying, "Conchubur, be quiet! You have brought me grief upon sorrow; as long as I live, surely, your love will be of no concern to me." Stung by her attitude, Conchubur asked, "What do you hate most that you see?" and was told, "Yourself, surely, and Éogan." Conchubur then told her that, in that case, she would spend the next year with Éogan, and he deliverd her to Noísiu's killer, tauntingly calling Derdriu a "ewe between two rams."

The next day, standing behind Éogan in his chariot, she saw a boulder beside the path and as they speedily approached it, leaned outward so that her head was smashed to fragments against the rock.

Derdriu's plight troubles for reasons perhaps beyond what the storyteller intended. The tale of Derdriu, like all myths created or transcribed by men, is really about men. Women in myths are symbolic and that is to be expected. But they are symbolic in a way that men in myths are not, reflective of a general objectifying or metaphorizing of women.

In Celtic stories, and in myths from most cultures, women are transformative vehicles for cyclic change. This sounds like a major role—a powerful role—but it is, like motherhood, at the sacrifice of autonomy. This is fine as far as it goes, but why is it limited to women and why is it the encompassing female role? In myth and in life, women are seen as the means, the vehicle, the context; the passage, not the passenger; the archetype, not the individual; the other, not the self—or even the comrade.

Women are dealt with as polarized projections: Madonnas or

whores, beautiful dream maidens or nightmarish hags. When, in myth or in life, does a woman represent everyman—the universal human? Instead, and almost invariably, she is man's catalyst; man's vessel; man's cauldron, womb, or ideal; man's fear or temptation; man's quickening. Femininity is seen as the chalice, and masculinity, the dagger. The function of a cup is to hold something, to receive and contain—passively useful. The blade is active, keen, formidable—singular and self-defined.

Historically, women leaders were relatively rare; they were exceptions and their deeds were pointedly considered in reference to their gender. In the sagas, when Maeve eventually failed in her dispute with Conchubur, her warriors lamented, "This is what we get for following behind the rump of a woman." It is sure that Conchubur's warriors would not have remarked on the folly of being led by a man had it been the king who lost. Male leaders are leaders and women leaders are women. This was so in most, if not all, cultures and eras in history. Native American women traditionally were not leaders; Wilma Mankiller, modern day chief of the Cherokee Nation, is an exception. Sitting Bull, Crazy Horse, Chief Joseph, Red Cloud, Tecumsah were individuals, but White Buffalo Calf Woman is portrayed as an archetype. Pocahontas was famous for what she did for John Smith (an inaccurately romantic story), and Sacajawea for helping Lewis and Clark—again, the means by which men pursued their goals or achieved transcendence.

This brings us to a second Celtic story, that of Emer's Only Jealousy. It is a tale actually about a man, Cú Chulainn, the most heroic of ancient Ireland's warriors. This saga (more often known as The Wasting Sickness of Cú Chulainn) is a long complex tale, and I won't tell most of it. We enter the story after Cú Chulainn had lain sick, away from home, for a year, his illness the result of a vision he had on Samhain of being beaten by two sidhe women.

Cú Chulainn was a most attractive man, and Emer, his wife, was well aware that Cú Chulainn sometimes slept with other women when he was off and about the countryside being a hero. She was not dismayed by this, realizing it was inevitable for Cú, being so splendid and so frequently off and about, to desire and be desired by other women. Emer was not insecure, having full confidence in Cú's love, and was a busy and capable person in her own right. When Emer finally got word of her husband's illness, she went and urged him to stir out of his sickbed and do what needed to be done. "Shame on you," she said, " lying there for love of a woman—long lying will make you sick."

Cú Chulainn got up, then, and after some dithering went to Fand, the sidhe woman he had fallen in love with, and helped her sister's husband win a battle in the Otherworld. Cú stayed with Fand for a month; they had a great passion for one another and Cú Chulainn gave no thought at all to Emer.

For the first time, Emer was jealous. Mortal women were one thing, but sidhe women another. The mundane world could never compare with the magical beauty of the faery realm. Emer sharpened her knives and went looking for Fand. Fifty women went along with her, a show of solidarity.

At their approach, Cú Chulainn assured Fand of his protection and addressed his wife arrogantly, saying, "I avoid you, woman, as every man avoids the one he loves. I will not strike your hard spear, held with trembling hand; neither do you threaten me with your thin, feeble knife and weak, restrained anger, for the strength of women is insufficient to demand my full power."

Well! Emer asked why he had dishonored her and Cú Chulainn waxed eloquent on the subject of Fand and her admirable qualities. Emer then gave what was a pithy psychological analysis of the situation: "Perhaps this woman you have chosen is no better than I. But what's red is beautiful, what's new is bright, what's tall is fair, what's familiar is stale. The unknown is honored, the known is neglected—until all is known. Lad, we lived together in harmony once, and we could do so again if only I still pleased you."

Cú Chulainn was affected by this and said, "By my word, you do please me, and you will as long as you live."

"Leave me, then," Fand told him. "Better to leave me," Emer decided, but Fand persisted, grieving at the shame of Cú Chulainn's vacillation. Fand went home to the Otherworld, but her love for Cú Chulainn continued to trouble her.

Fand's husband, Manandán mac Ler, hearing that she had been forsaken by Cú, came to offer companionship, saying, "Well, woman, are you waiting for Cú Chulainn or will you go with me?" Fand replied with an honesty most men would find crushing: "By my word, there is a man I would prefer as husband. But it is with you I will go; I will not wait for Cú Chulainn, for he has betrayed me. Another thing, good person, you have no other worthy queens, but Cú Chulainn does."

But Cú was not reconciled to going home. When he realized Fand had *returned to her husband he was wild with grief and went off to the mountains where he neither ate nor drank for days. Emer enlisted the aid of the Druids and poets to find Cú; the crazed warrior tried to kill them but the Druids sang spells over him and managed to bind his hands and feet.*

When he came to his senses, the Druids gave Cú Chulainn a drink that caused forgetfulness, which they gave to Emer as well, and Manandán shook his cloak between Cú Chulainn and Fand that they might never meet again.

I told this story of Emer's Only Jealousy to a male friend and he was agitated—he did not like it. Asked why, he said it was the infidelity that bothered him—Cú's forgetting Emer when he was in the arms of Fand, and Fand's neglect of Manandán. On the other hand, he was also bothered that Cú Chulainn could not just turn away from mortal life and become a full-time lotus eater in sidhe paradise. The forces of fate—as usual, embodied in women's forms—had their way with our hero, and this was upsetting to both Cú Chulainn and my male friend. And yet, Cú was not quite willing to take spiritual initiative when it was offered. Throughout the long tale, Cú Chulainn displayed an atypical absence of impetus and vigor, except during the battle (always his most comfortable venue). He was in over his head with the rest of the situation, and even his faithful charioteer got impatient with him. It was man's evolutionary journey that was described and, again, women—whether earthly or otherworldly—were present to serve the process and prod the journeyer.

The magical figure in Celtic religion most embodying the explicitly dark female forces was the Mórrígan. Epona, Britain's horse goddess; Irish Brigid, the triple-aspected patroness of smithcraft, healing, and poetry; Welsh goddesses Ceridwen, with her cauldron of rebirth; powerful Arianrhod; poignant, beautiful Rhiannon; and the great Irish mother-goddess Danu all reveal facets of Celtic relationship to the feminine, but it was the Mórrígan who danced the shadow. She gave form to a recurring perception of the feminine.

The Mórrígan, in classic Celtic style, was triple-aspected; she had two sisters, Macha and Babd. The Mórrígan was ostensibly a war goddess: predicting and inciting bloody crisis; amplifying and feeding off it; influencing its outcome, sometimes supporting, and sometimes mocking various mortal participants. She was an extremist, though not without subtlety, or, certainly, guile.

She often appeared as a crow, and took other shapes as well. When the Mórrígan and her sisters visited an army the night before battle, such horror fell over the men that a third of the army died of fright. These were ferocious Celtic warriors the likes of whose dauntlessness even impressed Alexander the Great. What could be so scary about the Mórrígan?

She was not necessarily deathly looking. Quite often she took the form of a gorgeous young woman, though not a shy, pensive creature. Cú Chulainn was intercepted by her in this guise—she was tooling along in her chariot and offered to have sex with him. Cú told her that the last thing he needed was a roll in the hay; he had just finished one of his heroic, fatiguing deeds and was too tired to get it up. About to fight another battle, he wanted to go take a restorative snooze somewhere. The Mórrígan offered, in that case, to support him in the upcoming fight. Cú foolishly turned this down also, and the Mórrígan revealed who she was, saying he would be seeing her again soon (in the form of a giant eel, it turned out), helping those he opposed. (Cú seemed to be the prototype of the hero whose power remains solitary and unneedful of others, though he was trained to herohood by women.)

At other times the Mórrígan took the appearance of a hag, the archetype of death and dissolution. But, as can be seen in the variety of shapes the Mórrígan assumed, it was not the aged crone that was what was fearsome about the Mórrígan. It was her particular femaleness— an unmitigated capacity. She had no mate or consort; she had sisters. She had appetites. She made even the strong and brave confront their naked mortality, the abyss beneath endeavor's shine. She was the carrion crow picking bare their notions of glory. How different she was from the war gods!

Celts were not known as death-fearing people. They dared much, made the committed gesture, believed in a beautiful afterlife and, probably, in reincarnation. The fear the Mórrígan invoked was, perhaps, a fear of chaos, meaninglessness, voided ego, personal insignificance. In ordinary life, men sometimes seem to suspect a fundamental insignificance in relation to their projected sense of woman and the power of her sex. The typical reaction to this is to try to control, subjugate, or diminish that power. In ancient times, Celts did not seem to have minded admitting fear of the Mórrígan, and she was not construed to be evil, she was simply an acknowledged force in their lives. She was the reminder of their vulnerability, of the

vanity of deeds; and this was a fear, perhaps, making Celts suscep-
tible to Christianity's promises of certainty, a shadowless safety in
God's paternal hand.

Being in my mid-forties, living alone, my son grown, offers a
strange sensation of fluid age, where I sometimes feel very old, sometimes youthful, and often both simultaneously. There is a Mórríganish
shapeshifting quality to having a body that can be vamp or viper,
dancer or dodderer. My family has the genetic gift of looking younger
than we are, and this, too, has a shapeshifter feel to it, sometimes
disconcerting, a joggling of assumptions. Maiden, mother, crone—I
perhaps contain all of them but, while appreciating these perspectives of embodiment, feel a more primary yet transcendent identity
having far more to do with consciousness itself, and I ponder what
this has to do with gender.

The Celts had no goddess of love, as such, unlike the Romans and
Greeks. This is interesting in the same way Celtic lack of phallic art is
interesting; both seem indicative of an integrated outlook. The Celts
were not unconcerned with love (or sex); quite to the contrary, their
integration of love into all aspects of divinity and as an essential medium of life experience was a stellar attribute of Celtic consciousness.
It gave their literature and art a particular luminosity, complexity,
and, often, fine humor. Love, sex, sensitivity, and beauty were all
embraced as naturally as breath. Heart, for Celts, was not separate
from or lesser than mind, body, and spirit. This integrated experience
is a measure of the degree to which the culture manifested integration of women and men.

Florence Farr, an early member of England's Golden Dawn Society, said that:

> Pure being is indivisible and unalterable motion. We stop the
> rush of Being and form the visible world by cutting Eternity
> up into Time and Space. Earth is the consciousness of *experi-
> ence*, by which we self-reflect. *Through love* [italics mine] we
> awaken to the ultimate state in which the Earth is insepa-
> rable from consciousness. Then we begin to know the con-
> sciousness of invisible natures. (Greer)

The Celts were acutely aware of "invisible natures," which is why
the sidhe and their Otherworld figured so largely in Celtic life, even,
to some extent, in modern times. Interrelationship is where we prac-

tice love; love is where we practice interrelationship—the awakening of consciousness, the integration of what is awakened. Love extending into each strata of experience fully engages life's potential. Love moves us to know the divine.

Another provocative thing Florence Farr said was, "The power of laughing at ourselves is the germ of all wisdom and enlightenment," something also typical of Celts: wonderfully incorporated in myths, music, art, and general temperament. Jeffrey Gantz refers to the characteristic Irish saga as having "a mythic subtext, a heroic competition, visits to and from the Otherworld, elements of humour and parody and a rambling, patchwork structure."

Without the ability to laugh at ourselves, lines are drawn and rigidity sets in—constriction, loss of perspective, stagnation. Humorless societies compartmentalize consciousness; one of the major ills of this is sexism. It is terrifying when such absurdity is not perceived; results of this are travesties such as the Inquisition and the Salem witch trials. Laughing at ourselves is not a luxury; it is the germ of decent, sustainable coexistence as well as enlightenment.

Looking again at Farr's statement that "Earth is the consciousness of *experience*, by which we self-reflect," leads to consideration of a basis for experience. The more circumscribed one's experience, the more limited is the self that is reflected, and vice versa. Being a man or woman are possible orientations for experience, but the heavier the investment in their specificity, the more they predicate and limit self-identification and experience. Additionally circumscribing are cultural and religious boundaries predefining each sex's experience. These notions assign value and describe capacity, and so, if Woman is prerated 2 and Man is prerated 4, Woman will never equal Man.

Some perspectives see male and female in terms of a bipolar balance (balance considered a hoped-to-be-realized ideal), each sex being the repository of opposite but complementary attributes. The Jungian variation has each sex also possessing the unrealized or underdeveloped anima or animus of their complement.

All this seems a muddled preoccupation with how to measure a narrow option. Farr's hypothesis opens a much broader arena. She says, "Earth is the consciousness of *experience*," not, "Earth is the consciousness of gender experience." In the larger arena, self can reflect any number of perspectives. Equality then takes on different implications altogether; it then simply means mutuality of respect and opportunity. It ceases to be a numbers game (childbearing rated 5, muscle mass rated 3, and so on) where we divide the human pie and get the gender totals to come out equal—or unequal for partisans. The vast capacity of consciousness—of experience—is mocked by such constrictive strategies. Equality, like family, should be another given. People whose self-reflection mirrors inclusive identification have the truest sense of equality—and an ever expanding experience.

In the course of research I jotted down a quote from a Scotswoman of the late 1800s. She said, "In the beauty of the world lies the ultimate redemption of our mortality. When we shall become at one with nature in a sense profounder than even the poetic imaginings of most of us, we shall understand what now we fail to discern."

Some months later I came across startling information about Fiona MacLeod, the author of this quote. It turned out "she" was actually a Scotsman named William Sharp! This was a switch from women of that era using male pseudonyms when writing. But Fiona MacLeod was not just a name; she was a personality alternate to Sharp's own. Bizarre as this arrangement may seem, and objectionably misty as much of MacLeod's writing was, as the quote shows, MacLeod (and, we assume, Sharp) had a keenly sensitive and exploratory mind.

The quote itself appealed to me, but the story behind Fiona MacLeod had its own interest, part of which was the possibility of canceling any gender identification attached to ideas expressed in MacLeod's/Sharp's writings. Whether regarded as androgynous, or as a woman's writings "channeled" by a man, or as the writings of a man suffering from multiple personality disorder, there is a disruption of conventional pigeonholing.

During the latter part of World War II, my mother worked at a radio station. Word of the armistice in Europe was received during one of Barbara's stints at the microphone, but the station manager would not let my mother make the momentous announcement. He insisted a man must be the one to read this important news to the public, to provide proper gravity and authority. Barbara keenly recalls her disappointment at being displaced from that opportunity to proclaim peace. Her brother—her only sibling—was killed in that war.

Almost five decades later, twelve-year old Gia, my land partner's daughter, complained that the series of historical documentaries shown in her classroom was entirely narrated by pompous-sounding men. Some things are slow to change. Gradually, however, perception of our human spectrum widens beyond a narrow conception of what is present both in potential and in manifestation. The at-one-ment that Fiona MacLeod spoke of may indeed offer understanding of many things we now fail to discern.

If women are often excluded in matters of war and peace, there are still some examples of courageous women mentioned in conventional history, those stories of men's battles and governments: Scotswomen such as Isobel of Fife, the Countess of Buchan, who dared, in 1306, to set the crown of Scotland on the head of Robert the Bruce when her brother, whose right it was, feared to do so. And Black Agnes, Randolph's daughter, who resolutely defended the castle at Dunbar against the powerful English in the 1340s. In fact, Agnes deliberately invited seige in order to give Scottish forces time to gather. For nineteen weeks the English battered her gates, then sent for heavy seige engines and catapults to continue the assault. Agnes would stroll along the castle walls, infuriating the attackers—like a cat out of reach of dogs—dusting off the parapet's missile gouges with her white hanky. Eventually the English gave up and sulked off. As they said: "Came I early, came I late, I found Agnes at the gate."

And, of course, there was the cool and committed Flora Mac-Donald, who helped smuggle Prince Charlie out of Scotland after the defeat at Culloden. Flora, born on the outer Herbridean island of South Uist, lived from 1722 to 1790. In June of 1746, twenty-four-year-old Flora was visiting her brother and, in the custom of the day, took his cattle to the upland shielings for summer grazing. It was in this setting that she was asked to help the prince, who was in eminent danger of capture by the English military and Scots militias patrolling the isles. Flora's stepfather, Hugh MacDonald, was a captain in one of the militias searching for Charlie, but he managed to send warning of troop movements to friends of the prince, thus abetting Charlie's elusivity. With Charlie was Neil MacEachain MacDonald, Flora's cousin.

A scheme was concocted for disguising Charlie as Flora's Irish maid, Betty Burke. Preparatory to this, Flora and a servant set out for Clanranald's house, but on the way were arrested for having no passports. They were taken to the militia commander who, luckily, was Hugh MacDonald, and he issued passes for Flora, the servant, and "Betty Burke," so opening the way for the prince's travel in disguise. Once again at liberty, Flora proceeded to Clanranald's and was there provided with suitable garments for the prince. After much rearranging of plans, Charlie at last set sail for Skye in an eight-oared boat with Flora and five men. At first tempestuous seas, then fog, impeded progress and, coming into Skye, the boat was fired upon by soldiers on shore. Managing safe landfall farther on, Flora hid the prince among rocks and hurried to her friend Lady Margaret MacDonald's house, there to dismayingly discover a militia lieutenant at dinner with Lady Margaret and Sir Alexander. She heard that Lady Clanranald and her husband, back on Uist, had been arrested and transported to London to stand trial for supporting Charlie. But with characteristic poise Flora engaged in casual conversation with the lieutenant who, with his men, was on Skye in pursuit of the prince.

A decision was made that Charlie go overland the fifteen miles to Portree and from there cross to the Isle of Raasay where a Jacobite sympathizer, MacLeod of Raasay, might offer sanctuary. Flora caught up to the prince during this overland leg of the journey. Charlie boldly strode along in his skirts, kilting them up to cross streams, and did not attempt to play his part with much skill, causing astonished and highly critical remarks to be made about this forward, uncouth "Irishwoman" by onlookers. At one stop, the lady of the house was afraid to go into her own hall because "I saw such an odd muckle trallup of a carlin, making lang wide steps through the hall that I could not like her appearance at all." Soon after Charlie departed this house, his host and host's daughter were arrested and imprisoned. But the prince, once more in male attire, arrived at Portree and there said good-bye to Flora, Charlie going on to Raasay and eventually being rescued to France. Flora, we are told by historian David Daiches, "was a hard-headed, highly competent young woman who managed her part of the affair very successfully." There was no hint of romance between her and the prince.

Flora was arrested in Armadale and confined aboard a ship, though treated decently. She was then imprisoned in the Tower of London for about seven months, and released in accordance with the Act of Indemnity of 1747. She married and in 1774 emigrated to North Carolina, there to actively support the Royalist cause during the American Revolution. In 1779 she returned to the Hebrides, dying on Skye at age sixty-eight.

Charlie never rewarded Flora for the risks taken on his behalf; royalty often assumes those sacrifices from others. Engraved on Flora's tombstone is Samuel Johnson's remark that "Her name will be mentioned in history, and if courage and fidelity be virtues, mentioned with honour."

But, as so often is the case, the story of a woman "mentioned in history" is told because of its supportive relation to a man—though, thankfully, in Flora's case the woman is not construed as having risked herself out of romantic attachment. Flora's convictions, and the actions taken on their account, were consistent throughout her life. But scores of Jacobites imperiled themselves for Charlie; why is Flora MacDonald famed? It would seem simply because of her gender. The paradox that excludes women from historical notice also puts them in the fore when it highlights male purpose.

The Bonnie Prince was popular among Scotswomen, not only for his dashing appearance but also due to other appealing qualities: he was known to be honorable; gracious and lenient to enemies; brave but not bloodthirsty; congenial with the common soldiers, as concerned for their well-being as his own, and so on. While her husband—who held a commission in the government's Black Watch—was away, Lady MacIntosh raised the MacIntosh clan for Charlie and was at Moy when the battle of Culloden was fought. She was arrested but survived threat of hanging to die in bed an unrepentant Jacobite. Women in conventional history-telling are usually invisible or incidental, or, like Flora MacDonald and Lady MacIntosh, precious ornaments on the cloaks of men's causes. What and where, I wonder, is the larger story of Highland clanswomen? Fanny Wright, from Dundee, was a radical feminist of the early 1800s, also advocating labor rights and free, equal, universal education. Suffragettes Maude Younger, Jean and Kate Gordon, Nettie Shuler, and Harriet Upton were Scots; Anita McGee, founder of the Army Nurse Corps, and ferocious Carrie Nation of the Temperance movement, were of Scots descent. Celtic women have never been content with merely being helpmeets. A few hundred years ago a Spanish ambassador to Britain, though shocked by the "boldness" of Scotswomen, noted that they were "honest and courteous, graceful and handsome, absolute mistresses of their houses, and even of their husbands, in all things concerning the administration of their property, income as well as expenditure." As in resisting the Clearances, women were in the forefront of the rent strikes in Glasgow in 1915 during the shipyard's strike, making that action more than the usual token walkout.

I met a Highland Council member—the mother of seven children—whose husband drowned; she cared for her huge brood of children, dealt with her tragedy, and, with admirable commitment and good humor, served on the Council. Hundreds of people attended her husband's funeral—people in Scotland do not live isolated existences, though this has been changing in remote areas of the Highlands. Remoteness did not used to deter Highlanders from regularly walking miles to visit one another, to gather for ceilidhs, and to work together. Social bonds were preeminent. Today, in Sutherland, Caithness, and the Outer Isles, venues for these bonds to be exercised have largely been lost to television. Unemployment, cultural wounding, and the exodus of the young have dispirited rural communities. In those communities, pubs often become contexts for alcoholism rather than being places to socialize, make music, and strengthen communal bonds. That local people talk of this as a problem means that perspective is still rooted enough in traditional culture to recognize the change and its negative implications.

A strong facet of cultural tradition for Celts, unlike in many societies, is gender equality, embedded in history and remaining an undercurrent in Celtic countries today. Equality and freedom go with, not against, the flow of Celtic culture. Life in Scotland still moves at a human—not machinelike—pace. Shops are mainly family owned and small; often shops are multipurpose, one wee space combining a restaurant and yarn business, for instance, or crafts and hairdressing. I bought clothes and music tapes at a post office. The orientation is still to human relationships and social concerns. People still talk about real people, not about people on TV. They gossip in the shops, yet have a courtesy toward one another I find lacking in America.

"This is my friend Mrs. Scully," I heard a woman on my bus say, introducing one friend to another. Old-fashioned forms of respect are still in evidence, subtle but influential. Much of this human pace and communal reference in Scottish society is a result of gender integration. Sensitivity, strength, love of beauty, hardihood, courage, depth of heart are not separated into male and female categories; they are simply qualities of the people. The assertiveness of Scotswomen does not have to be learned in recovery workshops. It naturally arises and is naturally accepted.

In Newtonmore, south of Inverness, Robin and I went to a pub for a farewell whiskey on our last night in Scotland. It was a small place— no tourists—with a juke box playing oldies. A hulking, inebriated young man shambled over to our table and thrust a meaty hand in my face. "Dance," he commanded with Tarzan-ish succinctness. It brought to mind an image of the "big youth" listed in historical descriptions of chiefs' retinues.

"No thanks," I said, worried at the thought of those shambling feet. Robin also demurred. A local woman at the next table came over and chastised our suitor: "These ladies are here minding their own business; now you just leave them alone," she said sternly. We smiled; our tartan Tarzan retreated to the snookers table. The woman introduced herself: "I'm Darlene." She did a few eye-blinkingly sexy moves to the Righteous Brothers tune playing on the juke box. "I'm in here drinking because I'm pining for my boyfriend," Darlene confided. "But I'm not pining too much, because he's English." A fitting note for departure. *Scotland forever,* I thought; *may your women never lose their strength and panache.*

There is a Highland story about selkies—those beings who are sometimes seals, sometimes humans—that is striking in its lessons about relationship between the sexes, and about traditional Celtic views.

Fionagalla and her sister selkies were singing and combing their long hair among the rocks one full-moon night when three brothers crept up and stole their seal pelts. Selkies cannot return to seal form without their pelts and are compelled to go with whomever has possession of those skins. Two of the brothers went triumphantly home with their newly acquired selkie wives, but the third felt badly about his deed—the selkies cried so desperately for their pelts—so instead of claiming his bride, the young man gave Fionagalla back her sealskin, and she promptly disappeared into the midnight sea.

The youth could not, however, put the selkie out of his mind. On the ninth night (a multiple of the Celtic magic number three) he went to the seal rocks and, sure enough, there was Fionagalla, this time with her father. The father led Fionagalla to the young man, saying to her, "You must thank him for his good deed, and do right by him."

The upshot was, Fiongalla went home with the youth and all that night they busied around his house cleaning, making food, arranging the sparse furnishings, and companionably chatting. They so enjoyed this shared domestic activity that every ninth night Fionagalla returned and they worked together and both were happy.

Meanwhile, the other two brothers grew weak and lazy. Their wives did all the work, raised the children, and provided family comfort and nourishment. One day, the wife of one of these brothers found her seal pelt

*and vanished back into the wild ocean. The other brother, panicking, tried
to burn his wife's pelt; it exploded and the man ran from his burning
house, but his wife died within the fire.*

This is a different kind of tale altogether from those Greek and
Roman myths deifying rape and kidnapping and glorifying male
dominance. Selkies were not always women in Celtic stories, but were
beings who moved between the realms of autonomy's freedom (and
risk) and the benefits and bonds of relationship. Willingness is a key
factor in these matters; and in those stories where a selkie is compelled to relationship—even when that relationship turns out well,
even when beloved children are a result—the selkie invariably returns to the sea if the chance to do so arises. The mystery and wild
beauty that so often stirs possessive desire ever yearns away from
that grasp, ever tending back toward integrity, freedom.

Christianity (and chivalry, the most tempting synthesis of Celtic
and Christian gender attitudes) was responsible for most of the
changes in the status of Celtic women. It is interesting that Catholicism, though it undermined women's freedom and equality, came
under fire during the Protestant Reformation for its tolerance of female monarchs. John Knox, leader of the Reformation in Scotland,
despised women. In his "First Blast of the Trumpet Against the Mon-
strous Regiment of Women," Knox asserted that, "To promote a
woman, to bear rule, superiority, dominion, or empire above any
realm, nation, or city is repugnant to Nature; is contumely to God."
This sort of attitude had a fatal effect on Mary, Queen of Scots.

The Reformation, backlash against a manifestly corrupt Catholic
Church and its distancing of people from direct approach to both
church administration and to the divine, nonetheless belittled women.
In both Protestantism and Catholicism women lost essential ground
in the realm of equality. If religion and society are hens and eggs, one
continually hatching the other, can there be the possibility of a truly
egalitarian chick emerging from a cycle that persistently excludes
sexual equality—whether the hens are Catholic, Protestant, Muslim,
Hindu, Buddhist, or New Age?

Some modern-day women answer this question by turning to separatism or to neopagan Goddess spirituality. Separatism is a response
to pain but not a solution, except for individuals for whom it may
offer a position of both strength and some measure of safety.

What of Goddess spirituality? There is much claim to feminism as well as Celticism in modern Wicca, neopaganism, and Dianic theology. The issue of Celticism in neopaganism is discussed in part two; the question of feminism in Goddess spirituality is controversial. Some of the disagreement is based on a supposed opposition between introverted religion and social or political activism, a disagreement that must be viewed through individual approaches in the long run: spirituality can be as active a forum for feminist expression as politics for some women—Starhawk is a modern example. Other feminist objections point out Goddess religion's tendency to project images of women that recast them in stereotypical biological roles. Once self-respect for Maiden-Mother-Crone is reclaimed, it is tempting to settle into the metaphor, if not the experience, of separate female empowerment in those roles. Without dismissing this, and bypassing consideration of whether or not the world is Goddess-created (or a Goddess embodiment), there still seems to be a limiting psychology in operation when gender is made the primary basis for anything. Genderfying spirituality seems especially perilous, putting an invested numinosity on duality. This is not to say that sex, and the sexes, aren't expressions of the sacred, but is duality—especially when based on biological assets, spiritualized or not—a focus that really leads to equality? And is duality the ultimate reach of experience, much less the extent of consciousness' potential?

In ancient Ireland, household authority resided with whichever spouse had the most wealth, mainly measured in cattle. This was the issue that began the most famous of the Irish sagas, the Táin Bó Cúailnge (the Cattle Raid of Cooley).

Queen Maeve and King Ailill were in bed, reflecting on their relationship. (Ailill, incidentally, not Maeve, was the province's ruler, but Maeve was acknowledged as making the decisions that actively guided the course of things, as everyone in Ireland knew.) The pillow talk between Maeve and Ailill led to sharp dispute about which of the two had the most household wealth. For Maeve this was a crucial issue. She insisted an inventory be conducted. Everything—everything!—was counted and evaluated, from cattle, sheep, pigs, and horses to cups, plates, raw gold, and personal ornaments. The tally came out completely balanced, except for one thing. Ailill had the better bull.

[Bulls are an evocative subject. The bulls in the Táin were not ordinary creatures; they were actually characters from another saga, and at this point in the story could be considered transformed gods.]

Maeve, at the realization of Ailill's advantage due to his possessing the superior bull, set about trying to acquire the Brown Bull of Cúailnge, the only thing that would equalize her position with her husband's. The saga became an epic encompassing war between the provinces in which fortunes and alliances were overturned, gessa and honor were invoked and violated, supernatural events unfolded at every turn, gods and goddesses and banshees (not to mention the other sidhe) made appearances, and hundreds of warriors died, eventually including Ireland's greatest and dearest hero, Cú Chulainn—ostensibly, all because Maeve needed a better bull.

In the end, Maeve lost the war and the brown bull she'd stolen. The prized beast of Cúailnge died after killing Ailill's bull in a shuddering, earth-tearing battle between two gods in awesome animal form. Mortals and their desires and struggles suddenly seemed puny in comparison. Maeve and Aillil went home—their marriage philosophy encompassed these ups and downs—and the surviving warriors retired to lick their wounds and contemplate the devastation wrought.

Which brings us back to equality and duality: even Maeve, whom many said was truly a goddess (though in North American terms I see her more as a heyoka or Coyote figure) could not achieve equality by the duality route. Whether assets are monetary or biological, mundane or spiritual, it still becomes a valuing of what is less intrinsic than being itself, and so is always subject to vagaries of attitude and possession. Women do not need a better bull, or even one as good as the king's, or a cow who is as good or better than a bull.

Goddess spirituality, at its clearest, has a strength and veracity that endures and renews itself through endless generations and endless variations of form and resonance. It is a path having the shimmer of magic and a bedrock of planetary well-being. But that does not prevent questioning of how, in this generation, it informs perspectives on equality. Does the vocabulary it offers and the images it promotes better serve as a traveler's homeward beacon, or as a valued illumination of where we began the journey and perhaps are, in our own ways and to expanded ends, beginning again?

There is an appealing measure of gratification available in neo-pagan women's roles: the priestess, the witch, the diviner, the shaman, and a rainbow of goddesses for inspiration. For women growing up in societies and religions where patriarchy hemmed them in like phallic cage bars, neopaganism and Wicca at first appear as ecstatic releases into women's paradise. There are, of course, shadows lurking—societal patterns seeking to assert themselves under pagan guise. Even when conditioned structures are eluded, it is difficult to shake off conditioned relational patterning—instead of cage bars, women may find themselves confined by the enveloping circle.

Reaching a point where gratification loses its stimulation, much of neopaganism's glamor may fade, leaving women pondering what direction to take in unfolding a path of integrity, equality, and spiritual depth. Those things may indeed be found in contemporary Goddess religion, but there tends more often to be a gleaning than a harvest. Amid Jungianism, earth stewardism, leftover sexual frustration from the sixties, technopaganism, and other themes influencing modern Goddess spirituality, what is Celticism's contribution?

Celtic myths, in relation to Celtic spirituality, are not allegories, metaphors, or tales of a linear past. They are the literal immediacy of cosmic enactment as it includes human beings and their endeavors. Goddesses in Celtic spirituality are present in both the way summer or winter can be present and, occasionally, in the way a seldom-seen visitor can be present. What happens, then, if Derdriu, Maeve, Emer, and Fand stride out from between book covers, and the Mórrígan's black wings actually brush past the window on a dark night? What happens when women cease to be symbols and projections, and their spirituality becomes concrete?

There is speculation that women in ancient Britain became fed up with Druidism's male predominance, and doubtless many Irish and Scots women became fed up with the paternalism of chiefs—it was women who resisted evictions during the Clearances; the men seemed dazed by the "father's" betrayal. Even the ancient myths plainly portrayed women, whether they were queens, goddesses, or farm wives, as disadvantaged by and often dissatisfied with male-favored social structures and modes of relationship. The difference between how Celtic myths portrayed this and how modern society looks at women's lack of freedom is that the Celts made no attempt to justify inequality.

This was not out of obliviousness or a sense that the status quo was suitable; it was because myths are contemporaneous forces in motion—not static symbols, moral stories, or packaged, analyzed history. As such, they are dynamic contexts for social change as well as renewal, and it is this that is missing in modern use and understanding of Celtic myths and spirituality.

Concepts of women, concepts of nature, and concepts projecting one onto the other to create archetypes in human subconscious have been around for millennia. Whether goddesses are entities, natural forces, or vitalized collective projections—or something else altogether, human relationship to them has changed, as has human relationship with the land—though both have remained mirrors of relationship to the feminine. Would this fade in the light of true freedom and equality? Or would it intensify? Or might it become something else?

Climbing a steep hillside in the northwest Highlands, along a quick-tumbling stream, the rocks were slick and the heather vigorous and dewy. I followed a sheep path; Robin and Catherine had almost disappeared ahead among rocks and heights. The wind was sea-strong, chill from the previous night's rain. If there was a goddess there she was atmospheric and moody.

My response to land is sensual, observant but rarely cerebral; and more than that—emotional, maybe—but like a sea both stirred and, in its depths, still. Land, or nature, does not seem "mother" to me, but simply and powerfully alive and vivid. Home. Itself, no matter shorn grass, or too many sheep. Scotland is to me a sweet sharp breaking of the heart, like Celtic music—intimate and wild and beautiful.

Robin came down the rocky slope; Catherine appeared in an angling descent through the heather. Young Gia, as always in the streambed, was selecting stones to take home. Four people on a hillside, a place we could be—and were—happy. I thought of Derdriu with Noísiu and his brothers, liberated, content in the craggy island wilderness.

We are literal within the myth. What, in our times, will be the transformative telling?

Gneiss

Rock 3000 million years old—
backhoes shove it, exhume it,
tear it naked to thin light on this
island Skye, stone of Sleat.
From peat-black pools—eyes
in moorland sockets—the ageless
monster may rise, shiver and break
an unwinking surface, snatch
sheep snugged in heather beside
blackwater bogs—what was
before sheep, before names.
The single-track road
does not divide.
In the garden of Sleat
unbordered yesterday is simplified—
endless variation of a song
composed 3000 million years ago—
unforgetting.

PART IV

LAND AND PEOPLE

First Thought Mountain

The land describes itself to me
 in winter, in quiet,
in the way each snowflake
touches it.
Contoured by moonlight,
by clouds filling the low places,
by wind in the heights,
taking of the rock, grain by grain,
there is no mistake in
these shapes that guide the flow of light
like riverbanks, the sky moving
in crevices, valleys, along
the bluffs, then waiting
in stillness upon the fields,
nourishing the land
even in winter.

IN WINTER I PARK THE TRUCK AT THE BOTTOM of First Thought
Mountain and walk home, a trek of several miles. My land partner,
Robin, does this also, her cabin a half mile closer to our parking spot.
We pull laundry, groceries, and supplies on sleds or backpack them

"like mules," as Robin says one day, toiling under a bulky load.

The driveway is at first a one-lane clay ribbon hugging the mountain's flank, rising, winding, dropping sheer on one side. It forks, and our branch is a two-track crossing 120 acres—fields, cattail marsh, bluffs, hills and ridges with their steepled fir and pine, and the swift icy creek crowded by cedars, larch, yew, and silver birch.

In winter the driveway narrows to a footpath trod by deer, coyotes, rabbits, grouse, sometimes a bobcat, as well as humans. Our walking staffs punch holes in the snow; sleds standardize the path's width. Two shortcuts reduce the distance home, but the first of them is a challenge—a dauntingly high, steep hillside. Going down is often accomplished, like it or not, on one's backside. Going up often requires bracing and scrambling with hands as well as feet. Each time I choose the shortcut, with or without a pack, eyeing its uncompromising angle and height, I affirm, "It is a good day to die." Once, breathlessly hauling ourselves over the crest, Gabriel set down the gallon jug of milk he carried and it instantly sledded to the bottom of the hill. We were stunned, frozen between hilarity and weeping; Gabriel shed his pack and retrieved the milk jug.

On new moon, dark cold gathers beneath the trees. Walking home, using no flashlight, attention is concentrated in booted feet as they search out the path. The snow is faintly luminous, but under the trees darkness rules. The breath is loud; footsteps crunch; I waver, sometimes slip and stumble. Branches startle with sharp pokes or lightly whip my cheek as I pass, awkward, hurried, sweaty under the pack, cold in my extremities.

A pause; the mountain's presence surrounds. Sensing it, imagination imposes fear and fantasy, or the mind tries to discount and override the sense of presence or sometimes, within receptive awareness, attunes to it. However this presence is defined—as an entity, a web of energy, an aspect of pervasive consciousness—it breathes around me.

In winter the mountain's surface quiets: animals, trees and bushes, insects, snakes, all seem dreaming. Those awake—deer, raven, coyote, owl—are delineated by the stillness and smooth frozen whiteness, a suspended context. But the mountain's depths, its mountainness, seem more awake than at any other time. Winter is its venue: stone; bone; abiding power, crystallized and lucid. I stand in darkness through which light floats, diffuse, fine . . . living. It is the mountain's exhalation; I breathe it, vision adjusting as inner and outer habitats reach equanimity, as though the mountain and I become of one thought, mystery's idea. Life.

The Stones of Clava, in Scotland, are an astronomically aligned grouping of cairns made by the Picts. Sitting beside the inner wall of one of those cairns, I saw it was comprised of hundreds of small and middle sized stones, reddish brown, smooth grained. The Highlands have some of the oldest rock in the world; I did not know how old these stones were, but cupping one in my hand, I knew the hand that first lifted and moved this stone, that placed it with intention and awareness on this cairn, turned to dust thousands of years ago. A hand formed like mine, warm, alive, strong-gripped. The stone remains, little changed by those thousands of cycles. Tourists wandered among the cairns as I sat, the stone weighting and cooling my hand. We are—and are not—just passing through.

On the mountain I begin walking again, slowly and more quietly, more surely, body less stiff. Somewhere a cougar stalks between straight towers of ponderosas, a grouse hunches within the pocket of a snow cave. Coyote's voice lifts over us, wailing for the moon's return; I dissolve in spaces between molecules, becoming the mountain's breath, finding myself home.

What is memory but knowledge of patterns? Time is thought of as context but it is not—relationship is, its dimensions and arrangements. Winter, the frozen lake, memories solid enough to walk on—crystallized. We study the patterns, the tracks in the snow.

Mind skates on the surface of cold stillness, gradually losing momentum, slowing, listening. Beneath stillness is life—a pulse, a song quiet as starlight at this distance, solstitial. It is a cat's stillness, complete but aware, surrounding the heated core. Starlight in proximity becomes sun, unimaginable fire, the relentless eye of day—also solstitial. We live in ignorance or denial of the sources and ends of things; consumerism depends on this oblivion and on acceptance of blind technologies and tamperings. To live in denial of cycles, consequences, natural processes is to live in denial of relationship—context, memory—ruled by habits and conditioning, yet severed from awareness of source and consequence.

Where do the tracks in the snow lead? Where do they begin? Who makes them? It is not linear: nothing on this curving earth, in this spiraling galaxy, is linear. Where do we come from? Where do we go? Who are we? *It is not linear.* Unmoving, the mountain constantly changes, present as an experience, patterns of consciousness—life formed and transformed, an expressive vocabulary. Can I be a foreign word here?

When Neil Armstrong and Alan Bean went to the moon they carried clan tartans. On the mountain grow mullein, yarrow, St. John's-wort, dandelion, and other naturalized European plants. The plants and I are not indigenous to this mountain, but abide with rootedness, sensitive to vagaries of context, part of a web of habitat, give and receive, at the mercy of larger cycles that arbitrate balance and change. My life is the land's. In winter, commitment is explicit—the migrators and hibernators offer example, then leave me to the chosen path—awake, vulnerable, in love with a druid-robed mountain, and the shortcut is no mercy.

My brother Stu, Gabriel, and I trudged toward home after a long drive north from my dad's house in Oregon. It was evening, late in December, blizzardous, and I had a migraine. At the shortcut I decided to climb, carrying one of the cats and a backpack. Gabriel and Stu, lugging most of the baggage and the other cat, sensibly chose the roundabout way. Snow on the hillside was knee-deep; I lunged through it, floundering, the protesting cat occupying both hands. The migraine medication—which had not diminished the headache—constricted blood vessels, making the struggle even more grim.

Near the top a harsh pain tore across my chest and I collapsed in the snow, a dark weight pressing so I could hardly breathe. The primary thought was to confine the cat; lying in the snow I was not afraid, but did wonder about survival. "Help," I mentally implored. Nothing happened except the cat squirmed and snow whirled down. The mountain helped as it always does, by showing what is present with impartial clarity. Not impervious, but impartial—more teacher than parent. Resource was present; I had to move.

Crawling, clutching the surly cat, I reached Robin's cabin and dragged myself onto her porch but could not call out. Robin and Gia were talking inside, the sound homey, as was the glow of lamplight from their windows. This is absurd, I thought, chagrined at the melodrama. Ineffectually I thumped the side of the house with the flat of my hand. No one heard. I did it again; genial chatter ceased. "Who is it?" Robin demanded. Gia opened the door—and screamed, as I feared she might. "She's dying!"

Of embarrassment. They hauled us inside: the cat finally achieved freedom and I lay on the floor trying not to look terminal. Robin offered water, Gia stifled sobs; eventually I was propped in the rocking chair to await Stu and Gabriel's arrival. For weeks afterward there was a strange depression, a ghostlike exhaustion. "Maybe I'm not strong enough to live here," I told the mountain. It answered, "Are you not alive?"

"What's it like to be a recluse?" a Lakota man, fellow author, wrote one winter. I told him about the land, community of diversity, silences in which to hear, solitude in which to feel, intimacy of consciousness in which to know and be known. The mountain never lies, never cheats, never hates; I told him there is peace here, healing. In Wendell Berry's words, "I come into the peace of wild things." The Lakota man sent a twenty-dollar bill: "I spend more money on my kid's hockey than you earn in a year; buy some stamps and envelopes and keep writing. You talk like an Indian."

There was an episode in Agallamh na Seanórach when Caoilte told the Christian nobles about a division made of Ireland by the two sons of King Feradhach Fechtnach after the King's death. One son took Ireland's wealth and treasure, herds of cattle, settled dwellings, and fortresses. The other son's portion was Ireland's cliffs and estuaries, the fruits of the woods and sea, and the salmon and game. Caoilte's listeners were indignant at this division, saying it was grossly unequal, the first son getting the far better portion. Caoilte replied that the portion they disparaged was the one he and his companions much preferred.

Celts and Indians are like-minded in this preference for land, a living, nourishing alliance. Each morning when I go outside, encountering the day's weather, seeing what is about—a raven over the bluffs, a deer raising her elegant head among the cedars, the land's familiar aspects and those newly revealed—there is a sense of awe and gratitude. There is a wealth of beauty, and stones that speak of beauty's endurance in presence and renewal. In Scotland, a lorry driver picked me up hitchhiking in Perthshire and said, "It's great getting paid for driving around all day admiring the hills." When beauty is not taken for granted it remains a resource of joy. At the hostel where I stayed

in southern Skye the stillness of early morning would lure me outside. Roe deer browsed on the moor; cattle grazed in July's cool damp-
ness; across the Sound of Sleat, Knoydart was all soft shades of blue
in successive mountain humps reflected in the mirror of the sound.
Tara, Peter's border collie, would be snoozing on the kitchen floor,
and the hostelers still asleep in their bunks. I loved that morning time
when beauty made the gift of life most quietly and simply known.

The mountain where I live is not paradise: in spring appear ticks
and mosquitoes and the clay road turns to treacherous mire; in summer the dust, talc-fine, is everywhere, and there are rattlers coiling,
muscular, atavistic; lightning slams dry mountainsides and fires rage;
in autumn the days fly with the geese during our scramble for stove
wood and winter supplies; then comes the cold: hardship, frozen
drains and rationed water, the long haul until spring. But these are
not drawbacks to an otherwise good life. They are sinews of the
mountain's strength, and thus of ours; dimensions of experience that
deepen capacity, exercise faculty, helping us live more fully and know
beauty more wholly.

In winter I mainly see two people: Robin and the postmistress.
Robin treks over about once a week, and once or twice a week I hike
down the mountain, driving into town to pick up my mail. The postmistress, from Alberta, calls me "Luv." She is, for months, my primary social encounter. Sometimes I buy a newspaper from the box
outside the general store. Once a month is a seventy-mile round-trip
to a larger town to replenish supplies. Water is heated in a kettle on
the woodstove for washing and laundry. It is a sometimes arduous
but unhurried way of life.

Full moons in winter bring primal wakefulness; I stand outside in
cold, gleaming stillness or sit inside, moonlight pouring through windows and skylights, bringing owl-feathered thoughts, an old magic.
Sometimes on such nights, Robin and Gia ski in their field in moonlight or lie on their backs in the snow, watching the jeweled sky. My
friend Vlodya lives in Canada, 165 mountainous miles north; he visits once a month, sometimes less. In winter I am housebound, protecting canned goods and produce from freezing. The woodstove is
an altar of well-being, fed with offerings—trees with their cellular
memories of heat and light, elemental medicine, the life of connection. When Vlodya visits, nestled beside me in the frozen night, I push
two blankets from the bed; he, too, is an altar of warmth.

There is little wind on the mountain in winter, and during cold snaps the sky is deep sapphire, the snow brilliant, pure. One year my birthday fell on such a vivid, frigid day. No packages or cards arrived; I was alone as I was alone most days, and decided to hike down to check the post box, suddenly wishing for something to make the day special. It was Gabriel's second year in college and solitude was explicit.

Below-zero air pinched the nostrils. Dazzling snow squeaked underfoot, its shingled surface looking like soap flakes. My mother, like the Inuit, names distinct variations of snow such as that which causes one to slip back three inches at each step forward, and that which seems crusted but gives way when you rock forward for the next step, and so on. On that day, glittery snow concealed the ice, and I paced flatfooted like a bear. Reaching the truck, I thumped the door a few times to loosen the lock, climbed inside, and murmured a prayer before trying the ignition. Amazingly, it started. With a kiss to the steering wheel and a pat to the dashboard, I set off. But the mailbox turned out to be empty, and in front of the general store the newspaper dispenser was empty too. Robin's truck was parked behind the school; I peeked inside and—voila!—saw that she had picked up my packages and letters.

No matter how cold it is, climbing home always works up a sweat. I summited the shortcut and angled across Robin's field, sprawling midway to rest and lob ice chunks at Leo, Gabriel's dog, who leaped and snapped at them. I read the birthday letters. Alex, hearing I was hying off to Scotland in a few months despite inadequate income, had sent $500 and kindly commented that my trip could not possibly be impractical because I was going in June when long daylight hours would assure full experiential value.

Dazed by this largess, I slid the letters back into the pack and trudged onward—it was too cold to sit long. At the top of the hill beyond Robin's spring was a pause to catch breath, leaning forward with hands propped on knees to relieve my shoulders of the pack's weight. Standing thus, I thought about the gift from my brother, and was visited by anxiety. If the check was deposited, the money would evaporate into mundane necessities. I decided to cash it and stash the bills in the desk. *What if the house burned?* I stared at my boots, stricken by the imagination of money going up in smoke.

It was my forty-fourth birthday; my pack was crammed with gifts, loving wishes, remembrances from family and friends, support and goodwill. Connection. Absurd, the loneliness that made me dwell, instead, on loss and calamity. Eighteen years before, my house burned—no insurance, no savings; there was another, less visible, backpack carried, its weight fear within happiness.

Something penetrated awareness in spite of preoccupation and I looked up, straightening beneath the load. An eagle was circling above, splendidly sailing in the sunlight, in the richly blue sky against which its black and white form was a singular authority of presence. It circled lower, directly above, tarrying, giving its company—eaglelike—without undue familiarity. I cried, standing there, glad to no longer be worrying about imaginary burned money. The eagle's voice, high and poignant, pierced the brilliant day with its own fierce shine, then the bird glided over the trees and Leo and I walked home.

The final winter before Gabriel went to college—two years before my books started being published—the car broke down in November and there was no money for fixing it. Gabriel was teaching photography and doing office work at a school in town, thirty-five miles away, so had to find rides with other rural commuters. Each workday he left the house to descend the mountain before daybreak and later hiked home in the dark, usually bearing groceries, pet food, and other supplies; we had no stocked reserves—a lean year.

Midwinter he got pneumonia, and was wrackingly ill for eight weeks. Regardless, he continued his crepuscular treks up and down the mountain, to and from work. His rangy body thinned frighteningly, though his pack loads sometimes reached eighty pounds. "Do you want a doctor?" I asked, in despair at our insufficient inventory of medicinal herbs. "No," he said. Then, during the worst of it: "I don't know," but by then he was too sick to get down the mountain. Illness lingered. Gabriel contrived a harness and travois for Leo, and she helped with hauling. He rebuilt our vehicle's carburetor but the car still refused to run.

Even on moonless nights, Gabriel hiked without a flashlight, walking home using awareness and memory. "Are you ever afraid?" I asked after his arrival one night when shadows were so dense I could not imagine how he kept to the path. "Early in winter, there were a few times," he admitted. "One night, I saw little clusters of dancing lights, and I haven't been afraid since. I feel at home with the mountain, peaceful and confident."

I would never want to repeat that difficult year, but it is remembered as a time of initiation and passage, when I saw my son willingly, and through great challenge, open to the maturation and deepening offered by such adversity. To be at home with a mountain was one of the gifts of that deepening.

Each year there is a strange reluctance to letting go of winter, despite the season's hardships. Winter's stillness and absolute beauty are enchantments within which there is nowhere else to be and nothing else to be done, its spell gracefully adamant. Its power arrests, midstep in a climb, between one armload of wood and the next; waking from dreams of fertile blooming meadows, I am held by silence in which light can be heard, eternal and unnamed.

> *Hummingbird at my window*
> *telling me, the lily blooms,*
> *elk are in the heights,*
> *swallows skim the rocks*
> *as though hearts will never cease.*

Our first spring on the mountain, a bear visited the tepee, our abode during house construction. We were not home to receive the visitor—I think the bear counted on this, on the absence of the vigilant dog. We returned to find the doorflap muddily paw-printed and flung into the bushes, but the bear proceeded no farther than the inside doormat, also rumpled and muddy. The tepee's interior was otherwise undisturbed. We immortalized the perfect bearprint on the doorflap with paint, increasing the tepee's medicine.

Bears periodically come calling, once toppling the compost pile, once venturing into the house (a natural progression from the tepee). Leo slept through a bear visit to the patio. Despite the traffic of wildlife in and around the house, it is not the same as having only canvas between oneself and the vast, teeming outdoors. For six months Gabriel and I lived in the twenty-foot tepee, a circularity of home with a fire at its heart.

Habitat, habit, habitation: a pattern of relationship to context—being with, being in context. Despite years of rural experience, I had never lived with a habitat like this mountain before; the tepee helped our adaptation to this new land. Oregon grape poked its head under the edge of the canvas; caterpillars nested in our clothes; a garter snake slithered through the entrance and we were never sure where it was; spiders tickled our noses at night; starlight peeped through the smoke hole. Storms were awesome—one night the wind snapped off a tepee pole, sometimes the canvas vibrated like a ship's sails. In stillness we heard owl calling, the rustle of deer, coyote's wild song. Once, wolf howled, a long sliding siren raising Leo's hackles and fluffing the cats like hedgehogs.

We were humble and vulnerable in the tepee, but also appropriate, as though properly attired for the occasion as we presented ourselves to our habitat. With separation minimized, we began to learn what would enable intimacy with place, directly experiencing textures, temperatures, moods and rhythms, light and shadow, the land's touch, voice, perils and elemental powers, its other inhabitants.

In early spring, at age twenty-one, I crossed Scotland's moors during an afternoon and evening of sleety rain and hypnotic mist. As darkness thickened, I pulled the car off the road and stopped. There had been no traffic. I had no clear idea where I was, and could see nothing but mist and nearby puddles glimmering on the pavement. Eerie— the wild haunted moor. I walked a few paces from the road and squatted to relieve my bladder. I couldn't see the car. So easy to wander and be forever lost, a keening ghost in the mist. The very things making it scary were what pleased me.

Camping in Mexico, I took a hike into the desert with Gabriel and my husband. We carried food and water but consumed both well before reaching what turned out to be a dry oasis. I was reeling from heat and dehydration by the time we got back to our vehicle. But there is something reassuring about such places—a sense of abiding power and integrity; places that hold their own.

That night on the moors I slept in the car, at dawn waking under observation. The mist had slithered away, and perched on rocks beside the car and completely surrounding the vehicle were mountain goats peering through the windows. The moors were treeless, empty; the goats seemed to have materialized like curious faeries that vanished when I eased out of the car, the moor not as exposing as it appeared.

Each context of habitat is eloquent, each in a different way. As a child in Florida there was Swamp, Hurricane, Ocean, Tornado, and Humidity to learn from; a landscape of palmettos, pines, mosquitoes, sandspurs; flat and, in those days, still teeming with wildlife. Memory of childhood is memory of habitat's pattern. We moved north to New York when I was ten; I remember swooping through the mountains of North Carolina with my father, exhilarated as George ringingly recited "The Charge of the Light Brigade," and a churning thunderstorm flashed and rolled down on us from the peaks.

Desert, Lake, River, Prairie, Valley, Forest—everywhere can astonish, enlarge us with particularities of revelation. One is unremittingly drawn to reading these environmental messages, as though the earth's habitats comprise a text whose totality includes each scrolling vine, each runic branch and swirling script of river eddy. Watching the flickering northern lights, their silent, enigmatic code is a language one feels forever on the edge of translating, with no frustration in failure—only joy that heaven and earth speak.

The wild is a nativity, an origin of what we have and what we are, but the wild, if cherished at all these days, is mainly perceived as metaphor, not actuality. Some strangers from the city, a woman and her companion, turned up at my house one day. The woman had purchased acreage at the bottom of the mountain and wanted to view our straw-bale house preparatory to perhaps building one herself. She was a bubbling fountain of enthusiasm and inquiry, foreseeing her rural abode as a parklike haven, a placid setting for a tidy herb garden, exotic dogs, perhaps some llamas. She was charmed by the dirt road until hearing that it potholes and washboards badly in winter and spring. Concern with her naiveté demanded I also alert her to the local presence of bears, cougars, and coyotes; poor soil, knapweed, and forest fires. Her rural dream staggered. Inevitably, rattlesnakes had to be mentioned, and she almost burst into tears. "What do you do?" she implored.

"Watch where you put your hands and feet," I suggested.

What, indeed? Why did she think land prices were low and population sparse here? I was sympathetic to her dream but had witnessed the shattering of its like over and over in rural areas. Perhaps more injurious in the long run is what that dream does to wilderness: a pattern of colonization and eradication; urban designs, facilities, and attitudes imposed on whatever is encountered. Habitat is soon overrun and polluted, sterilized of predators; roads bring death to wildlife and disruption to age-old survival rhythms and movements, and allow accessibility into habitat needing to remain inviolate from logging, ranching, mining, recreation, and other intrusions. Electricity, bulldozed forests, heli-skiing, strip malls, golf courses, all-terrain joyrides, logging trucks in ruthless parade to the mills—the rural nightmare. When the dreamers are finished there will be no wilderness. Would that potholes gave more pause.

"Why don't they just add more lanes?" young Gia innocently

asked, as we negotiated the stop-and-pass method of single-lane traffic in the northern Highlands, where getting from place to place is a co-operative venture. My reply to her was unneccessarily sharp and emphatic, pointing out that more lanes meant more land paved, more facilities for cars and drivers, more pollution and dead wildlife: "more" was San Diego's sixteen-lane freeway, and look at where that had gotten us. But "underdevelopment" in the Highlands is not just a wise sense of proportion and the valuing of a simple-paced, land-based way of life. It also reflects the area's forced depopulation and continuing economic problems. John Prebble, in *The Highland Clearances,* reminds us that in the Highlands "The hills are still empty. In all Britain only among them can one find real solitude, and if their history is known there is no satisfaction to be got from the experience." The Highlands' wilderness is an anomaly in densely populated Europe, and as such attracts tourists, hill walkers, rock climbers, and fishing enthusiasts worldwide. Beautiful and precious, that wilderness, but unseverable from the suffering in its history and the questions, still unresolved, of its people's future.

Environmental consciousness was present in the Celtic World long before it appeared in the rest of Europe, but environmentalism in its modern form is often at odds with modern Celtic culture. The basic problem seems to be that environmentalism has come to mean isolating habitat to be preserved, whereas Celtic culture has always been an integrated identification with habitat. The forced removal of Highland people and the destruction of ancient communities has made these divergent perspectives even more an issue.

Land that traditionally was inhabited does not become a true wilderness when it is converted to sheep walks and deer parks—barrens where trees and natural vegetation are destroyed. Deforestation in Scotland has been in progress for a long time, often due to human activity and land-use policies. There has been a tremendous, grievous loss of wildlife species: lynx, bear, elk, reindeer, beaver, wild ox, wild boar, wolf, crane, sea eagle, auk, goshawk, bittern, and others. Even traditional agriculture had its environmental drawbacks. But the flooding of the Highlands with sheep and deer far eclipsed anything previous in its adverse effect on the land—and sheep farming ceased to be profitable about one hundred years ago, but sheep farms continue to be encouraged by government subsidies. Any healing of the land will necessitate huge reductions in the numbers of sheep and deer in the Highlands.

James Hunter suggests this quintessentially Celtic approach combining social rehabilitation and ecological restoration of the glens:

> It proved possible in the nineteenth century to reinstate an-
> cient notions concerning land tenure. Might it not prove just
> as possible in the future to incorporate other equally long-
> lived ideas into strategies for the Highland environment? . . .
> Because of the bureaucratic way in which we organize our
> national affairs . . . policy for the corncrake tends to be kept
> in one hermetically sealed compartment of our public life,
> while policy for Gaelic is kept in another. . . . Suppose that we
> were to knock the different boxes into one. Suppose that we
> were to integrate our various environmental, agricultural,
> social, cultural, linguistic, and other objectives into a single
> strategy for the future of the Scottish Highlands. And sup-
> pose, finally, that we were to be successful. We should then
> have made a very worthwhile contribution to solving the ever
> more insistent question of how to sustain life on earth.

Every spring the little rock dam slowing the creek's flow where my
water pipe sits is tumbled apart by spring melt. The cascade's havoc
is temporary; when the spring rush subsides I restack the stones
around my little pool. Each spring I also repair the one-inch plastic
pipe, which is often perforated in places by the sharp teeth of large
animals. What induces them to bite the pipe makes for speculation as
I wrap duct tape around the plastic, fingering the holes and imagin-
ing fierce jaws (probably bear's) that made them. I think about human relationship with the wild.

Coyotes are an interesting case in point. Wary as only an animal
so persecuted can be, coyote nevertheless seems inclined to interaction. Gabriel, walking from tepee to outhouse one evening, let rip a
ululation inspired by the moment's mood and was unnerved by an
immediate, deafening cacophony in return, from a congregation of
coyotes concealed so near as to seem ready to spring into view. Coyote seems interested.

Late one night, a coyote darted across the road in front of the truck
and descended the embankment. I stopped, rolled down the window,
and softly called. Coyote's head popped up from the ditch. I shut the

engine off and continued talking; Leo, tethered in back, remained silent. Coyote rose from the embankment and approached the truck;
only a few yards separated us. Suddenly I was worried that another
vehicle might arrive; it seemed irresponsible to invite the animal into
possible hazard. Telling coyote thanks and good-bye, I started the truck
and coyote melted into the forested night.

Barriers between species are not so impenetrable as tends to be
assumed. Aid given drowning humans by dolphins is more than just
legend; communication and sympathetic interaction is possible among
all species. In Oregon a male grizzly bear was seen, not only allowing
a starving domestic cat to share his food, but deliberately offering the
cat choice morsels. Motherless baby rabbits were nursed by a Dober-
man, orphan squirrels by a cat, baby geese and owls were raised by
an eagle. In India, two young girls were found living with a pack of
wolves. Examples abound of encounters between species that hint at
potentials of communication and relationship.

A trap-crippled, starving bobcat came to the house, throwing herself against my window despite the presence of the dog, desperate
for help. She had chewed off half of two legs in order to escape the
trap. The bobcat did not survive, but my mother wrote after I told her
of this tragedy, saying, "That such a creature for shunning human
beings came to your door—a creature harmed so by human beings—
at your *door*—shows that our paths *can* cross, ours and the wild ones!
That's if the human loves. . . . The message of the bobcat is so unarguable. There it is. You couldn't have prolonged its life in the wild even
if you'd been able to feed it, but what it did must not die. Somehow
we will write in such a way that the love of nature will be adopted by
those who need it. Somehow the point will get across. It will be the
bobcat's message."

Walking home across the lush spring mountain; it was the first day of
sunshine after weeks of rain—inordinate rain. Wind and sun; liquid
birdsong; lupines blooming in the meadow, mirroring the sky. Red-
tail hawk rose from the pine so close I felt its size and confident sleek
power in the pit of my stomach, like having an orca rise beside one
from the sea. The hawk floated, scanning the ground, catching the
wind with a tilt of wings, sliding across the air, circling higher. I raised
an arm in salute and called, hearing the fierce, harsh descent of the
hawk's cry in return. Chickadees burst from a fir tree like a shower of

sparks; a grouse drummed, determined, vulnerable; we were all of the mountain, the wind and sun.

I sat on the Perthshire moors in the lee of a sheltering rock as cold April wind streamed over the land. The folded brown stems of the previous year's bracken, along with cushiony heather and grasses, made a kind nest for my body. A burn gurgled over rocks, winding past rectangles of planted forest, past stone walls and stony hills, through peat bogs, to the river below. An occasional flood of sunlight broke through low, heavy clouds; high bare hills rose in the distance. I lay in the heather as though waiting for a lover. A buzzard soared and hovered over the moor. I talked to the land through prayer and the resting of my body there; in a sinking and soaring of awareness into and above the land, I listened to the wind and the burn and the singing birds, and there was no other voice or sound.

"Guess what!" Gabriel wrote from college. "I've got a kilt!" His Highland dance teacher, appropriately named Heather, had found a used kilt for him. "All I need are the proper socks and shoes and I'll be able to dance at the Highland Games in Seattle."

Seattle? Celts have always been a restless, exploratory people. Celt-Iberians were famed seafarers; traces in New Hampshire suggest Celts settled there long before other non-Native arrivals in North America. Highland Games in Seattle. . . . What does homeland mean for Celtic descendants no longer living in Celtic lands—no longer having purely Celtic cultures to return to? Standing on the mountain in the spring sunlight was an experience of home that is love's at-one-ment. Lying on the Perthshire moors or peering over the misty cliffs outside Cruden Bay were experiences of land speaking through spirit and blood, through memory as present as my red hair and second sight. It has to do with people and community as well as land; with the unfoldment and relationship of history and heritage in certain places.

Celtic Americans are offspring; we are not Celts. Like most offspring we wander and explore and become something a little different from our ancestors. Celtic lands and history become a sort of Otherworld coexistent with where we are, sometimes accessed. It is not out of character for homeland to become as fluid—available, but not static in time and space—as other aspects of Celtic reality. Highland Games in Seattle; offspring learning intimacy with faraway lands. But the places where our history abides in the rocks and glens, in the lochs and braes and sea-battered islands, where people still live whose names and visages and temperaments we share, are irreplaceable. Without them we are orphaned.

This realization was most compelling when I went to Scotland, where I felt an at-homeness I had never experienced anywhere else. "We'll give you honorary citizenship when Scotland gets its independence," my friend Gavin, on Skye, kindly offered. I remembered being in Wales with Catherine, Robin, and Gia. We were walking in the twilight; a horse frisked on the hill, tossing mane, quick clatter of hooves. We heard sheep calling, saw cats and rabbits tucked into the protection of hedges. It was a lovely, poignant evening.

A herd of sheep came toward us, filling the narrow lane like a bobbing, frothy river. They were driven by two men and a dog. The sheep spooked at the presence of us four strangers facing them, and turned aside. The dog quickly pursued. One man shouted at the dog in Welsh; I felt his eyes on us, disapproving, and his judgment: dumb tourists—and I wanted to say, "Give us a chance; the distance between us may not be so great as you think."

Everything about being in Scotland moved me—tears and restless yearnings easily surfaced. The sensible, ironic, scrutinizing part of my nature was met with pure music, as if the heart had finally been answered. I felt like an ardent, awkward lover and wished for some grace of character, shy within a lover's deep, aching hunger.

One day in April I climbed higher and higher on the Perthshire moors until a sheer force of wind stopped me. Charcoal clouds tumbled across the sky; I could hardly stand. It was easy to feel how, as in myths, the elements could impregnate a woman. I turned, exhilarated, opening my arms. Clouds parted and sunlight shafted through, spreading a warmth over me. Sinking to the ground, I leaned against a stone, into its seductive silence and steadfastness. A dark rippling burn sang riverward at my feet: moss, primroses, textures that beguiled, fluid and sensuous. Would the land have me?

The Highlands feel especially thin-skinned, the land's body vibrantly alive, though the rock is unimaginably ancient. It is strange—despite history's tragedies and bloody conflicts, history so infusing the land that I often felt invisible presences walking beside me in the hills and glens, the land remains innocent. It does not feel burdened or tarnished or worn-out. At Kylerhea, on Skye, Robin, Catherine, Gia, and I made solstice prayers by the Kyle channel, out of the wind with our backs to a shelf of rock. Catherine began reading aloud our Potawatomie friend's vision-quest song:

Awaken you lands
All you people out there, live.
Live strong.
The power is still here.
Live strongly and true, you birds,
animals, creeping and swimming ones.
Awaken, my people
Return to the old ways;
it is not too late.
Remember and live again.
Live strongly.

As Catherine read, a gray seal burst from the sea with a fish flapping in his jaws. All during our prayers seals undulated through the channel in front of us, rising, diving, graceful and confident. Afterward, we drove to a hostel near the Cuillin Hills. A crowd of beer-drinking rock climbers monopolized the hostel kitchen, preparing a mess of fresh fish. I was not sure that what those guys were about was what Lewis Sawaquat meant by "Live strongly." But, reflecting on the image of the seal bursting from the sea, and juxtaposing it with the sight of the hulking fellows lustily whacking off fish heads in the kitchen, I had to smile.

On Skye with my sister Leigh, we drove to Sleat during a moody Hebridean day of wind, clouds, sprinkling rain, and sunbreaks. During the morning the hills were mist-shrouded and mysterious: "a dream of mountains," Leigh called it. In the afternoon we discovered the ruins of Dunsgaith Castle, a long-ago seat of MacDonald chiefs. The wind gusted hard, bending the massed clumps of nettles flourishing within the ruins. Sun and cloud patterned the hills and sea, a silver sheen running across the water, a silver band on the horizon. Mountains rose, fantastically rugged, across Loch Eishort. Stories say the castle was built in a single night by a faery woman. Such tales abound on Skye, a spell-casting island.

At the north end of Skye, in Trotternish, we explored another ruin: Duntulm Castle, whose history included but also predated the MacDonald chiefs. A cairn in front of the ruins is dedicated to the MacArthurs, hereditary pipers to the MacDonalds during the

eighteenth century. The cairn's inscription reads, in Gaelic and English: "This world will end / But love and music endureth." A Celtic
sentiment indeed.

Before walking to the ruins, which cling to a headland overlooking the Minch, I was drawn into conversation with a piper skirling
tunes into a shrieking coastal wind, hoping to glean coins from visitors to Duntulm. He spoke of the many places he had lived in Scotland and the many piping masters he had studied under. "I lost my
music to the whiskey for ten years," he said frankly, "but now I'm
working at getting the music back." I asked where in Scotland he
liked best. "Here," he said, pointing to a hill not far from where we
stood. "On Skye is inspiration for any kind of thing you want to do."

One June Catherine, Robin, and I hiked in Skye's Cuillin Moutains, a
place that is the heart of Skye's enduring mythophysicality. We hiked
for four hours of vigorous, wind-slammed joy between the rounded
red Cuillins and the jagged black Cuillins. The path was rocky, often
boggy, a world of sheep-grazed heather beside a shining ribbon of
river. We stopped before reaching the end of the long glen, and I left
a stone from the mountain at home at our turn-around spot. The cease-
less wind and the image of the small stone sitting year upon year
amid trembling grasses, rain, and sun brought an uprising of grief at
what I knew of wholeness and what I felt of being stretched between
two lands. I was and yet could not be that stone.

Near the end of our traipse out of the glen, I looked up to see
Catherine and Robin well ahead of me, side by side, turning for a
moment to smile at each other, striding with the wind whipping their
long hair; and that was an affecting image also—shared moments
amid the clean simplicity of the elements. A year later Robin joined
me for three weeks during my stay in Scotland, and we took a ferry
from Skye to the outer isles of Harris and Lewis.

The two are not separate islands, though in many ways, both historical and geographical, they are separate places. Harris instantly
captivated me with its absolute rockiness, the likes of which I had
never before seen. Land without trees, so dominated by stone, has an
underlying silence despite the sweeping voice of the wind. The energy of consciousness is present, but not the speech of growth and
decay. Harris sounded like forever.

Waiting at Tarbert for our ride from the ferry landing to the hostel, we struck up a conversation with a traffic warden, a lovely greying man who spoke with the characteristic sharp intakes of breath and soft exclamations of the outer islanders. He talked about school closings and his sister-in-law, who, at age seventy-two, was the sole dweller left in a township that used to number seven hundred inhabitants. He spoke regretfully of clam dredgers ruining the abundant fishing outside Tarbert's harbor. There were no ceilidhs on Harris anymore, he said; just TV. You had to go to Benbecula or the Uists—isles south of Harris—to find a ceilidh.

Most inhabitants brought up in the outer isles speak Gaelic. Roddy Campbell, at whose hostel we stayed, said that newcomers use English, so local children feel like part of a "prehistoric culture" if they use their native language. Roddy's comment to us—that in the previous sixty years the population of Harris had gone from 6000 to 1800 inhabitants—was offered in a quiet tone, but we heard sadness, felt it ourselves, driving past tumbled stone houses and empty townships.

During an evening of misty rain we walked through the stillness of Drinishader village, the sea calm, pewter colored under a grey sky. From one house came the slow cadences of a hymn sung in Gaelic, the language of our ancestors, flowing into the darkening evening like sand from an hourglass.

In the morning Roddy took us back to Tarbert to catch the bus to Lewis. In one of northern Harris' bays was moored Greenpeace's ship, there to protest oil drilling in the outer Hebrides. Highlanders and Islanders, like indigenous people of North America, are struggling with the dilemma of being Earth-cherishing people faced with resource extraction as the most available basis for economic survival. Tourism, now a primary industry in the Highlands and Islands, brings with it a dual pressure for scenic preservation and service facilities, a push and pull with cultural and environmental continuities both the price and the prize. Tourists wanting helicopter rides in the Cuillins of Skye vie with hikers wanting pristine quiet. Locals both resent and depend on tourists, summer residents, and estate owners. Ecological wisdom is often sacrificed for short-term gain or long-term mismanagement because of economic fear, bureaucratic distancing from reality, ignorance, or greed. Local people feel little control and little confidence—fruits of centuries of disempowerment.

On Lewis I felt as though standing on the edge of the world. The rock of Lewis is ancient beyond imagination or cognizance, and that ancientness influences the very atmosphere of Lewis. It is a place where people live side by side with antiquity, with standing stones, the roofless remains of blackhouses, the works of their ancestors. It is a place ruled by wind and wave and stone, almost treeless, with primordial mountains in the south and miles of flat peat-plain in the north, where the wind is like an unarguable arm that could sweep all it encounters into the sea, if not into an Otherworld dimension. Peat digs are numerous, the people rural, old-fashioned, informal, and unpretentious. A woman at the bus station in Stornoway smiled when I noted that on the Lewis buses they did things the opposite of how they are done in the rest of Scotland. The outer isles are far removed, almost transparent in some magical way despite harsh realities; Lewis felt dreamlike, as though I could stay and forget all else, years passing unnoticed. I did not want to leave.

The bus dropped us off on the northwest coast and we hiked down a long, straight road toward the sea. Each house we passed had its peat stack and border collie. We were offered a ride in a cart full of rocks, pulled by a tractor—the crofter turned out to be the owner of the hostel. After settling in we walked to the shore, down a lane between sheep pastures. The day was warm and calm, the ocean blue, rocks shelving into kelp beds, the beach cobbled with multicolored swirl-patterned stones. We clambered on rock ledges and sat hypnotized by rolling waves, wheeling seabirds, endless distances. Walking back, I saw a shepherd in the pasture, dressed as shepherds always are in jeans, rubber boots, sweater, jacket, and cap, carrying a walking stick. He stood and moved as shepherds always do, a kind of Highland tai chi—patient, a thrift of motion, slouched and alert, subtle and purposeful.

Next day we visited the Callanais (or Callanish) Stones, which stand like graceful dancers in a mineral choreography perhaps six thousand years old. The stones themselves are 3000 million years old, beautiful, with soft swirled patterns of dawn colors amid their gray. Unlike heavily touristed Stonehenge, Callanais is a quiet, low-key place; there were intervals during our visit when we had the circle to ourselves. The stones are tall and impressive but the place's atmosphere has a lightness to it, though when I rested my hand against one stone I felt an intoxicating abidance of power. I did not delve into the energy there, but I walked among the stones and made prayers for the dead, including friends who had passed that year. On Lewis, the living and dead seem to commune in close and congenial proximity.

It was grey, windy, raining—a typical Lewis day—when Robin and I ventured into the mountains near Uig on the western side of the island. We traveled by post bus—a van carrying mail and passengers into remote areas—a slow mode of travel, but friendly. The mountains silenced us—rocks and sea lochs, standing stones, mist curling around primordial crags. We were absorbed, fascinated, magnetized. Each dwelling we stopped at to deliver mail had a different home-made receptacle with a unique latch, each of which the mail carrier knew the secret of. There were converted ovens and fridge boxes, wooden cubbies, all kinds of sturdy arrangements. At houses where mail was delivered to the door, our driver sometimes returned to the van munching a pancake or biscuit—people care for one another in basic, nourishing ways that are the culture's foundation. I had seen people on city buses in Scotland handing sweets to drivers, too.

Hearing Gaelic spoken on Lewis, I was content. It was enough to hear it, though I wished I could speak it also. The only secondary school on Lewis is in Stornoway. "Once the kids go off to school in Stornoway they're gone," I was told. "They leave the island after that." Incomers to the Hebrides speak English; children growing up in Gaelic-speaking families go off to an English-speaking world. On Lewis is both the abidance and tenuousness of Celtic culture. Everywhere are war memorials, as throughout the Highlands, but Islanders lost a stunning proportion of their male population in Britain's wars. Clearances, wars, the disappearance of the young—I wondered what could stem and turn the tide of loss. As the ferry pulled away from Tarbert, returning us to Skye, I sang a lament written by a Lewisman in Canada. Mist and dusk blurred the island's outlines and waves came between boat and land until there was nothing to sing to but night and sea.

Back in America, Celtomania continued to foment. I came home to workshop students enthusing about "Celtic shamanism" and friends listening to Dougie MacLean CDs and watching Riverdance videos. It seemed, on the whole, a good excitement, one of discovery and resonance, and one that would have an elevating effect on the tourist economies of Celtic countries, and on their arts. Heritage interest from outside stimulates heritage valuation from inside. As always, this yields a mix of commercialized invention and exploitation, and genuine preservation and evolution. In the midst of this reconnection with

roots a future germinates, though in the case of the Isle of Eigg perhaps it would be more appropriate to say a future is hatching.

Eigg is a 7400-acre island near Skye—about ten miles off mainland Scotland—that made history in June 1997. Land rights and land
reforms are, along with parliamentary devolution, the most essential
issues in Scotland as it reaches toward a future that will renew and
sustain its lands and people. As an editorial in the *West Highland Free
Press* simply stated in 1997, "the only room for political maneouvre is
in the Highlands and Islands and the only issue that counts is the
land." Eigg is a microcosm of the evolution of relationship between
Celtic people and land.

The island was first inhabited by Mesolithic hunter-gatherers from
around 8000 B.C. and then by Neolithic farmers three thousand years
later, before receiving its Bronze Age and Iron Age Celts. That Celtic
culture was influenced by Viking incomers—a Gaelic-Norse kingdom
that was dominant from the eighth to twelfth centuries. Land was
held in tribal units represented by the clan aristocracy, with smaller
farmers having joint tenancy, sharing rights to the seaweed on the
shores, the birds on the cliffs, and common pasture land. There were
also individual portions of land distributed by casting lots each year
so that good and bad farmland was equally shared. Tacksmen were
relatives of clan chiefs, holding "tacks" of land in exchange for a share
of the crops, hospitality to the chief and his retinue, and, most importantly, for military service. Chiefs counted their wealth in terms of
warriors. Scotland had a cattle economy, traditionally Celtic, with its
women taking herds up to the shielings each summer while men
tended oat and barley crops in the townships. There was a happy,
effective balance in the rhythms of relationship with the land.

This changed when feudalism ate into Gaelic culture, eroding its
values and changing clan chiefs to landlords whose rent-racking forced
many tacksmen to emigrate, taking their people with them. The kelp
boom during the Napoleonic wars stemmed that emigration from
the Hebrides, as chiefs pressured parliament to prohibit the people's
leaving. This was reversed when the kelp industry died, and tenants
were evicted to make room for sheep. Emigration increased again
with the devastating potato famine in 1846.

In 1879, Michael Davitt, in Ireland's County Mayo, founded what
became the Irish Land League, and within two years secured the Irish
Land Act, giving Irish tenant farmers and smallholders some security
of tenure. On Skye, crofting tenants adopted Davitt's tactics, using rent

strikes to force return of such things as grazing rights taken away during the Clearances. These tactics spread to the rest of the Highlands and Islands, and the Highland Land League was formed, modeled on Davitt's organization. In 1886, the Crofter's War resulted in the Crofting Act that protected tenure and fair rents, though it did not return land and homes to people earlier evicted during the Clearances.

Twenty percent of the Highlands and Islands are now crofted, mainly in the western isles, Orkney, Shetland, and on the northwest coast. Eighty-five percent of the crofts are tenanted rather than owned, though there is always the option to buy. Government grants encourage sheep and cattle farming, unfortunately, instead of a variety of agricultural endeavors more appropriate to the land and economy. Arable land is often used for hay, potatoes, turnips, or sometimes rape or kale for fodder. The crofts provide far more diversity of land use than does agribusiness, but fewer than five percent of crofters are able to support themselves on crofting alone.

Most of the Isle of Eigg did not fall under crofting protection. Residents of Eigg, in 1997, still were officially described as "vassals," and the island's owner (who in 1997 was Marlin Eckhardt Maruma, a German artist) was officially the "feudal superior." When Maruma put the island up for sale, these "vassals" decided to put an end to feudalism's oppressions and neglects on Eigg. As a community, they bought their island, ending seven generations of landlordism.

It took almost a year to raise the money. The community formed a partnership with the Scottish Wildlife Trust and the Highland Council. One million five hundred thousand pounds came from public donations sent from around the world, as Eigg became a focal point of struggle for reestablishment of communal relationship with land.

Simon Fraser, a solicitor from Lewis who also helped in the crofter's successful land-control bid in Assynt, said, "This is a triumph for all that is good in humanity and is certainly one in the eye for everything that is mean-spirited and self-seeking. It is my opinion that what has been achieved would have been unthinkable 30 or 40 years ago. . . . The outside world regarded us in the Highlands as living in some Ealingesque twilight. Such agencies as existed would lay their plans down for our future with little reference to us. Such crumbs as may have fallen from their table, or the table of the local toff, we were supposed to be grateful for. The very notion that we could be trusted to run things ourselves would've been laughed off the park. This change will now continue."

Alastair McIntosh added, "Let history record that the women of this 'Island of the Big Women' have played an absolutely central role. . . . The vision that grafted fresh life to the taproot of old Highland culture can now shine out from a new dawn. This, for the good of community; for the benefit of wildlife; and for the enrichment of the wide world out there that has shown it cares and for which we give profound thanks."

In true Celtic fashion, the buyout's success, finalized on June 12, 1997, was ecstatically celebrated with a marathon ceilidh and the installment of a commemorative standing stone. Whiskey and music flowed and the people danced. Several weeks after this event, Robin and I were invited to Eigg by our friend Gavin, who had grown up on the island, though he now lived on Skye.

Getting to Eigg involved several boats: a ferry from Skye to the mainland; a smaller ferry from the mainland to a patch of sea off Eigg; and a wee transport boat from there to shore. At the pier was a café that filled and emptied with the tides of the ferry schedule. During intervals of activity the little building contained a din of conversation and rattling coffee cups; the windows were fogged with a combination of kitchen steam, cigarette smoke, and evaporation from wet wool sweaters; children caroused, ecotourists piled rucksacks in the corner and studied maps, bacon sizzled, and congratulatory cards dangled from walls.

On Eigg is no electricity or water system except what is harnessed or generated by individual crofts. There is no pub, no service station, no police force, and little TV. The current population is about sixty-three, though there were once five hundred or so people living on Eigg. The four-mile stretch of road gives passage to vehicles lacking amenities such as headlights, hubcaps, shock absorbers, and mufflers. On the other hand, the island is rich in wildlife, including birds such as eagles, kestrels, peregrines, and buzzards, who feed on the abundant supply of rabbits and small mammals. The profusion of wildlife has meant that more than half the island is considered of particular scientific interest and is monitored by the Scottish Wildlife Trust. There are red-throated divers, otters, dolphins, and whales; Europe's smallest bat, rare alpine plants, and breeding colonies of butterflies. More than 170 species of birds and 430 species of plants abide on Eigg, a diversity that makes the island unique.

We stayed in a musty but accommodating house on Eigg called the Crow's Nest, surrounded by lush flowering greenery in the garden part of the island near the laird's lodge. On the foggy day of our arrival, Gavin led us down to the shore to see the cave in which 395 MacDonalds were suffocated by vengeful MacLeods. The place still seemed to reek of fear and death; our flashlight beams lingered on sheep bones and the finality of stone walls. But the shore was fascinating—multitextures and colors of rock along a fractured coast of headlands and beaches. Back at the house I changed out of saturated shoes, socks, and jeans, and sat in front of the fire nursing a glass of whiskey, pondering the brutality in Scottish history.

Clouds opened the next morning, uncurtaining the island, and we spent the day walking, mainly through the northern amphitheater of towering escarpments that curve to contain an area of pastoral croftland. Pastures gently led to a generous curve of beach—one of the most beautiful places I have ever seen, with its smooth white sand, primordial rock, and the Isle of Rhum's rugged, mysterious bulk rising from the sea a few miles away.

As we waded in the turquoise water a golden eagle, wings stroking mightily above the weight of a rabbit, was harassed into dropping his meal by two hooded crows. Laig Beach is famous for its cattle strolling across the sands like people on holiday, or standing knee-deep in the ocean, their calves scampering in chase games along the beach. The shoreline rock extends in basalt dykes and sculpted limestone scallops; waterfalls spill from the green rim of pastures.

In Gavin's company we often paused in our wanders, accepting tea and biscuits at homes of people who knew Gavin as a boy or from their later dealings with him. Robin and I replied to inquiries about where we were from (and our surnames, of course) but mostly we listened to island gossip—infidelities and runnings-away; who was living where and doing what with their crofts; deaths and births; reminiscences. It was comfortable talk—warm, subtle, sometimes pointed but always courteous in its own way, even to those absent. Between stops to visit, we told Gavin we were finding it ludicrous to continually be referred to as "young ladies," considering we were in our mid-forties. "Ach," he said, "You should be flattered; well then, what shall I call you?" Robin suggested "women" but Gavin protested that that would be too formal. "How about 'bonnie lasses'?" he suggested, which of course we thought was fine.

Camille Dressler, Eigg's unofficial historian, a dynamic Frenchwoman-turned-Scot, gave us a tour of the estate lodge and its gracious surroundings—trees and flowers both native and exotic. The lodge had deteriorated and was, unlike the grounds, in a challenging state of neglect. The islanders had not yet settled on what use to make of the once detested bastion of lairdship. I wandered from room to room perusing newspaper clippings tacked to walls; it was as though stiff and humorless grown-ups had been chased away by a band of intrepid, merry youths. What would they do now? Many of Eigg's inhabitants are not young, but the spirit of victory over feudalism was young, even in its attendance to mundane realities. What will its maturing bring?

Sitting at the pier on Eigg, watching children in their intense play among stacks of shipping crates, I was struck by the sense of natural freedom apparent in those children; their good manners but lack of inhibition, how they looked me in the eyes when addressed, their joy, their outdoor—not TV—orientation. It is free children who will make a free world. The day we left Eigg the ferry was bringing in musicians and storytellers for the island's feis, the cultivation and celebration of traditional culture that focuses on learning as well as performing. It is music that will sing the future into being.

What is land sense? I think of my son climbing home up the mountain in winter darkness, knowing his way, unafraid. I think of Indians and Celts, their sacred geographies, place-names reflecting relationship, the shape of experience, spiritual immanence. I think of a spokesperson for the Scottish Crofter's Union saying, "Crofting is a type of production that is entirely in tune with nature." Land sense is attunement to place, an extension of awareness and identity. "What worries us," a Highland woman told me, regarding incomers and estate owners, "is that these people have no sense of the land." Land sense guides a people's action, the form of what is done and the realization of being. It is why urban paganism is essentially an oxymoron. It is why loss of land sense is loss of sustainable community or communalness.

I live on a mountain that teaches land sense, in its dangers and demands, in the elementalness of survival there, in my primal interdependency with its life forms and its cycles, rhythms, patterns, and distinctions that guide my actions. My life is the mountain's life, it is of the mountain. My land sense is like a sense of my own body, my own temperament and consciousness—not mirrored but known, an integration.

In Scotland, in 1996, I stood in morning light at a campground in the Highlands. The wind had softened to a breeze that floated away the strands of hair I pulled from my brush. Sheep called in the pasture. Grey loch, grey sky, grey stone, and luminous green hills. Light gleamed in horizontal bands above the land; swallows threaded the cool air. I was not ready to leave. The previous day, stopping where a stream spilled down a steep mountainside, I looked up from preoccupation with the rocks to find two sheep peering down from a ledge. "What are you doing?" they seemed to ask. And I was not sure.

Later that day, gazing at an ancient, grey-streaked mountain, I had a sudden sensation of vertigo, as if passing through a veil into clarity of apprehension. The world within the world, ever present, where all things speak. I wanted to listen there longer. A year later I returned—and stayed. It takes time, the knowing, even when resonance is immediate; it is not a one-night stand.

Land sense is a resource that is not "managed." It is not extracted; it is not even stewarded. It is lived.

At the Falls of Shin, in Easter Ross, I stood above the rushing water and watched Atlantic salmon surge homeward. The falls poured with relentless force over the rocks, and every now and then a salmon hurled itself at the foamy cascade. It seemed inconceivable that any of them made it—the rapids and falls were so intense. I reflected that I have never tried as hard at anything as those fish did at getting upriver.

Celts are a salmonlike people, casting themselves bravely, gallantly, precipitously upon life's currents. Without the river and all its griefs and challenges, there is no path home, no depth of experience, no clearing and strengthening within movement. Watching the salmon, I thought of William Wallace and others who knew that freedom is vital, the way home. As we left the falls a car pulled up, and three nattily dressed vacationers climbed out with their fishing equipment. "Live strongly, Salmon," I prayed. "Live free."

On one of my last mornings on Skye before returning to America, I rose at dawn and went outside the hostel. As I walked down the lane between pastures I sang to the morning—to the Highland cows, the misty mountains, the calm sea. I scratched the necks of the Eriskey horses and sang to them, too. They stood dozing, companionable, not yet ready to cavort. I roused the border collie sleeping in the kitchen and carried my bowl of muesli outside to a bench overlooking the sound. A flock of chickens pecked gravel at my feet and hens hopped up on either side of me on the bench. My little clan of animal friends, awake while the world slept. I sat, happy and sad at once— grateful, and feeling sorry for myself because of impending departure, and filling myself with the morning's beatitude.

If you do not wake, dear friend,
these heron-blue mountains
poised between washed sky
and satin sea; the whale-backed
islands in intimate faraway foreverness;
Scotland in July dawning damp
as a newborn, still as the dream
at life's end; a single white sail
on the kyle's invisible current;
cattle grazing the heathered braes;
will disappear.

As day's light strengthened, I heard people stir.

Here

It is a still night—so clear

with smooth snowdrifts under the moon

Even indoors I feel the stillness

Over everything

Over my boots standing by the chair

Over the cats each in a spell of sleep

There's only the radio playing small instrumentals

like flowers resting on velvet

I think about the day

the love, disagreement, teamwork nonetheless

Thoughts are soft flowers

carried to a shelf somewhere

I wish I could tell you the silence

around trees deepening into dark sky

It has always been here

How strange that silence speaks

untarnished by our interchange

It is the silence of love loving

beyond ricocheting sound

It seems to me to say

Yes I am here

Barbara Cruden

CONCLUSION

W HAT IS IT IN CELTIC ANCESTRY that calls for reclamation? What
vital continuities can nourish and enlighten our lives and those
of our children? It is not re-creation or repetition of the past that is
needed, but connection, and the kind of wise cherishing that tends
both root and flower. It is not form that should be looked to, but rather
the distinct living force that fluidly cloaks itself in form, like a knot-
work pattern, ever changing. Celticism's form, for our times, will
rightly be unique in its expression; so many strands of continuity have
been broken or lost, but in so many small and ordinary ways we still
have been handed a legacy.

What are some of this gift's components? One face of Celtic spirit
is kinship consciousness, with many worthy attributes that can be
applied to modern lives:

- It is a communal system in which no one is insignificant;
  everyone has respectful place and access to support and
  affiliation.
- It encourages cooperative activity; traditional Celtic pastoral,
  agricultural, and societal systems operated on a participatory
  basis.
- It asserts that relationships are important, through a wealth
  of interactive and celebratory customs; people do not live
  disconnected lives.

- Hospitality is imperative; no one is excluded from being received and sheltered—even absolute enemies may find occasion to come to terms—and generous hospitality is considered standard conduct, not an extraordinary or optional virtue.
- Kinship consciousness promotes honorable personal behavior and communal responsibility; justice is based on reparation that falls on the entire communal unit. Community and individual are accountable to and for each other; an enlargement of identity, priority, and commitment.
- Social patterning in a kinship society encourages care with words and names, for their implications and powers.
- Kinship orients to family and land, not to authoritarian politics or religious ascendancy; freedom and choice are emphasized, balanced by responsibility and tolerance.
- Lands are held communally and in trust; personal greed and grasping are minimized, as is a view of land as a commodity. The clan relationship to land was traditionally "classless."
- Community spirit fosters a sense of how each person's contributions serve the larger good, based on an interdependent reality.
- It affirms that living beings are more valuable than the conventional trappings of wealth. (There is a story of a MacLeod chief, Alasdair Crotach, who, after visiting the affluent King James V—who was proud of his royal dining hall and candlesticks—wagered that he could outdo the king's splendor. When James V visited the Highland chief to judge the Highlander's relative splendor, he was escorted to an outdoor feast on a high, flat-topped hill called MacLeod's Tables, where the "candlesticks" were tartaned clansmen holding torches. The king conceded the wager.)

A second face of Celtic spirit is that of equality between women and men, which is part of a general commitment to freedom. A particularly Celtic aspect of sexual equality is that it is not an attempted balance of compartmentalized polarities but is rather a respectful acceptance of individual capacity's range, and social provisioning for its expression. Also important is consideration of sex as a natural, wholesome activity, and sexual desire as something equally experienced and properly expressed and acted upon by both women and men.

Good relationship between the sexes was crucial to Celts, carrying through in relationship with the land and reflected in the faring of individuals, clans, and tribes. The well-being of women and household harmony were traditionally barometers of general well-being, an awareness dismayingly absent in modern cultures.

A third face of our triadic Celtic spirit is relationship to nature, characterized by attention to a multidimensional, integrated reality, the constant fluid interplay of spirit and form. This nongrasping awareness accepts transformative and supernatural occurrence as part of daily life. Celtic relationship to nature suggests that death need not be feared in an interdependent and interpenetrative universe. The coexistence of an Otherworld interwoven through the mundane natural world persuasively informs Celtic consciousness; spiritual and temporal affairs are co-influential.

Celts love the land. They are ardently engaged with locality, with a sense of place. It is a vigorous relationship, the land not something to be subdued or made servant of—relationship requiring appropriate attitude and conduct, those things that come naturally when there is love.

Archeologists found that the most beautiful and finely crafted Celtic artifacts were those discovered in places of sacred offering. The Celts gave their best to spirit—art, spirit, and land were undivided. The high valuing of beauty in art, music, dance, poetry, and learning that is so characteristic of Celts—where craftspeople, bards, and Druids were honored as much or more than warriors and nobility—is rooted in immanence of spirit.

Awareness of and participation in a complexly interrelated well-being is the common denominator in all these faces of Celtic spirit, a continuity available—calling—to be embodied in today's world. The heart of Celticism is the freedom and wholeness of women and men, humans and nature, spirit and form, individuals and community. Frank Delaney, in *The Celts,* describes it thus:

> At the height of their development the Celts constituted an archetypal European people: tribal, familial, hierarchal, agricultural. They were a brilliant people, of the oral tradition. A superstitious people, who actively sought deeper beliefs. A practical people, but producing penetrating intellectual concepts. Not a political people, although they enjoyed many sophisticated legal structures. They did not achieve or desire

a cohesive political nationhood, although their motivation, the unity of the tribe, might have been the perfect political model. Nor were they an imperial people, although they colonized many lands, and in some cases left a dominant cultural imprint forever. . . . They appreciated beauty and eroticism and they wedded the practical to the exquisite. In their art they proceeded from the geometric patterns of the primitive tribe to the abstract expression of their civilisation. They exercised a philosophy which saw truth as a diamond, many-faceted and precious. And thereby they celebrated one quality of life vital to them—personal, spiritual freedom.

Comparisons between Celtic and American Indian traditional ways have been lightly touched upon throughout our look at the Celts, as catalysts for further thought rather than as attempts to present an in-depth study of similarities and differences. Among branches of Celtic peoples themselves are cultural variations not delved into here, such as the territorial emphasis of Irish tuatha in comparison to the more kin-oriented Scottish clans, and so on. Generalizations eventually and inevitably yield to myriad distinctions and controversies of perspective, but for today's people of Celtic or American Indian ancestry it may be helpful to consider some of the parallels contained within those cultural roots. It is a consideration that can broaden the understanding of resonance felt by many Celtic Americans in relation to Indian spirituality, and clarify or redirect the exploration of Celtic Americans drawn to indigenous outlooks. The journey through Celtic heritage, like journeys through Scotland, is a peregrination of heights and glens, a winding road of many branches under shifting light in which perception yields surety in order to better encompass possibility, a more subtle infiltration of vision.

Homeland is referent to both history and heart. When Rome-born Prince Charlie was advised by the chiefs to go home, he testily replied, "I *am* home," an enviable certainty despite the price the clans paid for its assertion. The spirit of Celticism is also a matter of both history and heart—one without the other is of little practical value in terms of evolution or continuity, or even reinvention.

As modern Americans we have neither a comparable rurality nor aristocracy as lenses of consciousness through which to experience or understand pagan religion or the life context of ancient Celts. Much of what we know about Gaelic perspective is seen against a backdrop of

Celtic struggle with invasive colonizing forces, and that view is distorted by psychological as well as physical and chronological distance. When I was in Scotland, I tried to pinpoint what it was about Americans that made us so easily identifiable to local people, beyond our accents—and even when we were not being particularly ignorant or pushy. Two observations emerged. One was that Americans are socially conditioned to project self-image, constantly, through clothing, egoistic preoccupation, verbal competitiveness, and other "This is me; aren't I great?" strategies. Celtic warriors did this too; but it is not a social behavior that belongs in ordinary contexts of interaction.

The second distinguishing feature of Americans is that we walk around—wherever we are—like we own the place. Every Scot I talked to about this nodded and said, "Exactly." Even *humble* tourists tend to do this. I attribute it to the fact that the United States has never been invaded (except from the perspective of Native American experience) and, as a nation, has not experienced the suffering of that or other collective disasters, such as famine or cultural proscription. Those things make a difference in your outlook and how you move in the world.

In reconnecting with heritage, whether at home or abroad, knowing your people's history, the sufferings and shadows as well as the triumphs and joys, informs self-perception in a way that sensitizes you to context. It broadens and deepens perspective so that knowing yourself is not such a "me"-centered affair; it is knowing of relationship. And that is a very Celtic perspective.

Resonance with Celtic heritage is often sought through genealogy, through identifying with aspects of heritage and partisan feelings or subscription to cultural traditions both old and newly created, and through nurturing elements of Celticism that seem worthwhile. The four sections of this book suggest additonal arenas in which resonance can be explored and applied in contemporary life.

But for experience to be more than sentimental affectation or cultural veneer, continuity of spirit needs to flow from deeper wellsprings, resonance's source. From this comes a *direct* participation informed not only by heritage but by that which shaped ancestral consciousness. The land we stand on—relationship to place—is always available to those who seek the experience and understanding of land sense. If this orientation lacks its original, indigenous culture and mindset, it still offers an evolution of land-based awareness.

We are not our ancestors, but in Celtic view, our ancestors created us, and they were beings both of flesh and of Otherworld magic; they were light and tree and ocean wave and living stone; they were mystery embraced within desire to be. Whether transcendent or transformative, being finds its path through embodied relationship. History is in the ground, and as long as that terrain is sustained in sacred fertility, integrity, and endurance of beauty, we will have resource for both continuity and creation, essential reflections of spirit.

Notable Historic Dates for Ireland and Scotland

400 B.C.	Celts crossing to Britain from Gaul
350 B.C.	Celts entering Ireland
55 B.C.–A.D. 43	Conquest of Britain by Rome
A.D. 80	Julius Agricola invades Scottish Lowlands
121	Hadrian's Wall built
400	Saint Ninian brings Christianity to southern Picts
409	Rome abandons Britain
410	Alaric the Goth sacks Rome
432	Patrick brings Christianity to Ireland
500	Dal Riada (now Argyll) settled by Irish
563	Columba and his monks on Iona
793	Vikings begin coastal invasions of Ireland and Scotland
843	Kenneth MacAlpine unites Picts and Scots
1014	Vikings defeated in Ireland by Brian Boru
1153	Somerled, indigenous leader of Scotland's western isles, challenges Norse supremacy and wins battles from 1156–1158; Norse concede his position as Lord of the Isles. Somerled's descendents become clans Donald and MacDougall.

1170 Anglo-Norman invasion of Ireland; Normans merge with Irish Celts

1263 Scotland's Alexander III defeats Haakon IV of Norway in the Hebrides

1290–1292 First Interregnum. Scotland falls under English rule to avoid civil war.

1296 Scottish revolt against English rule, led by John Balliol. Edward I wins, takes Scottish Stone of Destiny (on which Scottish kings are crowned) and exiles Balliol.

1297 William Wallace leads an extraordinary rebellion but is defeated in 1298 (more by the treachery of Scots nobles than by the English). He is captured in 1305 and executed by England.

1306 Robert the Bruce, outlawed by England, begins a guerilla campaign that eventually pushes England out of Scotland. In 1314 Bruce secures Scotland as a result of the battle of Bannockburn.

1326 First Scottish Parliament meets

1328 Treaty between Bruce and Edward II recognizes Scottish independence, but battles continue for decades, both civil and with England, complicated by religious as well as political alliances

1468 Scotland acquires Shetland and Orkney Islands from Norway

1560 "Confession of Faith" passed by Scottish Parliament. Reformed ideas gaining ground in Scotland since at least the 1520s, consequent to resentment of French Catholic influence on monarchs

1561 Mary, Queen of Scots, returns from France and is allowed to continue her Catholicism

1567 Mary forced to abdicate in favor of her son, is imprisoned for nineteen years, then is executed by Elizabeth; Mary's half-brother, Earl of Moray, becomes Regent

1587 Act is passed for subduing the clans of the Borders, Highlands, and Isles

1597 As part of a campaign to bring clans under central authority, King James requires chiefs to produce land titles and guarantees of good conduct. The most powerful families get more power, further undermining clan integrity.

1603 England's Queen Elizabeth dies and Scotland's King

James VI, son of Mary, rules both Scotland and England, though the two remain independent

1638 Scottish Protestants sign National Covenant to oppose changes in the Scottish Church; battles follow from 1644–1645

1648 Charles I surrenders to Covenanters who hand him to the English Parliament; Charles continues negotiating with the Scottish Covenanters, agreeing to a limited restoration of Presbyterianism in return for armed support. The Scots consequently reenter war, on the side of Charles.

1650 Charles II crowned following his father's execution; he accepts the Covenant

1649 Cromwell (England) begins massacring Catholics in Ireland

1651 Cromwell crushes Scots (Covenanter army); Scotland becomes part of English Commonwealth and is later made a protectorate. Charles flees to the Continent.

1660 Charles returns and restores Scottish monarchy

1678 A Highland army is sent to suppress Covenant extremists in southwest Scotland; plundering leaves inhabitants with lasting hatred of Highlanders

1689 James VII, a Catholic who succeeds his brother Charles in 1655, removes penalties against Catholics that have been in effect since the 1660s, but William of Orange (James' brother-in-law) accepts English (Anglican) invitation to depose James. William and his wife, Mary, become corulers; the Scots declare James' throne forfeit because James flees, and invite William to be king of Scots. A Jacobite Highland rebellion against this is defeated.

1690 Battle of the Boyne in Ireland; "wild geese" (Irish nobility) flee their country

1692 Massacre at Glencoe: William's punative action against a branch of the MacDonalds, who seem slow to sign an oath of allegiance; thirty-eight MacDonalds are murdered by troops led by a Campbell, acting as William's agent in a violation of Gaelic laws of hospitality

1707 Scotland pressured into dependence on England during economic hardships; becomes part of the United Kingdom in a union of parliaments, despite Scottish resistance. Churches, education, and legal systems remain separate.

1715   Second Jacobite uprising; supporters of James, "the Old Pretender," attempt to restore Scotland's Stuart dynasty but fail

1719   Third Jacobite uprising defeated at Glen Shiel (the clans generally refuse to participate in this one)

1743   Potatoes introduced in Scotland

1745   Last Jacobite uprising: Charles Edward Stuart (Bonnie Prince Charlie), "the Young Pretender," with reluctant but courageous clan support, tries and fails to wrest Scotland from English rule. After some success, the Jacobites are crushed at Culloden Moor, and the clans are subjected to bloody repression. Highland music, dress, and language are banned by law. MacGregors are proscribed.

1759   Robert Burns born

1775   Penal statutes against MacGregors repealed

1782   Repeal of act proscribing Highland dress

1790   Highland Clearances "reorganize" Highland estates to allow sheep farming and English sport hunting at expense of arable land and local inhabitants; tenants evicted. Great hardship and much migration—approximately 150,000 Scots emigrate to North America in late 1700s.

1845   Famine in Ireland; population severely decimated. England gives no aid. Much starvation and immigration.

1886   Crofter's Holding Act in Scotland safeguards rights of small farms

1916   Easter Uprising in Ireland; Irish Republic proclaimed

1919–1921   Irish war of independence

1922   Treaty between Ireland and England establishes Irish Free State, except for six northern counties under British rule

1997   Scotland votes by referendum to again establish its own Parliament. Political reforms in Northern Ireland bring peace with the IRA.

Appendix II

Clan Names

C LANSHIP WAS A DISTINCT CHARACTERISTIC of Celtic culture. The word *clan* comes from the Gaelic *clanna,* meaning "children." Each clan was headed by a chief; if the chief was not adept in military leadership, there was also a *ceann-cath*—a war leader—usually a member of the chief's family. The tanist (*tainistear* in Gaelic) was the chosen heir to the chiefship, and the chief's immediate family formed a kind of council consisting of the nine senior descendants of a chiefly great-grandfather, who elected the tanist. Chiefs could nominate a successor, but it had to be within blood relationship. In Ireland, succession became restricted to the male line; in Scotland, electors and candidates could be female or connected by female lineage.

The cadet houses *(gilfines)* into which the clans were divided were headed by chieftains, known as *ceann-tighes.* In the course of clan involvement with land disputes and clan rights, a regulated system of heraldry evolved, distinguishing between chiefs and descendants of principal cadet houses. Occasionally cadet families would break away to form seperate clans. Over time chiefs became invested with both feudal and traditionally Celtic powers.

Clan members originally were descendants of a common ancestor, but as the clans developed and extended territorial bases, adopted and allied families living in those territories and having no blood kinship might become part of the clan. The system of septs or subclans emerged in part from that development, so that a clansperson became simply someone who professed allegiance to a chief, whether through descent from a common ancestor, adoption, or territiorial association. All clanspeople considered themselves noble—clan society was classless.

Various clans claim mythological roots or royal antecedents; the confederated clans of MacSweens, Lamonts, MacLeys, MacLachlans, and MacNeills can trace a single line of ancestry back to Neill of the Nine Hostages, Ireland's High King in the fifth century. The Mac-Kinnons and MacGregors boast direct descendance from Scotland's first royal family, the Alpins. But most clan origins cannot be authenticated earlier than the eleventh century, the lineages mainly becoming evident in the thirteenth and fourteenth centuries. When listing origins in terms of ethnicity, the influx of Anglo, Norman, and Flemish families into the Highlands becomes apparent. The feudal component of clanship that developed because of this influx and other non-Celtic influences led to certain clans being promoted over others by the Scottish Crown. This feudal component became what most differentiates Scottish clanship from indigenous tribalism.

The following list of clans and families is not comprehensive but is in accordance with the current Standing Council of Scottish Chiefs. If you are of Scottish origin you may find your family name listed here. There is no similar extant system providing groupings of family names for other Celtic nationalities, so if your ancestry is Breton, Irish, Welsh, Manx, or Cornish, tracing your particular Celtic connections may require a more individualized genealogical search.

Names like O'Malley, O'Neil, O'Donohue, and so on are usually Irish, "O" being the Irish equivalent of the Scottish "Mac," meaning "son of." Names beginning with "Mc" are often Irish, sometimes Scottish. ("Nic" was Gaelic for "daughter of.") If your ancestry is Lowland Scots you may not find your family name listed here either. Not even all Highland surnames are included in these lists; many Scots were not associated with clans as such.

Because of Irish immigration to Scotland in the time of the Dal Riadans, there is much crossover in Irish and Scottish family names—Irish Kennedys and Scottish Kennedys, for instance—which can be confusing if you are trying to trace your surname to a place of origin. Again the personal quest—talking to elders and exploring the family tree—may yield the most useful answers about your Celtic antecedents and where they came from.

The lists presented here are intended to serve those quests for connection—the sense of extended alliances and kinship, of continuity and perhaps a deepened feeling of relationship with your family name, a more meaningful identification with what it—and you—carry. Each name is a story, each generation a chapter, and now it is your turn. You are your name's tale in progress.

Celtic names have always been linked with specific places; tracing your own name to a certain locality is a kind of homecoming to where your ancestors walked and were buried, to the landscape that filled their senses and shaped their days and nights with its private and distinct spirit. This may be a place of resonance and belonging for you as well. Universality—all my relations—is most truly honored when there is also reality of honoring what is specifically present. The two create a wholeness of experience.

Clan plant badges—Celtic totems—and ethnic origins are noted in the clan list presented here; a few origins are designated as "territorial," meaning that association with regional name rather than family name was the clan's founding basis. Many of the clans listed were powerful Lowland or Border families who gained territorial dominance as feudal nobles and landowners. These families often strategically intermarried with Celts, but the Lowlands and Border did not have clans in the old Gaelic sense, as in the Highlands and Islands, and are more accurately referred to as families. The second list given is that of the so-called Armigerous Clans and Families of Scotland. These are not currently members of the Council of Scottish Chiefs, but each have a registered coat of arms, indicating clan organization.

Member Clans and Families of the Standing Council of Scottish Chiefs

Name	Plant badge	Ethnic origin
Agnew		Norman
Anstruther	olive	Norman
Arbuthnott		territorial
Bannerman		Lowland
Barclay		Norman
Borthwick	rose	perhaps Saxon
Boyd		Norman
Boyle		Norman
Brodie	lesser periwinkle	possibly Pictish

Name	Plant badge	Ethnic origin
Bruce	rosemary	Norman
Buchan	sunflower	territiorial
Burnett	holly	Norman or Saxon
Cameron	oak or crowberry	debated
Campbell	bog myrtle	debated
Carmichael		Lowland
Carnegie		debated
Cathcart		Lowland
Charteris		Norman
Chattan*	red whortleberry	Celtic
Chisholm	fern	Norman
Cochrane		Norse
Colquhoun	hazel	territorial
Colville		Norman
Cranstoun	strawberry	territorial
Crichton		Lowland
Dewar		Lowland
Drummond	holly	possibly Saxon
Dunbar		Celtic
Dundas		Northumberland
Durie		Norman
Eliott	white hawthorne	debated
Elphinstone		debated
Erskine		Norman
Farquharson	Scots fir	Celtic
Fergusson	poplar	Celtic
Forbes	broom	Lowland
Forsyth	forsythia	debated
Fraser	yew	France
Fraser of Lovat		Norman
Gordon	rock ivy	Anglo-Norman
Graham	spurge laurel	Anglo-Norman
Grant	Scots pine	Norman
Grierson	bluebell	debated

---

*Clan Chattan evolved from a confederation of families: MacPhersons, Cattanachs, MacBeans, MacPhails, MacKintoshes and their cadet branches, MacGillivrays, Davidsons, MacLeans of Dochgarroch, MacQueens of Pollochaig, Macintyres of Badenoch, and MacAndrews.

Name	Plant badge	Ethnic origin
Guthrie		uncertain
Haig		Norman
Haldane		Norman
Hamilton		Norman
Hannay	periwinkle	Celtic
Hay	mistletoe	Norman
Henderson	cotton grass	Lowland
Home	broom	Saxon
Hope		France
Hunter	thrift	Norman
Irvine		Celtic
Jardine	apple	Norman
Johnstone	red hawthorne	Lowland
Keith	white rose	Norman
Kennedy	oak	Saxon or Norman
Kerr		Norman
Kincaid	territorial	
Lamont	crabapple	Celtic
Leask		debated
Lennox	rose	debated
Leslie	rue	Saxon
Lindsay	lime tree	England
Lockhart		England
Lumsden	hazel	Lowlands
Lyon		France
Macalister	heath	Celtic
MacBain	boxwood	Celtic
MacDonald	heather	Norse-Celtic
MacDonnell	heath	Celtic
MacDougall	bell heather	Norse-Celtic
MacDowall	oak	Celtic
MacGregor	Scots pine	Celtic
MacIntyre	heather	Norse-Celtic
MacKay	great bullrush	Celtic
MacKenzie	staghorn moss	Celtic
MacKinnon	pine	Norse-Celtic
MacKintosh	red whortleberry	Celtic
MacLachlan	rowan	Norse-Celtic
MacLean	crowberry or holly	Celtic

Name	Plant badge	Ethnic origin
MacLaren	laurel or bay	Celtic
MacLennan	furze	Celtic
MacLeod	juniper	Norse
MacMillan	holly	Celtic
MacNab	stone bramble	Celtic
MacNaughten	azalea	Pictish
MacNeacail		Norse
MacNeil	dryas	Celtic
MacPherson	heather	Celtic
MacThomas	snowberry	Celtic
Maitland	honeysuckle	Norman
Makgill		Lowland
Malcolm / MacCallum	rowan	Celtic
Mar		Celtic
Marjoribanks		Norman
Matheson	rose	Norse-Celtic
Menzies	Menzies heath	Norman
Moffat		Norse
Moncreiffe	oak	Celtic
Montgomery		Norman
Morrison	driftweed	Celtic
Munro	club moss	Celtic
Murray	butcher's broom / juniper	possibly Flemish or Pictish
Napier		Celtic
Nesbitt		possibly Norman
Nicholson	juniper	Norse
Ogilvy	hawthorne	
Primrose	primrose	
Ramsey	harebell	Norman
Rattray		
Robertson	bracken	Celtic
Rollo		Norman
Rose	rosemary	Norman
Ross	juniper	Celtic
Ruthven		Norse
Sandilands		Northumberland
Scott	blueberry	possibly Saxon
Scrymgeour	rowan	Celtic

Name	Plant badge	Ethnic origin
Sempill		debated
Shaw	red whortleberry	Celtic
Sinclair	whin	Norman
Skine		Celtic
Spens		France
Stirling		Lowlands
Stuart	oak	Brittany
Sutherland	cotton sedge	Flemish
Swinton		Saxon
Urquhart	wallflower	Celtic
Wallace	oak	Welsh
Wedderburn	beech	Lowlands
Wemyss		Celtic

Armigerous Clans and Families of Scotland

Abercrombie
Abernethy
Adair
Adam
Aikenhead
Ainslie
Aiton
Allardice
Anderson
Armstrong
Arnott
Auchinleck
Baillie
Baird
Balfour
Bannatyne/
   Ballantyne
Baxter
Bell
Belshes
Bethune

Beveridge
Binning
Bisset
Blackadder
Blackstock
Blair
Blane
Blyth
Boswell
Brisbane
Broun
Buchanan
Butter
Byres
Cairns
Calder
Caldwell
Callender
Carruthers
Chalmers
Cheyne

Clelland
Clephane
Cockburn
Congilton
Criag
Crawford
Crosbie
Cumming
Cunningham
Dalrymple
Dalziel
Davidson
Dennistoun
Don
Douglas
Dunlop
Edmonstone
Fairlie
Falconer
Fenton
Fleming

Fletcher

Forrester

Fotheringham

Fullarton

Galbraith

Galloway

Garden

Gartshore

Gayre

Ged

Gibsone

Gladstains

Glas

Glen

Glendinning

Gray

Gunn

Haliburton

Halkerston

Halket

Hepburn

Heron

Herries

Hog

Hopkirk

Horsburgh

Houston

Hutton

Inglis

Innes

Kelly

Kinloch

Kinnaird

Kinnear

Kinnimont

Kirkcaldy

Kirkpatrick

Laing

Lammie

Langlands

Learmonth

Little

Livingstone

Logie

Lundin

Lyle

MacArthur

Macaulay

MacBrayne

MacDuff

MacEwan

MacFarlane

MacFie

MacGillevray

MacInnes

Mackie

MacLellan

MacQuarrie

MacQueen

MacRae

Masterson

Maule

Maxton

Maxwell

McCorquodale

McCulloch

McIver

McKerrell

Meldrum

Melville

Mercer

Middleton

Moncur

Monteith

Monypenny

Mouat

Moubray

Mow

Muir

Nairn

Nevoy

Newlands

Newton

Norvel

Ochterlony

Oliphant

Orrock

Paisley

Paterson

Pennycook

Pentland

Peter

Pitblade

Pitcairn

Pollock

Polwarth

Porterfield

Preston

Pringle

Purves

Rait

Ralston

Renton

Riddell

Roberton

Rossie

Russel

Rutherford

Schaw

Seton

Skirving

Somerville

Spalding

Spottiswood

Stewart

Strachan

Straiton

Strange

Sydserf

Symmers

Tailyour
Tait
Tennant
Trotter
Troup
Turnbull
Tweedie

Udny
Vans
Walkinshaw
Wardlaw
Watson
Wauchope

Weir
Whitefoord
Whitelaw
Wishart
Wood
Young

Scottish Names Associated with Clans and Families

Name	Associated Clan
Abbot	MacNab
Abbotson	MacNab
Addison	Gordon
Adie	Gordon
Airlie	Ogilvy
Airth	Graham
Aitcheson	Gordon
Aiken	Gordon
Alexander	Macalister, MacDonald
Alistair	Macalister
Allan	MacDonald, MacFarlane
Allanson	MacDonald, MacFarlane
Allison	Macalister
Arrol	Hay
Arthur	Macarthur
Askey	MacLeod
Austin	Keith
Ayson	MacKintosh
Bain	MacBain, MacKay
Balloch	MacDonald
Barrie	Farquharson, Gordon
Barron	Rose
Bartholomew	MacFarlane, Leslie
Bean	MacBain
Beath	MacDonald, Maclean
Beattie	MacBain
Begg	MacDonald
Berry	Forbes

Name	Associated Clan
Beton	MacLeod
Binnie	MacBain
Black	Lamont, MacGregor, MacLean
Blake	Lamont
Bonar	Graham
Bontein	Graham
Bowers	MacGregor
Bowie	MacDonald
Bowmaker	MacGregor
Bowman	Farquharson
Boyes	Forbes
Brebner	Farquharson
Brewer	Drummond, MacGregor
Brieve	Morrison
Brown	Lamont, MacMillan
Bryce	MacFarlane
Bryde	Brodie
Buntain	Graham
Burdon	Lamont
Burk	MacDonald
Burnes	Campbell
Burns	Campbell
Caddell	Campbell
Caird	Sinclair, MacGregor
Cariston	Skene
Carlyle	Bruce
Carr	Kerr
Carrick	Kennedy
Carson	MacPherson
Cassels	Kennedy
Cattanach	MacPherson
Caw	MacFarlane
Cessford	Kerr
Charles	MacKenzie
Christie	Farquharson
Clanachan	MacLean
Clark	Cameron MacPherson
Clement	Lamont
Clerk	Cameron, MacPherson

Name	Associated Clan
Cluny	MacPherson
Clyne	Sinclair
Cobb	Lindsay
Collier	Robertson
Colman	Buchanan
Colson	MacDonald
Colyer	Robertson
Combie	MacThomas
Comine	Comyn
Comrie	MacGregor
Conacher	MacDougall
Connall	MacDonald
Conochie	Campbell
Constable	Hay
Cook	Stewart
Corbett	Ross
Cormack	Buchanan
Coull	MacDonald
Coulson	MacDonald
Cousland	Buchanan
Coutts	Farquharson
Cowan	Colquhoun, MacDougall
Cowrie	Fraser
Crerar	Mackintosh
Crombie	MacDonald
Crookshanks	Stewart
Crum	MacDonald
Cullen	Gordon
Cumin	Comyn
Cushnie	Lumsden
Dallas	MacKintosh
Daniels	MacDonald
Davie	Davidson
Daivs	Davidson
Dawson	Davidson
Day	Davidson
Dean	Davidson
Denoon	Campbell
Deuchar	Lindsay

Name	Associated Clan
Dickson	Keith
Dingwall	Munro, Ross
Dinnes	Innes
Dis	Skene
Dixon	Keith
Dobbie	Robertson
Dobson	Robertson
Dochart	MacGregor
Docharty	MacGregor
Doig	Drummond
Doles	Mackintosh
Donachie	Robertson
Donaldson	MacDonald
Donillson	MacDonald
Donleavy	Buchanan
Donlevy	Buchanan
Donnellson	MacDonnell
Dove	Buchanan
Dow	Buchanan, Davidson
Downie	Lindsay
Drysdale	Douglas
Duff	MacDuff
Duffie	MacFie
Duffus	Sutherland
Duffy	MacFie
Duilach	Stewart
Duncanson	Robertson
Dunnachie	Robertson
Duthie	Ross
Dyce	Skene
Eadie	Gordon
Eaton	Home
Edie	Gordon
Elder	Mackintosh
Ennis	Innis
Enrick	Gunn
Esson	Mackintosh
Ewing	MacLachlan
Fair	Ross

Name	Associated Clan
Fairbairn	Armstrong
Federith	Sutherland
Fee	MacFie
Fergu	Ferguson
Ferries	Ferguson
Ferson	MacPherson
Fife	MacDuff
Findlater	Ogilvie
Findlay	Farquharson
Findlayson	Farquharson
Fisher	Campbell
Foulis	Munro
France	Stewart
Francis	Stewart
Frew	Fraser
Frissell	Fraser
Fife	MacDuff
Gallie	Gunn
Galt	MacDonald
Garrow	Stewart
Garvie	MacLean
Gaunson	Gunn
Geddes	Gordon
Georgeson	Gunn
Gibb	Buchanan
Gifford	Hay
Gilbert	Buchanan
Gilbride	MacDonald
Gilchrist	MacLachlan, Ogilvie
Gilfillan	MacNab
Gill	MacDonald
Gillanders	Ross
Gillespie	MacPherson
Gillies	MacPherson
Gillon	MacLean
Gilroy	Grant, MacGillivray
Glennie	Mackintosh
Gorrie	MacDonald
Goudie	MacPherson

Name	Associated Clan
Gow	MacPherson
Gowan	MacDonald
Gowrie	MacDonald
Greenlaw	Home
Gregorson	MacGregor
Gregopry	MacGregor
Greig	MacGregor
Greusach	Farquharson
Grewar	MacGregor, Drummond
Grier	MacGregor
Griesck	MacFarlane
Grigor	MacGregor
Gruamach	MacFarlane
Gruer	MacGregor, Drummond
Haddon	Graham
Haggart	Ross
Hallyard	Skene
Hardie	Farquharson, Mackintosh
Hardy	Farquharson, Mackintosh
Harold	MacLeod
Harper	Buchanan
Harperson	Buchanan
Harvey	Keith
Hastings	Campbell
Hawes	Campbell
Hawthorne	MacDonald
Hendrie	MacNaughton
Hendry	MacNaughton
Hewittson	MacDonald
Hewitt	MacDonald
Higginson	Mackintosh
Hobson	Robertson
Hossack	Mackintosh
Howe	Graham
Howie	Graham
Howieson	MacDonald
Hudson	MacDonald
Hughson	MacDonald
Huntly	Gordon

Name	Associated Clan
Hutchenson	MacDonald
Hutcheson	MacDonald
Hutchinson	MacDonald
Inches	Robertson
Ingram	Colquhoun
Innie	Innis
Isles	MacDonald
Jameson	Gunn, Stewart
Jamieson	Gunn, Stewart
Jeffrey	MacDonald
Kay	Davidson
Kean	Gunn, MacDonald
Kellie	MacDonald
Kendrick	MacNaughton
Kenneth	MacKenzie
Kerracher	Farquharson
Kilgour	MacDuff
King	Colquhoun
Kinnell	MacDonald
Kinnieson	MacFarlane
Knox	MacFarlane
Lachie	MacLachlan
Laidaw	Scott
Lair	Maclaren
Lamb	Lamont
Lambie	Lamont
Lammond	Lamont
Landers	Lamont
Lang	Leslie
Lansdale	Home
Lauchlan	MacLachlan
Lawrence	Maclaren
Lawrie	Maclaren
Lawson	Maclaren
Lean	MacLean
Leckie	MacGregor
Lecky	MacGregor
Lees	MacPherson
Leith	MacDonald

Name	Associated Clan
Lemond	Lamont
Lenny	Buchanan
Lewis	MacLeod
Limond	Lamont
Limont	Lamont
Linklater	Sinclair
Lobban	MacLennan
Lockerbie	Douglas
Lombard	Stewart
Lonie	Camerson
Lorne	Stewart, Cambell
Loudoun	Compbell
Low	Maclaren
Lowson	Maclaren
Lucas	Lamont
Luke	Lamont
Lyall	Sinclair
MacA'shallies	MacDonald
Macachounich	Colquhoun
Macadam	MacGregor
Macadie	Freguson
Macaindra	MacFarlane
Macaldonich	Buchanan
Macalduie	Lamont
Macallan	MacDonald, MacMarlane
Macalonie	Camerson
Macandeoir	Buchanan, MacNab
Macandrew	Mackintosh
Macangus	MacInnes
Macara	MacGregor, MacCrae
Macaree	MacGregor
Macaskill	MacLeod
Macaslan	Buchanan
Macauslan	Buchanan
Macay	Shaw
Macbaxter	MacMillan
Macbean	MacBain
Macbeath	MacBain, MacDonald, MacLean
Macbeolain	MacKenzie

Name	Associated Clan
Macbeth	MacBain, MacDonald, MacLean
Macbheath	MacBain, MacDonald, MacLean
Macbride	MacDonald
Macbrieve	Morrison
Macburie	MacDonald
Maccaa	MacFarlane
Maccabe	MacLeod
Maccaig	Farquharson, MacLeod
Maccaishe	MacDonald
Maccall	MacDonald
Maccalman	Buchanan
Maccamie	Stewart
Maccammond	Buchanan
Maccanish	MacInnes
Maccartney	Farquharson, Mackintosh
Maccartair	Campbell
Maccarter	Campbell
Maccash	MacDonald
Maccaskill	Macleod
Maccasland	Buchanan
Maccaul	MacDonald
Maccause	MacFarlane
Maccaw	MacFarlane
Maccay	MacKay
Macceallaich	MacDonald
Macclerich	Cameron
Macchlery	Cameron
Maccoiter	MacGregor
Macchruiter	Buchanan
Maccloy	Stewart
Macclure	MacLeod
Macluskie	MacDonald
Macclymont	Lamont
Maccodrum	MacDonald
Maccoll	MacDonald
Maccolman	Buchanan
Maccomas	MacThomas, Gunn
Maccombe	MacThomas
Maccombich	Stewart of Appin

Name	Associated Clan
Maccombie	MacThomas
Maccomie	MacThomas
Macconnacher	MacDougall
Macconachie	MacGregor, Robertson
Macconchy	Mackintosh
Maccondy	MacFarlane
Macconnach	MacKenzie
Macconnechy	Campbell, Robertson
Macconnell	MacDonald
Macconnochie	Campbell, Robertson
Maccooish	MacDonald
Maccook	MacDonald
Maccorkill	Gunn
Maccorkindale	MacLeod
Maccorkle	Gunn
Maccormack	Buchanan
Maccormick	MacLean of Lochbuie
Maccorrie	MacQuarrie
Maccosram	Macdonald
Maccoull	MacDougall
Maccowan	Colquhoun, Macdougall
Maccrae	MacRae
Maccrain	MacDonald
Maccracken	MacLean
Maccraw	MacRae
Maccreath	MacRae
Maccrie	MacKay
Maccrimmor	MacLeod
Maccrindle	MacDonald
Maccririe	MacDonald
Maccrouther	MacGregor, Drummond
Maccruithein	MacDonald
Maccuag	MacDonald
Maccuaig	Farquharson, MacLeod
Maccubbin	Buchanan
Maccuish	MacDonald
Maccune	MacEwan
Maccunn	MacPherson
Maccurrach	MacPherson
Maccutchen	MacDonald

Name	Associated Clan
Macdade	Davidson
Macdaniell	MacDonald
Macdavid	Davidson
Macdermid	Campbell
Macdiarmid	Campbell
Macdonachie	Robertson
Macdonleavy	Buchanan
Macdrain	MacDonald
Macduffie	MacFie
Macdulothe	MacDougall
Maceachan	MacDonald of Clanranald
Maceachern	MacDonald
Maceachin	MacDonald of Clanranald
Maceachran	MacDonald
Macearachar	Farquharson
Macelfrish	MacDonald
Macelheran	MacDonald
Maceoin	MacFarlane
Maceol	MacNaughton
Macerracher	MacFarlane
Macfadzean	MacLaine of Lochbuie
Macfall	MacPherson
Macfarquhar	Farquharson
Macfater	Maclaren
Macfeat	Maclaren
Macfergus	Ferguson
Macgaw	MacFarlane
Macgeachie	MacDonald of Clanranald
Macgeachin	MacDonald of Clanranald
Macgeoch	MacFarlane
Macghee	MacKay
Macghie	MacKay
Macgilbert	Buchanan
Macgilchrist	MacLachlan, Ogilvie
Macgill	MacDonald
Macgilledon	Lamont
Macgillegowie	Lamont
Macgillivantic	MacDonald
Macgillivour	MacGillivray
Macgillonie	Cameron

Name	Associated Clan
Macgilp	MacDonald
Macgilroy	Grant, MacGillivray
Macgilvernock	Graham
Macgilvra	MacGillivray, Maclaine of Lochbuie
Macgilvray	MacGillivray
Macglashan	Mackintosh, Stewart
Macglasrich	MacIver Campbell
Macgorrie	MacDonald
Macgoun	MacDonald, MacPherson
Macgowan	MacDonald, MacPherson
Macgown	MacDonald, MacPherson
Macgrath	MacRae
Macgreusich	Buchanan, MacFarlane
Macgrewar	MacGregor, Drummond
Macgrime	Graham
Macgrory	Maclaren
Macgrowther	MacGregor, Drummond
Macgruder	MacGregor, Drummond
Macgruer	Fraser
Macgruther	MacGregor, Drummond
Macguaran	MacQuarrie
Macguffie	MacFie
Macgugan	MacNeil
Macguire	MacQuarrie
Machaffie	MacFie
Machardie	Farquharson, Mackintosh
Macharold	MacLeod
Machendrie	MacNaughton
Machendry	MacNaughton, Macdonald
Machowell	MacDougall
Machugh	MacDonald
Machutchen	MacDonald
Macian	Gunn, MacDonald
Macildowie	Cameron
Macilduy	MacGregor, MacLean
Macilreach	MacDonald
Macilleriach	MacDonald
Macilrevie	MacDonald
Macilvain	MacBean
Macilvora	Maclaine of Lochbuie

Name	Associated Clan
Macilvrae	MacGillivray
Macilvride	MacDonald
Macilwhom	Lamont
Macilwraith	MacDonald
Macilzegowie	Lamont
Macimmey	Fraser
Macinally	Buchanan
Macindeor	Menzies
Macindoe	Buchanan
Macinroy	Robertson
Macinstalker	MacFallane
Maciock	MacFarlane
Macissac	Compbell, MacDonald
Maciver	MacIver, Campbell
Macivor	MacIver, Campbell
Macjames	MacFarlane
Mackail	Cameron
Mackames	Gunn
Mackaskill	MacLeod
Mackeachan	MacDonald
Mackeamish	Gunn
Mackean	Gunn, MacDonald
Mackechnie	MacDonald of Clanranald
Mackee	MacKay
Mackeggie	Mackintosh
Mackeith	MacPherson
Mackellachie	MacDonald
Mackellaig	MacDonald
Mackellar	Campbell
Mackelloch	MacDonald
Mackelvie	Campbell
Mackendrick	MacNaughton
Mackenrick	MacNaughton
Mackeochan	MacDonald of Clanranald
Mackerchar	Farquharson
Mackerlich	MacKenzie
Mackerracher	Farquharson
Mackerras	Ferguson
Mackersey	Ferguson
Mackessock	Campbell, MacDonald of Clanranald

Name	Associated Clan
Mackichan	MacDonald of Clanranald, MacDougall
Mackieson	Mackintosh
Mackiggan	MacDonald
Mackilligan	Mackintosh
Mackillop	Macdonald
Mackim	Fraser
Mackimmie	Fraser
Mackindlay	Farquharson
Mackinlay	Buchanan, Farquharson, MacFarlane, Stewart of Appin
Mackinnell	MacDonald
Mackinney	MacKinnon
Mackinning	MacKinnon
Mackinven	MacKinnon
Mackirdy	Stewart
Mackissock	Campbell, MacDonald of Clanranald
Macknight	MacNaughton
Maclae	Stewart of Appin
Maclagan	Robertson
Maclaghlan	MacLachlan
Maclairish	MacDonald
Maclamond	Lamont
Maclardie	MacDonald
Maclarty	MacDonald
Maclaverty	MacDonald
Maclaws	Campbell
Maclea	Stewart of Appin
Maclehose	Campbell
Macleish	MacPherson
Macleister	MacGregor
Maclergain	MacLean
Maclerie	Cameron, Mackintosh, MacPherson
Macleverty	MacDonald
Maclewis	MacLeod
Maclintock	MacDougall
Maclise	MacPherson
Macliver	MacGregor
Maclucas	Lamont, MacDougall
Maclugash	MacDougall
Maclulich	MacDougall, Munro, Ross

Name	Associated Clan
Maclure	MacLeod
Maclymont	Lamont
Macmanus	Colquhoun, Gunn
Macmartin	Cameron
Macmaster	Buchanan, MacInnis
Macmath	Matteson
Macmaurice	Buchanan
Macmenzies	Menzies
Macmichael	Stewart of Appin, Stewart
Macminn	Menzies
Macmonies	Menzies
Macmorran	MacKinnon
Macmunn	Stewart
Macmurchie	Buchanan, MacKenzie
Macmurdo	MacPherson
Macmurdoch	MacPherson
Macmurray	Murray
Macmurrich	MacDonald of Clanranald, MacPherson
Macmutrie	Stewart
Macnair	MacFarlane, MacNaughton
Macnamell	MacDougall
Macnayer	MacNaughton
Macnee	MacGregor
Macneilage	MacNeil
Macneilly	MacNeil
Macneish	MacGregor
Macneur	MacFarlane
Macney	MacGregor
Macnider	MacFarlane
Macnie	MacGregor
Macnish	MacGregor
Macniter	MacFarlane
Macniven	Cumming, Mackintosh, MacNaughton
Macnuir	MacNaughton
Macnuyer	Buchanan, MacNaughton
Macomie	MacThomas
Macomish	MacThomas
Maconie	Cameron
Macoran	Campbell
MacO'Shannaig	MacDonald

Name	Associated Clan
Macoull	MacDougall
Macourlic	Cameron
Macowen	Campbell
Macowl	MacDougall
Macpatrick	Lamont, Maclaran
Macpetrie	MacGregor
Macphadden	Maclaine of Lochbuie
Macphater	Maclaran
Macphedran	Campbell
Macphedron	Macauley
Macpheidiran	Macauley
Macphillip	MacDonald
Macphorich	Lamont
Macphun	Matheson, Campbell
Macquaire	MacQuarrie
MacQuartie	MacQuarrie
Macquey	MayKay
Macquhirr	MacQuarrie
Macquire	MacQuarrie
Macquistan	MacDonald
Macquoid	MacKay
Macra	MacRae
Macrach	MacRae
Macraild	MacLeod
Macraith	MacRae, MacDonald
Macritchie	Mackintosh
Macrob	Gunn, MacFarlane
Macrobb	MacFarlane
Macrobbie	Robertson, Durmmond
Macrobert	Robertson, Drummond
Macrobie	Robertson, Drummond
Macrorie	MacDonald
Macruer	MacDonald
Macrurie	Macdonald
Macshannachan	MacDonald
Macshimes	Fraser of Lovat
Macsimon	Fraser of Lovat
Macsorley	Cameron, MacDonald
Macsporran	MacDonald
Macswan	MacDonald

Name	Associated Clan
Macsween	MacDonald
Macswen	MacDonald
Macsymon	Fraser
Mactaggart	Ross
Mactary	Innes
Mactause	Campbell
Mactavish	Campbell
Mactear	Ross, MacIntrye
Mactier	Ross
Mactire	Ross
Maculric	Cameron
Macure	Campbell
Macvail	Cameron, MacKay
Macvanish	MacKenzie
Macvarish	MacDonald of Clanranald
Macveagh	MacLean
Macvean	MacBean
Macvey	MacLean
Macvicar	MacNaughton
Macvinish	MacKenzie
Macvurich	MacDonald of Clanranald, MacPherson
Macvurie	MacDonald of Clanranald
Macwalrick	Cameron
Macwalter	MacFarlane
Macwattie	Buchanan
Macwhannell	MacDonald
Macwhirr	MacQuarrie
Macwhirter	Buchanan
Macwilliam	Gunn, MacFarlane
Malcomson	Malcolm (Maccallum)
Malloch	MacGregor
Mann	Gunn
Manson	Gunn
Mark	MacDonald
Marnoch	Innes
Marshall	Keith
Martin	Cemeron, MacDonald
Mason	Sinclair
Massey	Matheson
Masterson	Buchanan

Name	Associated Clan
Mathie	Matheson
Mavor	Gordon
May	MacDonald
Means	Menzies
Meikleham	Lamont
Mein	Menzies
Meine	Menzies
Mennie	Menzies
Meyners	Menzies
Michie	Forbes
Miller	MacFarlane
Milne	Gordon, Ogilvy
Milfroy	MacGillivray
Minn	Menzies
Minnus	Menzies
Mitchell	Innes
Monach	MacFarlane
Monzie	Menzies
Moodie	Stewart
Moray	Murray
Morgan	Mackay
Morren	MacKinnon
Morris	Buchanan
Morton	Douglas
Munn	Stewart, Lamont
Murchie	Buchanan, Menzies
Murchison	Buchanan, Menzies
Murdoch	MacDonald, MacPherson
Murdoson	MacDonald, MacPherson
Murphy	MacDonald
Neil	MacNeil
Neil	MacNeil
Neill	MacNeil
Neilson	MacNeil
Nelson	Gunn, MacNeil
Neish	MacGregor
Nish	MacGregor
Niven	Cumming, Mackintosh
Nixon	Armstrong
Noble	Mackintosh

Name	*Associated Clan*
Norie	MacDonald
Norman	Sutherland
O'Drain	MacDonald
Oliver	Fraser
O'May	Sutherald
O'Shaig	MacDonald
O'Shannachan	MacDonald
O'Shannaig	MacDonald
Park	MacDonald
Parlene	MacFarlane
Paton	MacDonald, MacLean
Patrick	Lamont
Paul	Cameron, Mackintosh
Pearson	MacPherson
Peterkin	MacGregor
Petrie	MacGregor
Philipson	MacDonald
Pinkerton	Campbell
Piper	Murray
Pitullich	MacDonald
Pollard	MacKay
Polson	MacKay
Porter	MacNaughton
Pratt	Grant
Purcell	MacDonald
Raith	MacRae
Randolph	Bruce
Reidfurd	Innes
Reoch	Farquharson, MacDonald
Revie	MacDonald
Riach	Farquharson, MacDonald
Richardson	Ogilvie, Buchanan
Risk	Buchanan
Ritchie	Mackintosh Robb MacFarlane
Roberts	Robertson
Robinson	Gunn, Robertson
Robison	Gunn, Robertson
Robson	Gunn, Robertson
Rome	Johnstone
Ronald	MacDonald, Gunn

Name	Associated Clan
Ronaldson	MacDonald, Gunn
Rorison	MacDonald
Roy	Robertson
Rusk	Buchanan
Ruskin	Buchanan
Russell	Russell, Cumming
Sanderson	MacDonald
Sandison	Gunn
Saunders	Macalister
Scobie	MacKay
Shannon	MacDonald
Sharp	Stewart
Sherry	MacKinnon
Sim	Fraser of Lovat
Sime	Fraser of Lovat
Simon	Fraser of Lovat
Simpson	Fraser of Lovat
Simson	Fraser of Lovat
Skinner	MacGregor
Small	Murray
Smart	MacKenzie
Smith	MacPherson, Mackintosh
Sorely	Cameron, MacDonald
Spence	MacDuff
Spittal	Buchanan
Sporran	Buchanan
Stalker	MacFarlane
Stark	Robertson
Stenhouse	Burce
Stewart	Stewart
Storie	Ogilvie
Stringer	MacGregor
Summers	Lindsay
Suttie	Grant
Swan	Gunn
Swanson	Gunn
Syme	Fraser
Symon	Fraser
Taggart	Ross

Name	Associated Clan
Tarrill	Mackintosh
Tawesson	Campbell
Tawse	Farquharson
Thain	Innes, Mackintosh
Todd	Gordon
Tolmie	MacLeod
Tonnochy	Robertson
Torry	Campbell
Tosh	Mackintosh
Toward	Lamont
Towart	Lamont
Train	Ross
Turner	Lamont
Tyre	MacIntrye
Ure	Campbell
Vass	Munro, Ross
Wallis	Wallace
Walters	Forbes
Wass	Munro, Ross
Watt	Buchanan
Weaver	MacFarlane
Webster	MacFarlane
Whannell	MacDonald
Wharrie	MacQuarrie
Wheelan	MacDonald
White	MacGregor, Lamont
Whyte	MacGregor, Lamont
Wilke	MacDonald
Wilkinson	MacDonald
Will	Gunn
Williamson	Gunn, MacKay
Wilson	Gunn, Innes
Wright	MacIntrye
Wylie	Gunn, MacFarlane
Yuill	Buchanan
Yuille	Buchanan
Yule	Buchanan

RESOURCE ORGANIZATIONS FOR THE CONTINUITY OF CELTIC CULTURE

The International Celtic Congress

The Celtic Congress meets annually, rotating the meeting among the six Celtic countries. Its aims are to maintain Celtic language and culture.

Breton Branch

Breizh Ar C'hendalc'h Keltiek Etrevroadel
Loik Chapel, 5 Straed Berlioz
29245 Plourin Montroulez
FRANCE

Cornish branch

An Guntelles Keltek Kesgwlasek
Neil Plummer, 28 Peverill Road, Porthleven
Helston, Kernow
UNITED KINGDOM

Irish branch

An Chomhdhail Cheilteach
Rosin Ui Chuill, 179 Bothar Rath Maoinis
Baille Ath Cliath Dublin 6
IRELAND

Scottish branch

Celtic Congress
M. MacIver, 7 Teal Avenue
Inverness IV2 3TB
SCOTLAND

Other Resources

Centre De Recherche Bretonne Et Celtique

20 Rue Duquesne
29200 Brest
FRANCE

Breton Celtic resource/research center

World Manx Association
Peter Kelly, 52 Alberta Drive
Onchan, Douglas
UNITED KINGDOM
Open to anyone of Manx descent or association

Institute of Irish Studies

Queens Universtiy, 8 Fitzwilliam Street
Beal Feirste, Belfast BT9 6AW
NORTHERN IRELAND

Dalriada Celtic Heritage Trust

Dun na Beatha
2 Brathwic Place, Brodick
Isle of Arran KA27 8BN
SCOTLAND
Quarterly journal of Celtic studies; archives

BIBLIOGRAPHY

Bailyn, Bernard and Philip D. Morgan, eds. *Strangers Within the Realm: Cultural Margins of the First British Empire,* Chapel Hill, N.C.: University of North Carolina Press, 1991.

Bain, Robert. *The Clans and Tartans of Scotland.* London: William Collins, 1954.

Cahill, Thomas. *How the Irish Saved Civilization.* New York: Doubleday, 1995.

Caldicott, Moyra. *Women in Celtic Myth.* Rochester, Vt.: Destiny Books, 1988.

Campbell, Joseph P. *Popular Tales of the West Highlands,* 4 vols. Edinburgh: Wildwood, 1983.

Carmichael, Alexander. *Carmina Gadelica.* 6 vols. Edinburgh: Oliver & Boyd, 1928.

Chadwick, Nora. *The Celts.* New York: Penguin, 1977.

Chadwick, Nora and Myles Dillon. *The Celtic Realms.* London: Weidenfeld & Nicolson, 1967.

Cross, T. P. and C. H. Slover, eds. *Ancient Irish Tales.* New York: Barnes & Noble, 1969.

Daiches, David. *The Last Stuart: The Life and Times of Bonnie Prince Charlie.* New York: Putnam, 1973.

de Breffny, Brian. *The Irish World.* London: Thames & Hudson, 1986.

Delaney, Frank. *The Celts.* Boston: Little Brown, 1986.

Devine, Thomas M. *Clanship to Crofter's War, The Social Transformation of the Scottish Highlands.* Manchester: Manchester University Press, 1994.

Ellis, Peter Berresford. *The Druids.* Grand Rapids, Mich.: Wm. B. Eardman's, 1995.

Foster, Sally M. *Picts, Gaels, and Scots.* London: B. T. Batsford, 1996.

Gantz, Jeffrey. *Early Irish Myths and Sagas.* London: Penguin, 1981.

Goldstein, James. *The Matter of Scotland.* Lincoln: University of Nebraska Press, 1993.

Grant, Elizabeth. *Memoirs of a Highland Lady.* London: John Murray, 1978.

Grant, I. F. *Highland Folk Ways.* London: Routledge & Kegan Paul, 1961.

Green, Miranda, ed. *The Celtic World.* London: Routledge, 1995.

Greer, Mary K. *Women of the Golden Dawn: Rebels and Priestesses.* Rochester, Vt.: Inner Traditions, 1995.

Gonne, Maud. "Yeats and Ireland." In *Scattering Branches: Tributes to the Memory of W. B. Yeats,* edited by Stephen Gwynn. London: Macmillan, 1940.

Gunn, Neil. *Off in a Boat.* Glasgow: Richard Drew, 1988.

———. *Highland River.* Edinburgh: Canongate, 1991.

Herm, Gerhard. *The Celts.* New York: St. Martins, 1976.

Hewiston, Jim. *Tam Blake & Co: The Story of the Scots in America.* Edinburgh: n.p., 1995.

Hobsbawm, Eric and Terence Ranger, eds. *The Invention of Tradition.* Cambridge: Cambridge University Press, 1983.

Hunter, James. *A Dance Called America: The Scottish Highlands, the United States and Canada.* Edinburgh: Mainstream, 1994.

———. *On the Other Side of Sorrow: Nature and People in the Scottish Highlands.* Edinburgh: Mainstream, 1995.

Jackson, Kenneth Hurlstone. *A Celtic Miscellany.* Middlesex: Penguin, 1973.

Lynch, Michael. *Scotland: A New History.* London: Century, 1991.

MacCana, Proinsias. *Celtic Mythology.* London: Hamlyn, 1970.

MacKenzie, Alexander. *History of the Highland Clearances.* London: Melvin, 1986.

Mackie, J. D. *A History of Scotland.* London: Penguin, 1964.

MacLean, Fitzroy. *A Concise History of Scotland.* New York: Viking, 1970.

MacLennan, Hugh. *Scotchman's Return and Other Essays.* Toronto: New Canadian Library Edition, 1960.

MacManus, Seumas. *The Story of the Irish Race.* New York: Devin-Adair, 1944.

MacPhail, I. M. M. *The Crofter's War.* Stornoway, Scotland: Acair, 1989.

Magnusson, Magnus and Graham White, eds. *The Nature of Scotland: Landscape, Wildlife, and People.* Edinburgh: Canongate, 1991.

Markale, Jean. *Women of the Celts.* Rochester, Vt.: Inner Traditions, 1986.

Matthews, Caitlin and John. *Encyclopedia of Celtic Wisdom.* Dorset: Element Books, 1994.

McDonald, Lorraine. *Celtic Totem Animals.* Isle of Arran, Scotland: Dalriada, 1992.

McLaren, Moray. *Bonnie Prince Charlie.* New York: Saturday Review, 1972.

McNeill, Marion. *The Silver Bough.* 4 vols. William MacLellan

McPhee, John. *The Crofter and the Laird.* Toronto: Doubleday, 1969.

Meyer, Kuno. *Ancient Irish Poetry.* London: Constable, 1994.

O'Donohue, John. *Anam Cara: A Book of Celtic Wisdom.* New York: HarperCollins, 1997.

O'Rahilly, Thomas F. *Early Irish History and Mythology.* Dublin: Dublin Institute for Advanced Studies, 1976.

Piggot, Stuart. *The Druids.* New York: Penguin, 1978.

Pine, L. G. *The Highland Clans.* Rutland, Vt.: Tuttle, 1972.

Pittock, Murray H. G. *The Invention of Scotland: The Stuart Myth and the Scottish Identity, 1638 to the Present.* London: Routledge, 1991.

Porter, Jane. *The Scottish Chiefs.* New York: Charles Scribner's Sons, 1921.

Prebble, John. *The Highland Clearances.* London: Penguin, 1969.

———. *The Lion of the North.* London: Penguin, 1971.

———. *Mutiny: Highland Regiments in Revolt 1743–1804.* London: Penguin, 1975.

Proctor, Carolyn. *Caennas Nan Gàidheal: The Headship of the Gael.* Isle of Skye, Scotland: Clan Donald Lands Trust, 1985.

Rees, A and B. *Celtic Heritage.* London: Thames & Hudson, 1961.

Reese, Peter. *Wallace: A Biography.* Edinburgh: Canongate, 1996.

Richards, Eric. *A History of the Highland Clearances.* London: Croom Helm, 1982.

Rolleston, T. W. *Celtic Myths and Legends.* London: Studio Editions, 1994.

Ross, Anne. *Everyday Life of the Pagan Celts.* London: B. T. Batsford, 1970.

———. *Pagan Celtic Britain.* London: n.p., 1967.

———. *The Folklore of the Scottish Highlands.* New York: Barnes & Noble, 1976.

Ross, Anne and Don Robins, *The Life and Death of a Druid Prince.* New York: Simon & Schuster, 1989.

Rutherford, Ward. *The Druids and Their Heritage.* London: Gordon & Cremonese, 1978.

Sutherland, Elizabeth. *Ravens and Black Rain: The Story of Highland Second Sight.* London: Constable, 1985.

Van de Weyer, Robert. *Celtic Fire: An Anthology of Celtic Christian Literature.* London: Darton, Longman, & Todd, 1990.

Way of Plean, George, and Romilly Squire. *Scottish Clan and Family Encyclopedia.* Glasgow: HarperCollins, 1994.

Wentz, W. Y. Evans. *The Fairy Faith in Celtic Countries.* Oxford: Colin Smythe, 1911.